A HISTORY OF BRITISH EMPIRICAL SOCIOLOGY

A History of British Empirical Sociology

RAYMOND A. KENT
University of Stirling

Gower

078 136

Published by

Gower Publishing Company Limited,
Gower House, Croft Road,
Aldershot, Hants, GU11 3HR, England.

British Library Cataloguing in Publication Data

Kent, Raymond A.
   A history of British empirical sociology.
   1. Social surveys — Great Britain — History.
   I. Title
   361'.00723   HN29

HN
29
.K45
1981

ISBN 0 566 00520 4   Limp edition
ISBN 0 566 00415 1   Cased edition

Reproduced from copy supplied
Printed and bound in Great Britain
by Billing and Sons Limited and Kemp Hall Bindery
Guildford, London, Oxford, Worcester

Contents

Acknowledgements

I am grateful to David Bebbington of the Department of History, University of Stirling, for reading through the entire script of an earlier draft. I should also like to thank John Irwin of Gower Publishing for his many helpful comments and suggestions while the book was in preparation.

R.A. Kent

Introduction

> Modern sociology has two principal sources: the politico-social ideas or doctrines on the one hand, and the administrative statistics, surveys, and empirical investigations on the other . . . It is possible to argue that the empirical and quantitative sociology of today owes more to Quetelet and Le Play than it does to Montesquieu or Auguste Comte. But my tastes and abilities have predisposed me in the other direction.

This comment was made by Raymond Aron in the preface to the second volume of his *Main Currents in Sociological Thought* (1967). In declaring his personal interest Aron was, probably unintentionally, speaking for the vast majority of those sociologists who have written about the history of their discipline, which they have treated almost exclusively in terms of the development of social or sociological thought. One consequence of this has been that the difficulties experienced by theorists — even by those who have been regarded as key figures in the litany of 'founding fathers' — in relating their ideas to an empirical data base have been ignored or quietly overlooked.

It was Comte, a French philosopher, who coined the word 'sociology' in 1839. He offered an elaborate prospectus for the scientific study of society in a series of volumes published between 1830 and 1842. He was very clear about the techniques of inquiry that would be needed for his 'positive' method, namely observation, experiment and comparison. To single out observation as a 'method' may seem curious, even obvious, today; but Comte wanted to oppose previous tendencies for social theorising to be speculative, metaphysical or theological and thus beyond empirical verification. Not that Comte was for abandoning theory. On the contrary he argued that no real observation was possible 'except in as far as it is first directed, and finally interpreted, by some theory'.[1] He was well aware of the difficulties that this dual requirement imposed on sociology — that it would involve using in the first instance 'materials which have been badly elaborated, and doctrines which are ill-conceived'.[2] However, he failed to outline how the sociologist would break out of this vicious circle; indeed he did not indicate how observations were to be made and analysed — he only asserted that facts were 'plentiful'. It was their interpretation that was difficult. Direct experimentation was, of course, not possible in sociology, but indirect experimentation in the form of what nowadays would be called deviant case analysis was feasible. Comparison could take two main forms: the comparison of different co-existing states of human society so as to disclose different stages of evolution all at once, and comparison of societies at different consecutive stages in history.

The point needs to be made and emphasised, however, that Comte himself never actually engaged in any of these forms of empirical inquiry. In fact, he made very little use of empirical materials at all.

In Britain Herbert Spencer, who is best known for his evolutionary and functional theories of social institutions, was at least aware that his comparative method would need 'an immense accumulation of facts so classified and arranged as to facilitate generalisation'.[3] Accordingly, in 1867 he hired the first of three researchers who were to read and extract cultural data from ethnographic and historical sources, and to organise them according to a system of headings and sub-headings that Spencer had devised.[4] The results were eventually published in 17 large volumes under the general title of *Descriptive Sociology*.[5] The 'facts', however, were carefully selected so as to illustrate social evolution; like other great thinkers before him (and many afterwards), Spencer clearly considered history and existing social arrangements simply as a vast storehouse of examples with which to illustrate presumed truths. The idea of formulating testable statements which could then be validated or falsified by reference to factual data systematically collected for the purpose was not one that occurred to him.

Karl Marx was no less aware than Spencer of the need for empirical evidence. In his period of exile in London from 1849 he used secondary sources, particularly government 'Blue Books', to document the extent to which workers were being exploited by the capitalist system of

2

production. Once again, facts were being used for illustrative purposes, but Marx must have felt some dissatisfaction with data collected by others (particularly by those in the employment of the government itself), for in 1880 he drew up a lengthy questionnaire of over 100 items, 25,000 copies of which were distributed in France 'to all the workers' societies, to the socialist and democratic groups and circles, to the French newspapers, and to anyone else who asked for it'.[6] The idea was to extract 'exact and positive knowledge of the conditions in which the working class, the class to which the future belongs, lives and works'. It covered occupation and conditions of work, working hours and leisure activities, terms of employment, wages, the cost of living and the working class struggle for the improvement of conditions. However, very few replies were received and no results were ever published. Marx's attempt at primary empirical research was in short a flop.

In Germany Max Weber had been concerned with empirical research throughout most of his career. In the 1890s and in the first few years of the twentieth century he used questionnaires and direct observation in a number of large-scale social surveys of conditions of manual labour in Germany and of the effects of large-scale industry on the workers, and he made careful statistical analyses of the results.[7] He developed the idea of coding open-ended attitudinal responses in order to tabulate the results and he made systematic use of cross-tabulations (although curiously, not for the attitudinal variables). These researches, however, have not been the basis of Weber's influence in the field of sociology and they have been largely ignored by historians of the discipline. Weber was himself always ambivalent about the value of empirical research and the use of quantitative techniques and, like others in Germany at the time, seemed unable to integrate his empirical studies with efforts to build up general sociological theory.[8]

It was Durkheim in his study of suicide who came closest to the idea of testing specifically formulated hypotheses against empirical data, but in his case it was not data that he had himself collected. Although he was aware of the limitations of official statistics he never himself engaged in primary empirical research.[9] In short, although the key figures in the history of sociology as it has so far been told wanted to create a discipline that would apply the methods of the natural sciences (or some adaptation of them) to the study, and for Marx to the transformation, of society, they did not succeed in relating their abstract theories about social evolution, social structures and functions, social conflict and social behaviour to an empirical base in a way that contemporary sociologists would expect.

Aron's expressed preference for studying the development of social thought reveals yet another consequence of such a lopsided account of the history of sociology: the formulation of the alternative in terms of looking at the history of administrative statistics, surveys, and empirical investigations. The development of *techniques* of inquiry into social phenomena and the production of statistical data do indeed have a history, but one which is related not just to sociology but to social psychology, anthropology, market research, opinion polling, governmental inquiry, social administration, economics, statistics and so on. Sociologists do not have a monopoly over questionnaires, interview surveys and the systematic observation of social behaviour. The development of empirical sociology, however, is another matter. This is the real alternative to focusing attention on the origins of social thought and it is this which has been almost totally ignored by historians of sociology.[10]

The history of empirical sociology is more than just an account of early attempts at social fact gathering. Just as the empirical efforts (or lack of them) of theorists have been ignored so, too, have histories of sociology overlooked the attempts by a number of individuals, whose primary concern was indeed to collect facts about what they called 'the condition and progress of society', to build up inductive generalisations, and who often ended up explaining their findings in a surprisingly sociological manner. In their search for the 'causes' of poverty, crime, drunkenness and prostitution empirical sociologists came very close to a form of analysis with which contemporary analysis has more in common than have the theories of those more elegant thinkers who wanted to chart or to change the entire course of social history.

No doubt there are those who will argue that any subject matter needs to be sufficiently clearly defined before it will bear the weight of substantial analysis in historical narrative form. One cannot have a history of 'Europe' or of 'the West' without delimiting geographical boundaries. So, too, with 'sociology' or 'empirical sociology'. To argue thus, however, is to miss the point of much historical analysis. What counts as 'Europe', 'the West' or 'empirical sociology' will change over the years. Such developing perceptions and definitions of subject matter are themselves part of its history and must become part of the historical analysis. There would be many histories we could not write if clear-cut definitions were a prerequisite. Nor does history begin only when people are aware of the phenomenon under investigation or when they have a word for it. To argue that there was no sociology before Comte invented the word is like saying that neutrons did not exist before they were discovered and given a name. It is up to the historian to draw selected parallels between contemporary phenomena, however well or ill defined, and certain events in the past. The Domesday Inquiry of William the Conqueror in 1085 would almost certainly not be regarded as a piece of 'empirical sociology' as that term is used today, but that does not mean that similarities or comparisons between it and contemporary analysis cannot be pointed out or drawn.

The phenomenon which is the subject of this book may be loosely conceived as the story of those individuals who went out into the field to collect for themselves quantitative and qualitative data on social conditions in a manner that was professional, systematic and meticulous, and who made some attempt to summarise, interpret or explain what they found in terms of other social circumstances or general theories of society. The 'field', however, needs to be fairly broadly interpreted to include not only people's homes, their places of work, recreation, worship or misdemeanour, but also offices and libraries where documents may be stored and where statistics that were collected for purposes unrelated to sociological inquiry may be available. Secondary analysis — the re-analysis of existing data to develop or to test sociological theory — is thus part of empirical sociology in addition to what nowadays would be called 'primary' research.

Aron's admission that it is possible to argue that the empirical and quantitative sociology of today owes more to Quetelet and Le Play than it does to Montesquieu or Comte hints at yet another feature of histories of sociology: the view that Britain has had little to offer. None of the theorists that Aron considers is British. John Madge in the foreword to his influential *The Origins of Scientific Sociology* (1963) comments that the breakthrough of sociology, 'which has occurred in the United States and is now occurring in several European countries, seems in the Britain of the early 1960s to be as remote as it was 15 years ago'. In consequence, he felt unable to include a British work as the main subject of one of his chapters. More recent books by Hawthorn (1976) and Bottomore and Nisbet (1978) treat only Spencer and Hobhouse as major British theorists. Only Fletcher (1971) has concerned himself in more detail with the British scene. It may well be that Britain has not produced her Durkheim or her Weber, but it was in Britain that empirical sociology first developed. A tradition of social inquiry may be traced back to the seventeenth century and even further, but empirical sociology really began in embryo in the 1830s and 1840s — at the very time Comte in France was writing his major treatise on sociology.

Chapter 1 describes this early period of empirical sociology in which the 'social accountants' attempted to study social phenomena in a quantitative manner. They carried out social surveys or utilised official statistical information to produce aggregate numerical data which they perceived as 'the facts' that would not only speak louder than words, but would speak for themselves, would resolve debates and provide the basis for 'scientific' social reform. They saw their role as laying down the essential details on which others, more experienced in administrative matters than themselves, could devise some optimal solution to the social problems of the day. In the course of their investigations, however, these researchers often invented new techniques of data collection and data analysis, while their attempts to summarise, interpret or explain what they found often resulted in inductive generalisations that today might be described as 'grounded theory'. It was these men (and there is no record of any women being involved at the time) who first began testing specifically formulated hypotheses, and it was here that empirical sociology was born.

By the middle of the nineteenth century social accounting as a form of empirical sociology had almost disappeared. It was replaced by an early version of participant observation in which the researcher personally experienced the lives of the urban poor by temporarily becoming one of them. The results were typically presented as a narrative of a journey or exploration by a middle-class observer into the unknown culture of the British working classes. Chapter 2 shows how the 'social explorers' saw the urban poor as strange 'tribes' or 'wandering hoards' who inhabited a 'dark continent' or 'separate territory' that needed to be 'penetrated' like the darkest forests of Africa. It was Charles Booth who in the 1890s combined these two traditions to produce an inquiry unparalleled in its time and in many ways unsurpassed even by contemporary sociologists.

Chapter 3 explains how in the early twentieth century empirical sociology in Britain went through an extraordinary period in which the promise of a modern analytic and empirically based discipline looked as though it would emerge from several quarters; but each promise was to remain unfulfilled. The followers of Booth, like Rowntree, reverted to social accounting, while the formation of the Sociological Society in 1903 represented an unsteady alliance of town planners, eugenicists and social workers; but each developed in a different direction that was away from empirical sociology. The result was a protracted decline and eventual dissolution of the Society. Even the creation of the first chair in sociology in 1907 at the London School of Economics did little for the cause of empirical sociology. Chapter 4 turns to the inter-war period when empirical sociology showed few signs of making any progress. There were replications of earlier studies and a few large-scale social surveys, but these, if anything, were in many respects a step backwards from the inquiries of Booth and Rowntree. By 1943 one American observer of the British scene even felt that sociology as a whole was all but dead. However, a thread of social accounting was maintained, and it re-emerged with renewed vigour in the post-war years, which are considered in Chapter 5. The tradition of social

6

exploration had died away, but in its place came community studies which flourished in the 1950s and 1960s. The 1960s saw a proliferation of empirical sociology, particularly in more specialised substantive areas, but by the 1970s doubts were being raised about the value of the 'facts' derived from traditional methods. New approaches to empirical sociology were suggested, but what may loosely be labelled 'positivistic' approaches continued to be the staple diet of those who were publishing the results of empirical research.

The concluding chapter attempts to go beyond a simple descriptive history by showing how empirical sociology in Britain developed in a way that existing models of scientific growth cannot adequately explain. A new model, which emphasises the links between structures of norms and values for the conduct of empirical inquiry, the imperceptibility of innovation and the general social context in which a science is attempting to establish itself, is presented. It has been argued both that only at its peril does a science forget its history, and also that a science that hesitates to forget its founders is lost; but to forget something is to have known it in the first place, and a science ignorant of its founders and of its history does not know how far it has travelled nor in what direction. The chapter concludes that, in the absence of a balanced historical perspective, innovation in empirical sociology will remain hidden and long-term trends will be obscure.

The basic raw material for this study has been the published monographs and articles of those who may be regarded as having initiated or advanced the cause of empirical sociology. Biographies of some of the key individuals have also been drawn upon extensively. The selection of individuals probably requires some further comment at this stage. In contrast to the social theorists like Comte and Spencer few of the pioneers of empirical sociology in Britain — with the major exception of Sidney and Beatrice Webb — saw themselves as 'sociologists'. They might have regarded themselves as 'statisticians', 'reformers', 'humanitarians', 'philanthropists', or 'journalists'. Certainly there were also clergymen who produced 'statistical accounts' of their parishes in the 1790s and again in the 1830s and 1840s; there were businessmen like Booth and Rowntree who pursued their research activities as a kind of hobby carried out in their spare time; there were medical men like William Guy and Edwin Chadwick whose concern was largely with public health, and there were biologists, mathematicians and philosophers. In consequence it is not possible to avoid responsibility for making what must ultimately be a personal selection by including only those who saw themselves as 'empirical sociologists'. The work of five individuals has been chosen for detailed analysis in the following pages: Frederick Engels, Henry Mayhew, Charles Booth, and Sidney and Beatrice Webb. It is not that these five tower above all others in the size, significance and impact of their inquiries, but rather that they pioneered forms of inquiry that have subsequently become recognised as in the best of sociological traditions. If this study is not to degenerate into a list-like parade of all those whose work has some parallel with modern empirical sociology, then the selected individuals must to some extent stand for the others. This is inevitably at the expense of more contemporary researchers, but it may nevertheless help to emphasise that empirical sociology, too, has its 'founding fathers' just as much as sociological theory.

The commentary on the empirical inquiries included focuses on the methods and techniques of research used[11] and on the conclusions at which the empirical sociologists arrived. It does not dwell upon weaknesses and shortcomings; a critical analysis of each study would result in a very different — and much longer — book. Rather the focus is on achievement and innovation. It is in some ways a 'Whig interpretation of history' — a tendency of many historians 'to write on the side of the Protestants and Whigs, to praise revolutions provided they have been successful, to emphasise certain principles of progress in the past and to produce a story which is the ratification if not a glorification of the present'.[12] A more mature history would attempt to interpret events, practices and ideas in the way earlier researchers probably saw them at the time, and would relate them to the ideological, social, economic, political and literary context of the period. Some attempt has, however, been made to begin such an analysis. At the end of each chapter a brief commentary describes the contexts in which empirical sociology emerged and developed. This is no substitute for a thorough analysis of the relationships involved, but such is beyond the scope of this book. The epistemological assumptions made by the early empirical sociologists are clear enough: social reality was something that could be measured in the same way as the speed of falling bodies. Social facts had the same status as other scientific facts — they were truths to be discovered by patient and systematic observation. Their accumulation resulted in 'knowledge' about social circumstances — knowledge that could be utilised as a basis for effective social reform.

This interest in social reform was what united the pioneers of empirical sociology in Britain. Some saw their role as providing a factual base on which administrators could pursue more effective and more 'scientific' reforms. Some saw their role as 'king's adviser' — a kind of social technician who would use his skills to discover how changes desired by governments could be brought about. Others saw themselves as committed to certain social ends — a classless society, the reduction of inequality, the promotion of individualism or enlightened self-interest, the breeding of a superior human race, the creation of a welfare state — and were prepared to utilise empirical sociology to advocate or even actively promote them. Their commitment was to reform, not to the discipline of sociology as it was being advocated by Comte and Spencer, and later by Durkheim, Weber and Hobhouse. This is not to say that the empirical sociologists were uninfluenced by the theorists. Booth in his early years had been a follower of Comte and Beatrice Webb had certainly been influenced by her childhood relationship with Spencer. It was rather that the use of sociological inquiry as a contribution to sociological thought by developing theory or by testing existing theory was not one of their objectives. This by no means invalidates the work of the early empirical sociologists as 'non-sociological' as some writers have claimed.[13] Their empirical generalisations were inductively derived from their researches — but it was still theory, and it was more closely related to an empirical base than was the work of most of the theorists.

Notes

1   Quoted from Thompson, 1976, p.102. This contains an introductory essay on Comte followed by extracts from Comte's two major works, *Cours de Philosophie Positive* (1830—1844) in six volumes, and *Système de Politique Positive* (1848—1854) in four volumes. The extract containing the quotation is from a translation of the first of these works by Harriet Martineau, first published in 1853 by John Chapman and reprinted in 1913 by G. Bell.
2   Ibid., p.103.
3   There may have been an element of *post hoc* rationalisation here, since the quote comes from his *Autobiography*, 1904, p.171.
4   See Carneiro, 1968, for a brief but informative account of Spencer and his work.
5   Eight large folio volumes appeared between 1973 and 1881; the rest were published after his death in 1903. All 17 volumes have since been compiled and abstracted by Duncan, Scheppig and Collier, published by William and Norgate, 1934.
6   See Bottomore and Rubel, 1963, p.203, who also list all Marx's questions. The inquiry became known as the 'Enquête Ouvrière'.
7   See Lazarsfeld and Oberschall, 1965.
8   See Oberschall, 1965, for a full account.
9   See Clark, 1972, for an account of Durkheim's role in the French University.

10 Lazarsfeld, 1972, p.vii, has argued that the tradition of empirical social research has, until recently, been ignored in most countries, being neither studied in its own right, nor treated as part of the standard histories of sociology. Some progress has been made in exploring this tradition, in Germany by Oberschall, 1965, and Schad, 1972; in France by Clark, 1973, Lecuyer and Oberschall, 1968, and Lazarsfeld, 1972; and in the USA by Oberschall, 1972. Abrams, 1968, in an extended essay, traces the origins of British sociology as a whole between 1834 and 1914 by focusing on attempts to institutionalise sociology in this period. He examines the careers of three institutions — the Statistical Society of London, the National Association for the Promotion of Social Science, and the Sociological Society — and the work of seven individuals — Comte, Le Play, Spencer, Hobhouse, Galton, Booth and Geddes — as it interacted with these institutions. However, his interest is mainly in theory and he says little about the nature of the empirical sociology undertaken under the auspices of these organisations or carried out by Le Play, Booth or Geddes.

More specifically on the history of empirical sociology are the papers by Elesh, 1972, and Cole, 1972. Both focus on the failure of British empirical sociology to institutionalise, the former taking the case of the Manchester Statistical Society, while the latter concentrates on English criminology in the nineteenth century and in particular on a monograph by Thomas Plint, 1851, on crime in England. Cullen, 1975, looks at the men who between 1832 and 1852 were responsible for the development of governmental statistics and the formation of the London and various provincial statistical societies. Like Abrams, however, he concerns himself little with the techniques of research used or developed in that period, or with the ways in which the statistical movement laid the foundations for the development of empirical sociology in Britain. Keating, 1976, in attempting to illustrate a characteristic type of late nineteenth and early twentieth-century literature, in effect presents a commentary on the origins of participant observation. There are a few early studies of social surveys in Britain by Wells, 1935, Caradog Jones, 1948, and Abrams, 1951, which focus on the Booth—Rowntree—Bowley tradition. Finally, there are some biographies of individual nineteenth-century social researchers such as by Thompson and Yeo, 1971, and Humpheries, 1980, on Mayhew; Simey and Simey, 1960, and Pfautz, 1967, on Booth; Briggs, 1961, on Rowntree; and Cole, 1945, on the Webbs.

11 'Methods' refer to the general principles of scientific inquiry and the way in which 'knowledge' is to be derived. Examples of different methods are the historical method, the comparative method, the experimental method, the positivistic method and the interpretative method. 'Techniques' refer to the different tools of data collection and data

analysis such as the interview survey technique, the techniques of observation and participant observation, sampling techniques and statistical techniques.

12   Butterworth, 1931, Preface, p.v.

13   Banks, 1969, pp 3-4, for example, says of the surveys carried out by the Manchester and London Statistical Societies, that 'excellent though so many of these surveys are, they are not sociological as this term is understood today. Nor were they related to the main stream of sociological reasoning, stemming from Auguste Comte and Herbert Spencer, through Emile Durkheim and Max Weber, to the highly sophisticated theory builders of the present day . . . British empirical surveys have been strong on discovering isolated facts rather than patterns and weak in attempting to account for what they discovered. They are still worthy of attention as sources for any historically minded sociologist who seeks data to test a hypothesis, but they themselves make no contribution to such forms of knowledge. Where explanations have been offered at all they have been fabricated *post hoc*, and the only kinds of ideas they were explicitly formulated to falsify have been simple assertions of the all-or-nothing, more-or-less variety, such as the extent of poverty among the working classes in an urban area'.

It is hoped that this study will show that this is a very misconceived notion of what some of the early social researchers did. Mayhew and Booth, for example, were both concerned with the *causes* of poverty, and sought to show by empirical means that it was low wages rather than drink or idleness that was the main factor. These ideas were certainly not 'fabricated *post hoc*'. Both Mayhew's and Booth's analyses of prostitution in London, for example, show a very modern sociological touch. To accuse them of a 'lack of a sociological perspective', is to do considerable injustice to the work of these men.

1 The social accountants

Early surveys

The collection of statistical data about people has a long history in Britain. There were two main strands of development in what might be called the 'pre-history' of social accounting. One was the use of the survey to collect quantitative information by asking people questions and recording their answers, and the other involved the extraction of numerical data about demographic characteristics from records of births, marriages and deaths. The first strand may be traced back as far as 1085 when William the Conqueror initiated an inquiry into the extent and value both of the royal demesne and of the land held by the tenants-in-chief. Commissioners were sent into every shire, and the information, extracted on oath from the inhabitants, was written down and returned to the Royal Treasury at Winchester. The contemporary permanent record of this vast undertaking still survives in the two volumes of Domesday Book.[1]

The basic unit of analysis was the manor — who owned it, how big it was, how many people lived in it, whether they were villeins, cotters, slaves, or freemen, how much wood, meadow, pasture, how many mills and fishponds, how much it was worth and how much each freeman possessed. The information was organised by county, but it was not set out in tabular form as one might expect in a modern survey; rather, the 'statistics' were just numerical reports of possessions summarily presented in the text. An extract from Folio 87 on the Bishop of

Winchester's manor at Pipeminster in Somerset reads:

> The said bishop holds Pipeminster. Archbishop Stigand held it and paid geld for 15 hides. There is land for 20 ploughs, of it, 5 hides are in demesne and there are two ploughs and 17 villagers and 8 bordars with 14 ploughs. There are 6 acres of meadow and 400 acres of pasture and as many acres of wood. It is worth £13: now £16.[2]

The Domesday Survey, however, clearly dealt largely with economic matters. The earliest survey that was concerned more with social conditions was probably that conducted at the end of the eighteenth century by John Sinclair, an energetic and reform-minded Scottish agriculturalist. He sent to the ministers of religion in every parish in Scotland a questionnaire of over 160 items covering geology, geography and natural history of the parish, the age, sex, occupation and religion of its inhabitants, and the numbers of births, deaths, suicides, murders, unemployed, paupers and habitual drunkards. There were also questions about agricultural produce, animal husbandry and mineral wealth, about wages, prices and patterns of land tenure, and about comparisons of present conditions with earlier periods.[3] There ensued a lengthy correspondence that ran to some 20,000 letters, mostly to non-respondents, in which he begged, cajoled, argued, or threatened, and which extended over a period of 'seven years, seven months, and seven days'.[4] Detailed accounts of 938 parishes were obtained and were published largely as they were drawn up and written by the clergymen.

The result was *The Statistical Account of Scotland*, which appeared in 21 volumes between 1791 and 1799. The use of the word 'statistics' in the title prompted some historians to claim that Sinclair had introduced the word into English or at least had popularised its use. By the term Sinclair meant an 'inquiry into the state of a country for the purpose of ascertaining the quantum of happiness enjoyed by its inhabitants and the means to its future improvement'.[5] The assumptions implicit in such a definition — that statistics constituted a substantive area, not just a research technique, that 'happiness', or any other social condition, could be quantified or measured, and that the results could be used for reform — were all to become the hallmarks of the social statistician. Some 30 years later Sinclair published his *Analysis of the Statistical Account of Scotland*,[6] which was an abstract of the main findings and which was quite probably the earliest example of data presented in tabular form with computations of statistical averages and percentages.

In 1793 Sinclair, who had been in Parliament since 1780, persuaded Pitt to found a Board of Agriculture of which, naturally, he was to become President. The Board's first aim was to produce a statistical account of England on the same plan as the Scottish one. However, the English clergy were suspicious; they thought that the collection of statistics meant an attack on tithes and the plan had to be dropped.[7] It was Sir Frederick Eden, a businessman, who succeeded where Sinclair had failed. Eden adapted Sinclair's questionnaire and made use of the clergy as informants, but he also employed a research assistant in his field-work, an innovation not seen again until the 1830s. In addition he visited many of the parishes himself and 'procured on the spot, (from persons the most likely to supply useful information, and the least likely to be misinformed, or to mislead) the substance of several of the Reports'.[8] It may well be that he and his assistant were able to allay some of the fears that Sinclair had encountered (although it seems that some parish officers still refused to give any information).

In his three-volume *The State of the Poor* (1797) Eden claimed that his motives were 'benevolence and personal curiosity' following the difficulties the labouring classes had experienced from high prices during the years 1794—95. In a passage that anticipated the studies of Booth and Rowntree a century later he claimed that it was 'hardly possible to form any accurate judgement of the condition of the labouring classes . . . without first knowing what a labouring man can earn, and how much of the necessities of life he can purchase with his earnings'. After recounting the history of the poor from the conquest to the present period, Eden described the national establishments for the maintenance of the poor, the poor law system, the diet, dress, fuel and habitation of the labouring classes. The bulk of the material was, however, a series of 'parochial reports'. These represented a selection of parishes in every county in England and Wales in which (in similar fashion to Domesday) he simply recounted, for example, the number of acres, inhabitants, houses paying 'window tax', inns and farms. He described the principal agriculture, rents, land tax, wages and prices, and gave a general description of the state of the poor, how they fared and how they were treated. Some 112 parishes were covered in this way. He appeared to have had no definite method of selection, although almost every parish seemed to be chosen for some special characteristic or useful piece of information. The work just ended with a description of the last parish. However, one innovation was the detailed presentation of 43 family budgets of labourers, weavers, miners, masons, and other workers — an innovation not seen again for another 30 years.

The other strand in the pre-history of social accounting was the use of existing records to discover demographic regularities. The pioneer here was John Graunt, who published his *Natural and Political Observations . . . made upon Bills of Mortality* in 1662. Bills of Mortality were returns made by parish clerks of the deaths, causes of death and christenings that occurred in London and in some of the surrounding parishes.[9] From them he noted that some causes of death bore a constant relationship to the total number of deaths, that there was an excess of urban over rural deaths, that there was an excess of male over female births yet the numbers of the sexes remained roughly equal, and that there was a high rate of mortality during the early years of life. Graunt also estimated by several independent means the total population of London and noted its rapid recovery following outbreaks of the plague. Some of these regularities had been previously conjectured, but what Graunt offered was quantitative evidence derived from the compilation of numerous tables that he presented as an appendix and from which he made his observations. He was clearly aware of the limitations of the figures contained in the original Bills and he looked for evidence of 'sense' in the distinctions that were made as to 'causes' of death, and whether or not the individuals who reported the deaths (the 'searchers') offered grounds for the conclusions they came to.

Graunt had been a draper by training and became an opulent merchant of London. How he obtained his mathematical training and how he came to study population statistics is obscure. Indeed, after his death there was some controversy over whether it was Graunt or his friend William Petty who really deserved credit for this work. Parallels were found with some of Petty's earlier published writings, but the evidence was at best inconclusive.[10] Certainly the book represented the first recorded instance of the collection and use of statistical figures. Petty was full of the idea that numbers could elucidate all sorts of practical and political matters, and he gave his new science a name that it kept throughout the eighteenth century: 'political arithmetic'. In his book of that title (which he wrote in 1671, but it was not published until 1690) he said: 'Instead of using only comparative and superlative words, and intellectual arguments, I have taken the course . . . to express myself in Terms of Number, Weight, or Measure'. However, in what he wrote about trade, population, revenue, taxation and defence, he used any figures that came to hand, however defective; but he convinced his contemporaries of the value of a study that he had not himself the patience to pursue, and he was instrumental in gaining acceptance for the view that the collection of facts was an indispensable preliminary to practical and effective social reform. He applied quantitative analysis to political, social and economic conditions with such originality that he anticipated ideas that only recently would have been considered noteworthy intellectual innovations.[11]

In 1696 Gregory King published his *Natural and Political Observations and Conclusions Upon the State and Condition of England*. This was a bold approach to the question of estimating the size and structure of the population of England and Wales by taking certain figures of the number of houses in different areas and multiplying them by a series of factors relating to the number of persons per house.[12] King also provided what were almost certainly the earliest statistics on age and sex composition. No subsequent comparable figures were available until the 1821 Census was taken.

Though political arithmetic reached a degree of popularity in the eighteenth century, it never achieved the quantitative exactitude promised by Petty. A controversy over the size of the population of Great Britain and whether it was increasing or decreasing[13] brought discredit to the political arithmeticians, and the political economist Adam Smith declared in his *Wealth of Nations* (1776) that he had 'no great faith' in it. The term began to be invoked less and less, and by the end of the eighteenth century it had faded from the scene. Nearly 150 years later Lancelot Hogben resurrected political arithmetic in a book of that title, while as recently as 1980 Halsey was claiming that he was following the tradition of Petty and Graunt in his study of educational mobility.

The population controversy, however, did not go away, and the publication in 1798 of Malthus's *Essays on Population* led significant numbers of Members of Parliament to fear that the population would soon be increasing at a rate that would outstrip the means of subsistence; the only way to be definitely sure what was happening was to take a census. Accordingly, a Bill was put forward in Parliament in 1800 and it passed all its stages without opposition in the House of Commons, and the first census followed in 1801.

The responsibility for making the count of the population was given to the overseers of the poor or, in default of them, to 'some substantial householder in each parish, township, or place'. Three questions were put to them. First, they were asked 'How many inhabited houses are there in your parish, township, or place; by how many families are they occupied; and how many houses therein are unoccupied?' The second question was 'How many persons (including children of whatever age) are there actually found within the limits of your parish, township, or place, at the time of taking this account, distinguishing males from females, and exclusive of men actually serving in His Majesty's Service or belonging to registered vessels?' The last question was 'What number of persons in your parish, township or place are chiefly employed in agriculture; how many in trade, manufactures or handicraft; and how many are not comprised in any of the preceding classes?' The overseers were required to obtain this information 'by proceeding together or separately from house to house or otherwise' as they might judge expedient. No method or system for collecting the information was given or even suggested. When the returns were examined it was clear that there had been a number of misunderstandings. What was taken to be a 'house' and whether it was 'inhabited' was variously understood; for example, some houses were in the process of being built and, although almost ready to be occupied, may have been counted among the empty.[14] In consequence, when questions were framed for the next census an addition was made to the first, namely, 'How many houses are now being built and therefore not yet inhabited?' Similarly, it had been obscure whether 'employed' meant 'actively engaged in' or 'dependent upon' agriculture or industry. A Report on the Census in 1811 recognised that this question produced 'no result in 1811, if indeed an incorrect result be not worse than none, as giving colour and foundation to unfounded speculations'.

Political economy and statistics

The 1801 Census was only one manifestation in the early nineteenth century of a growing desire, certainly among the social and political elite, to know about the world and to collect all manner of facts that appeared to be relevant to a situation. The development of the natural sciences had provided a successful model of how painstaking observation and rational theory building could solve physical problems. Political economists felt that economic and social problems could be solved in a similar fashion. They believed not only that economic theory could be tested by the collection of empirical data, but also that problems and controversies that had for a long time remained unresolved could now be settled. There was much talk of the discovery of social scientific 'laws' through the processes of quantification. However, political economists derived their laws deductively from their theories, and had always been suspicious of the inductive proclivities of the political arithmeticians. Although political arithmetic had died away, the new science of 'statistics' was becoming increasingly popular; but political economists were jealous of their own success, of their influence and of their 'principles', and simply transferred their suspicion to the new science. They were careful to distinguish the two. While both were concerned with facts, 'the object of statisticians', wrote McCulloch in his *Principles of Political Economy* in 1825, was 'to describe the condition of a particular country at a particular period', while the goal of the political economist was 'to discover the causes which have brought it to that condition, and the means by which its wealth and riches may be indefinitely increased'.[15] At the same time the political economists, including McCulloch himself, were becoming increasingly interested in statistical matters. At the very least they were compelled to take statistical information seriously by the great political question of the day: was English society deteriorating and heading towards revolution as the Tories were prone to claim, or was it progressing as the Whigs would have it? The issue of the 'condition of England' could be settled only by statistical information. However, the political economists wished to keep their 'principles' intact and instead of using quantitative data to test their theories they insisted on a division of labour between the descriptive science of statistics and their own theoretically based discipline. Both would be geared to issue of public policy, but each would apply its own expertise. This separation of inductive and deductive processes was crucial and was maintained in Britain for well over a century.

Some of the political economists urged that the Census should be improved in order to provide more statistical information. Others, however, suggested the formation of a new society exclusively devoted to the collection of facts. The proposal lay dormant for a couple of years, but at a meeting of the British Association for the Advancement of Science in 1833 the presence of the Belgian statistician Quetelet along with Malthus and Charles Babbage precipitated the formation of a statistical section of the Association. This in turn became responsible for initiating a whole series of statistical societies that sprang up all over Britain. The earliest of these, the Manchester Society, had a strong and explicit reform interest. The first annual report of the Society averred that it owed its origin 'to a strong desire felt by its projectors to assist in promoting the progress of social improvement in the manufacturing population by which we are surrounded'.[16] The founders believed a precondition for this reform to be serious and extensive efforts to describe exactly the condition of the poor. It embarked on a number of pioneering inquiries whose form was to set the pattern for other statistical societies to follow. This was the house-to-house survey in which either members of the Society or 'paid agents' literally went from house to house along a street asking about working and living conditions.

The first such inquiry was into '4,102 Families of Working Men in Manchester'.[17] It was organised by a committee of the Society which prepared a questionnaire and employed an agent to go from door to door to collect the desired information. What was remarkable about this particular study, however, was that having selected an area highly populated by the working class, the agent apparently visited 'almost one in every two houses'.[18] This was a very early example of sampling — almost certainly the first — but its potential does not appear to have been recognised at the time even by other members of the Society. It is quite likely that they themselves did not perceive what they were doing as particularly significant or innovatory in terms of research techniques. No further reference to the idea of sampling occurs in any other of its reports, which tended to use complete enumerations. The development of sampling of respondents as a useful device in sociological research had to wait another 70 years.

A descriptive survey emerged with data on country of origin, rent paid, education of children, religion and type of dwelling. The results were apparently of such interest that they were read twice before the Statistical Section of the British Association at Edinburgh in 1834.[19] It was decided to extend the survey to other areas of Manchester and Salford and the outlying towns of Bury, Ashton, Stalybridge and Dukinfield. This time four agents were hired to make a house-to-house investigation, but instead of an interview schedule, they were given a list of questions which were modified to deal with contingencies in the course of the 17-month inquiry.[20] The Society's committee began by reading daily reports submitted by the agents to assess their accuracy by making comparisons with other data and by using informants. In some cases a second agent re-interviewed selected samples to check the reliability of the first interviews. In those instances where the interviewer made a rating, for example on the condition of the dwellings, he was provided with rough indices. A house was 'well furnished' if it contained 'a table and chairs, a clock, a chest of drawers, and a fair stock of necessary utensils' while a 'comfortable' house was 'clean, neatly arranged, and protected from the outside air, even where somewhat bare of furniture'.[21] The results were presented in tabular form and were discussed in a way that either qualified the findings or attempted to clarify potential misunderstandings of the categories used. The authors drew no conclusions; instead they stressed that more comparative data were needed before any inferences could be made.[22]

The Society also undertook a number of empirical studies of education between 1834 and 1841, again organised by a special committee. Whether or not this committee was composed of the same or some of the same individuals is obscure; the reports did not list the names of those involved. However, there were certainly marked differences between these studies and the ones concerning working-class conditions. The reports of these inquiries gave no explicit statements about how they were carried out except that the material was gathered by an agent of the Society. Most of the inquiries described the categories of schools, presented the tables without comment and concluded that the education of the working classes required great improvement. Lack of comparative data did not keep these researchers from drawing conclusions and suggesting policy reforms. One such report was on the condition of education in Pendleton. This was a house-to-house examination 'with a view to ascertain by that process the actual amount of schooling obtained by the people, and, if possible, to gather some information as to the results of such instruction'.[23] There appeared to be no questionnaire, for the authors of the report say: 'In conversing with the parents and children on this subject, the agent found that out of 2,657 cases of minors, who were either then or had been formerly at day or evening school, he could find nothing satisfactory regarding 716'.[24] The many quotes in the footnotes further suggest that the agent was simply noting what people told him in general conversation.

The Statistical Society of London

The statistical society that attracted most of the public attention, however, was the Statistical Society of London which was founded in 1834 as a result of a formal proposal by none other than Malthus. It was able to bring together government officials, party politicians and distinguished individuals. Abrams comments that 'in its early years the Council of the Society often looked like a sub-committee of a Whig Cabinet'.[25] However, because the Society was an offshoot of the Statistics Section of the British Association it had to represent statistics among the sciences as well as accomplish the goal set by Malthus: 'the collection and classification of all facts illustrative of the present condition and prospects of society'. The latter objective meant that statistics should be relevant to the needs of the day — a science of man that would be of direct service to the statesman and legislator. Statistics were seen as 'state-istics' or politically useful information needed by the statist. As such, statistics could hardly avoid becoming entangled in political issues. Nor could the Society limit itself purely to numerical facts to which the Statistics Section of the British Association was restricted. The solution it adopted was contained in the Prospectus of the Society:

> The Statistical Society will consider it to be the first and most essential rule of its conduct to exclude all Opinion from its transactions and publications and to confine its attention rigorously to facts, and as far as may be found possible, to facts which can be stated numerically and arranged in tables.[26]

In this way science was to be reconciled with politics and objectivity with relevance. Symbolising their vow to exclude all opinion was their motto — *aliis exterendum* — 'to be threshed out by others'. The aim was simply to gather the facts, leaving it to others to draw whatever conclusions might be warranted. The political economists had already accepted a distinction between political economy and statistical science, and their role in creating the philosophy of *aliis exterendum* was manifest in the first issue of the Society's journal which declared:

> The Science of Statistics differs from Political Economy because although it has the same end in view, it does not discuss causes, nor reason upon probable effects; it seeks only to collect, arrange, and compare, that class of facts which alone can form the basis of correct information with respect to social and political government.[27]

This philosophy implied that the facts, once collected, were unchallengeable. Their presentation and arrangement in tables of figures meant that it was a kind of scientific social bookkeeping or 'accounting'. Social accounting was thus a form of statistical science that had a clear subject matter — the condition of society — and a preferred form of presentation. The philosophy of excluding all opinion did not, however, exclude the search for causes and it was in this endeavour that sociological — as opposed to social — inquiry was to emerge.

The Society began its studies ambitiously with a programme of 'interrogatories'. Committees were appointed to pursue various investigations; one was 'for the purpose of prosecuting statistical enquiries into the state of education in a portion of the parishes of London' and another 'to collect a statistical account of the various strikes and combinations which have existed in different parts of the UK for the purpose of altering the rate of wages and of introducing new regulations between masters and men'.[28] The committee responsible for the latter study prepared a 'numerous list of queries' (some 57 in all) designed 'to elicit the complete impartial history of strikes'. Copies of these queries were 'transmitted to many intelligent individuals connected with, or interested in the welfare of manufacturers and other industrial pursuits in which large bodies of operators are employed'. These 'intelligent individuals', however, were not a general sample of the population, but the relevant authorities — the police, hospital and poor-law administrators, school managers, factory commissioners and so on. Returns were few and only a couple of reports were published.[29] The dangers of relying on self-completed questionnaires in a society not used to form filling had already been evident in Sinclair's abortive attempts to produce a Statistical Account of England in 1793. The only successful method was to send out 'agents' who collected information and interviewed informants themselves.

The Society began publishing its own journal in 1838 — the *Journal of the Statistical Society of London*. This was to be devoted to 'the collection of Facts which illuminate the condition of mankind, and tend to develop the principles by which the progress of society is determined'. In practice the development of 'principles' was not a major concern. Although less explicit than in the case of the Manchester Statistical Society, the London Society, too, was primarily interested in social reform. In the first volume, in an unsigned article presumably by the editor, the Society was classified along with other reform societies as having the purpose of improving the conditions of the labouring classes. It said:

> One of the distinguishing characteristics of the present era in this country is the increasing desire which exists on the part of the higher classes of society to improve the condition and to raise the character of the poor and labouring classes. . . . Benevolent individuals are united in numerous societies for the purpose of enquiring accurately into the state of the poor; of searching out the true character of their wants; and, lastly, of pointing out and endeavouring to remove the obstacles which at present hinder national improvement. Such, for instance, are the various Statistical Societies, and the Central Society of Education, for the purpose of enquiry; . . .

The Statistical Society of London differed, however, in one important respect from the Manchester one in that it thought of itself almost as a branch of government, and that one of its primary responsibilities was to provide the two Houses of Parliament and their many commissions with the data necessary to carry out rational and efficient social reform. In 1855 the Council of the Society reported that one of the functions of the Society was 'to prepare matters for that great assembly [Parliament], and that duty it appeared to be performing well'.[30] When Parliament had either passed the specific reform, or undertook the investigation itself, the members of the Society could see no reason for pursuing the topic any further. Social researchers were primarily interested in social reform, thought of themselves as reformers, and abandoned a problem when it was no longer significant for that purpose.

In its early years the Society prided itself on the degree to which it kept to its philosophy of social accounting. Many articles were limited to detailed description and presentation of numerical facts. Certainly every article presented numbers, usually arranged in tables, sometimes with very little comment. The facts were intended to speak for themselves and often consisted of minute details, for example of the number of people with particular diseases, or committing various offences, and even of the condition of the surface and sewerage of particular streets in Leeds. Yet opinions could scarcely be concealed. In an article entitled 'On the Establishment of County and District Schools for the Truancy of the Pauper Children maintained in Union Workhouses' Kay-Shuttleworth averred that children 'should not be taught to consider themselves as paupers'. Such a result could 'scarcely be avoided if those who had lost their natural guardians are trained in the workhouse, under the same roof, and in unavoidable contact with paupers'.[31]

Some researchers did, however, attempt to go beyond simple description to interpret or explain some of the data. The Reverend John Clay, in an article entitled 'Criminal Statistics of Preston',[32] was concerned with the causes of crime. Clay was chaplain to the Preston House of Correction and he used his position to interview the prisoners. However, his 'causes' were more a reflection of his moral standpoint than of any objective attempt to discover patterns of relationships between variables and included drinking, idleness, bad company, weak intellects, temptation and so on. He nevertheless did try to show from a table presenting age and sex by cause of crime the importance of each one of his causes, and later tried to account for the variation in crime rates from year to year.

Much data clearly already existed, enabling some of the early statisticians to confine themselves to secondary analysis. Some data were held by government departments but were not accessible to the public. An early feature of the Society's journal was that government officials would condense statistics from official sources and then simply present them to the Society. Others, however, attempted to go further by analysing and interpreting the data they had available. In 1839 Rawson presented 'An Inquiry into the Statistics of Crime in England and Wales' in which he set out to show that social phenomena were subject to general laws as evidenced by the regularity and uniformity of recorded social data. Using judicial statistics for the years 1835 to 1839 and material from the 1831 Census, he managed to show that crime prevailed to the greatest extent in large towns, that it was very much below the average in mining counties, in Wales and in the mountainous districts of the North of England.

Rawson was a prolific writer who covered topics ranging from the railways in Belgium to the then French colonies in north Africa. However, most of his work was based on secondary analysis of existing data rather than on data he had himself collected. This was also true for Joseph Fletcher, a barrister, who analysed the relationship between crime and education.[33] In an article on 'The Progress of Crime in the United Kingdom' he compared the education of criminals with the education of the general population, and concluded from data on the number of criminals who could write that there was 'an excess of instruction greatly on the side of crime, especially in the case of criminals'.[34] Later, in a very long article entitled 'Moral and Educational Statistics of England and Wales' (1849), he presented no fewer than 80 pages of minutely detailed comparative tables. Although, once again, he found that in some areas the criminal population appeared to be better educated than the population at large, he attempted to explain this 'paradox' by arguing that the indicator of education used — the percentage of signatures by marks in the marriage registers — could not always show a 'careful uprearing of the young . . . that is alone blessed to the good of righteous living in a Christian hope'.[35]

The earliest attempt specifically to set up and then test an hypothesis was probably that made by William Guy in 1843 in an article entitled 'An Attempt to determine the Influence of the Seasons and Weather on Sickness and Mortality'. He found that the atmospheric condition that exercised the most marked influence on sickness and mortality was temperature. Guy, who was Professor of Medicine at King's College, London, and Honorary Secretary to the Society, continued to publish a series of articles on the influence of various conditions on health, for example 'Influence of Employment upon Health' in which he summarised the main relationships between sex, sedentary occupations and certain diseases.[36]

Guy also wrote the earliest articles on quantitative techniques. In 1839 in 'On the Value of the Numerical Method as Applied to Science, but especially to Physiology and Medicine' he discussed the effect of increasing the number of observations made on the validity of the conclusions. Later in 1850 he wrote 'On the Relative Value of Averages derived from different numbers of observations' in which he formulated the bases for probability theory and sampling by showing that the larger the number of observations the less the variation in the averages calculated from successive groups.

The first attempt consciously to replicate an earlier study was reported by a committee of the Society in 1841 in an article entitled 'Report on the Condition of the Working Class in the Town of Kingston-upon-Hull'. The replication was of the pioneering study carried out by the Manchester Statistical Society in 1838 in an extensive manufacturing district in Manchester. The idea of replication as a deliberate research procedure, however, was not recognised at the time as a significant or useful 'innovation' and did not reappear until 1925 when Bowley and Hogg replicated Bowley's own earlier study of 1915.

Statistical societies were begun in many of the large industrial cities, in particular Bristol, Liverpool, Belfast, Birmingham, Leeds and Glasgow. Many others were mooted, but some never reached a formal level of existence. The Bristol Society was probably the most active and a number of its surveys were published in the *Journal of the Statistical Society of London*, which acted as an outlet for the publication of reports of those societies that lacked a journal.[37] Close connections with the British Association were maintained and the London journal continued to report papers read to the Statistical Section at their annual meetings. The British Association itself also supported surveys. For example in 1839 it gave £150 for studying the state of the working classes 'specified in the form of numerical tables' and £50 for inquiries into the statistics of collieries on the Tyne and Wear.

It was, too, in the same period that Sinclair's *Statistical Account of Scotland* was replicated. The original copy had been given to the Society for the Sons and Daughters of the Clergy. Its Secretary, Sir Henry Jardine, proposed to the Society that it should produce a *New Statistical Account of Scotland* and a committee was set up to achieve this end. The Committee's desire was intimated to the General Assembly of the Church of Scotland in 1832. The latter body 'was pleased to approve of the undertaking' and to 'recommend to the members of the Church to give all the aid in their power toward its completion'.[38] The work was completed in 1845 when it was published in 15 volumes. The *New Statistical Account* was almost exactly a replication of the one produced by Sinclair; the parochial clergy were asked to give a description of their respective parishes using a questionnaire along the same lines as Sinclair's. However, unlike the earlier work, this one was arranged by county. It was a little more statistical than the earlier version and perhaps for that reason had lost a little of its charm.

A growing number of people were able to undertake survey work, not the least of whom were those connected with the rise of the factory inspection system in England. Sizeable staffs were collected for the purpose of interviewing employers, local clergymen, other local authorities and the workers themselves.[39] In one study conducted between 1840 and 1842 the employers filled out 'tabular forms' so that the Commission could obtain a complete record of the number of children employed and of the conditions under which they worked. Some 20 sub-commissioners were used to investigate conditions at first hand and to take evidence. They did more than question witnesses: 'The Commissioners, in order that they might be better qualified to report on [the mines], thought it desirable that some of their body should see a few instances of underground labour, and make themselves acquainted with the nature of it, by personal observation'.[40] A number of them apparently became sick as a result of their work, but until these reports were written, there were simply no accounts of such labour.[41]

The Statistical Department of the Board of Trade was founded in 1832 to improve and collate the growing number of returns made to Parliament in a routine manner or called for by its members. George Porter and Rawson W. Rawson were appointed to be in charge of the work. Porter in particular had grandiose plans for the collection of all kinds of data, which amounted to little, while Rawson coveted taking over criminal statistics from the Home Office. By 1836 it was clear that there were limits to what could be achieved by a government body. The pattern that began to emerge in its annually published tables was the inclusion of statistics from three different types of sources. There was the reproduction of other official data with occasional additions from, for example, the Colonial and Home Offices. Second, information was collected from certain institutions of a semi-official character, and finally Porter was forced to rely on the 'co-operation of many intelligent and well-informed gentlemen in various parts of the Kingdom'.[42] Many such gentlemen, however, were unwilling to divulge what information they had. The annual tables grew in volume, but their main fault was their apparent aimlessness; everything that came to hand was printed. The collection of such useless material was accompanied by an inability to provide useful, even necessary, statistics.

Under the Registration Act of 1836 the General Register Office was set up to index the returns of births, deaths and marriages from a two-tiered system of registrars and superintendant registrars. Registration of deaths was compulsory, but not of births, which resulted in considerable and largely indeterminate under-registration of the latter. The compiler of the statistics was William Farr, who realised that the information was useful only in broad outline. There was little dross in the early reports and he cut out inessential detail.[43]

Developments in criminology

It was in the field of criminology, however, that some of the most sophisticated developments in research techniques took place. Cole, examining the continuity in this area, found six monographs making use of governmental statistics on crime (which had been available since 1836) and about 20 articles published between 1839 and 1857, and he concluded that the continuity between these years was 'rather impressive'.[44] Practically every author both criticised the work of other criminologists and used such work as support for his own. These studies were cumulative and significant progress was made, for example, in the use of age-specific rates of crime. The predominant mode of analysis was 'ecological', that is, the association between two or more variables would be compared within geographic areas, usually counties. Occasionally, comparisons were made over a period of time in a single area. A typical example was one in which population density was compared with crime rates in the 40 English counties. Symons, for example, arranged the counties in order of population density in one column, and in order of crime rate in another adjacent column. Not possessing a statistical tool such as the Spearman rank correlation co-efficient, he drew his conclusions on the basis of inspection. He concluded that the relationship was very close, but he failed to explain why population density caused crime.[45]

The culmination of this research activity was a remarkable but largely unknown monograph by Thomas Plint called *Crime in England*, which was published in 1851. Plint criticised the way Fletcher had grouped counties together and showed that the grouping was both arbitrary and, because averages were calculated, hid variations within counties. He pointed to the overall threefold increase in the number of convicted criminals per 100,000 of population between 1801 and 1845 in England, and argued that this did not show that the mass of the people were degenerating; rather, the growth and increasing wealth of the town population increased the opportunities for certain classes of offence against property. This produced an increase in the criminal class while the general population was growing in knowledge and morality. Criminals congregated where crimes were possible − in the big cities. As Plint himself put it: 'They congregate where there is plenty of plunder, and verge enough to hide'.[46] Plint then went on to show that crime was increasing much more slowly in the densely populated counties; that indeed in some it was actually declining. It was noticeable that the increase in crime was most rapid in the counties in which crime on the whole was the least. In counties densely popu-lated the incentives and occasions of crime had nearly reached their maximum.

Having demonstrated that it was not ignorance that was the cause of crime, Plint avoided substituting another monocausal theory; rather, crime was the result of a number of factors. He showed that 'certain variations in the price of food, and concomitant variations in the amount of employment of labour, are always accompanied by an increase in the number of criminals committed'.[47] In comparing crime in manufacturing and agricultural areas he used three-variable analysis to control for confounding variables; thus, when the population was split into age groups, there was no longer any relationship between type of county and crime. Plint explained that this was because 'whilst juvenile crime has been decreasing and the total crime either greatly retarded in its onward progress, or actually diminishing, the amount of crime committed by persons betwixt 20 and 30 years has augmented in a degree perfectly astounding'. If account was taken of the differing age structure between counties, of the differing proportions of the labouring classes, and of the crime committed by the migrant population who *came* to the manufacturing areas, then the 'moral condition' of the manufacturing areas as indicated by the 'corrected' crime rates was more favourable than that in the agricultural areas. In short, 'the morality of the manufacturing population ranks above the agricultural'.[48]

Plint, in effect, was saying that crime in towns was higher only because towns had a higher proportion of persons aged 15 to 30 and in the 'operative classes'. He deduced from this that it was not manufacturing as such that produced crime and immorality, but the socio-structural conditions in the towns. 'This', says Cole, 'is equivalent to controlling for all social differences between blacks and whites and then concluding that there is no difference in unemployment rates, or that whites in fact have higher unemployment than blacks'.[49] Cole concludes that Plint was using the new social science in defence of the industrial system and its accompanying social conditions, but this did not detract from the 'brilliant quality' of the book.[50]

Empirical sociology

Much of the empirical inquiry into social conditions that was carried out before 1851 had thus gone well beyond a simple descriptive sociography. It was more than just 'social' research — it was empirical sociology in embryo. There had been many developments in techniques and methods of inquiry: the use of parish and other records to derive demographic regularities and patterns, the introduction of tabular analysis with calculations of percentages and averages, the sampling of respondents, the use of 'paid agents' to conduct interviews using interview schedules and the use of mailed questionnaires. There had been replications of earlier studies and explicitly formulated hypotheses had been tested using quantitative data. There were cross-tabulations of variables, three-variable and multivariate analyses, some of a quite sophisticated kind, for the manipulation of data and the discovery of 'causes' while controlling for extraneous factors. The bases of probability theory for sampling procedures had been formulated, while the use of indicators to measure variables of more general conceptual and theoretical significance had been developed, particularly by the criminologists. There were careful analyses of secondary sources, and journal articles on quantitative techniques, while a concern for the accuracy of their data led many researchers to check their sources, for example by re-interviewing samples of respondents.

Unfortunately, except in the case of the English criminologists for a brief period, most of these developments were non-cumulative. Researchers seldom built upon the work of their predecessors and were as likely to begin again from scratch. Progress was very uneven with later research in some cases being less sophisticated and inferior to earlier studies. There were no norms and values for the conduct of empirical inquiry and there was no growing or accumulating body of 'principles' of research, so that everything the researchers did was in a sense 'new'; at the same time nothing was *recognised* as an 'innovation' or as a 'development' since that presupposed an acknowledged set of previously agreed practices. The result was that once the initial enthusiasm had worn off, research became ossified and unable to progress in any new directions. Innovations tended to be isolated events, unrecognised and unperceived as such by contemporaries and successors alike. Many were forgotten, perhaps only to be 'rediscovered' decades later as if nothing like them had been known before. The social accountants never were committed to the development of a science of society; their objective was social reform. Empirical investigation seemed to be a promising way of laying the basis for it, yet it soon became apparent that collecting social facts was expensive, time-consuming, and did not always — if ever — provide the basis for discovering systematically what were the 'best' ways to alleviate social evils. Collecting facts about illiteracy and schooling could not, for example, determine whether or not education should be a national system controlled by the church.

Researchers still believed that copious details were necessary for the efficient administration of reform, even though they themselves did not see what reforms followed from their inquiries. Many, like Eden, believed it was simply a matter of its being beyond their competence to formulate such policies. To others — and this was still true of Booth in the 1890s — if appropriate policies did not suggest themselves from systematic inquiry, then what was lacking was more information. To fellows of the Statistical Society of London what was needed was the exclusion of opinion entirely from their transactions in order to be able to concentrate upon the task of obtaining more and more accurate information. When policies were suggested they were more frequently based on a restatement of one or more current and fashionable conventional wisdoms than on the data so copiously collected. Facts did not and could not speak for themselves, nor could they really be separated from opinion. The collection and presentation of even the simplest numerical distributions was clearly influenced at every level by implicit theory and unspoken opinion. The assumption that the gradual accumulation of massive statistical information would, of its own accord and in due course, provide sufficient evidence to prove or to disprove social theories was a crucial mistake. The techniques of causal analysis were woefully inadequate to the task of demonstrating what *were* the efficient causes. Selection of 'causes' like drink, idleness, and 'bad company' were more a manifestation of researchers' own opinions and prejudices than the outcome of systematic analysis of the facts.

At the same time the development of government institutions to gather statistics and the creation of royal commissions to investigate such subjects as the poor laws, factory conditions, the Irish poor and religious instruction, meant that there were opportunities of a seductive kind to reform-minded individuals to avail themselves of a more direct path to reform than by conducting social research on their own. In the two decades between 1841 and 1860 some 130 commissions were appointed. On occasions, members of the London and Manchester Statistical Societies were employed as assistant commissioners to gather the data. The most notable example was the appointment of Sir James Kay-Shuttleworth to the position of Assistant Poor Law Commissioner in 1835. In 1839 he became secretary to the Committee of Council for Education, and High Sheriff of Lancashire in 1863. Five members of the Manchester Society were elected to Parliament in the period of the early surveys, three of whom had been involved in the surveys. It also happened at this time that the most active phases of the Anti-Corn Law League and the agitation for local government reform occurred, so interests, money, and manpower became further diverted into other causes.

The result of all these factors was that by the late 1840s there was already a decline in social research activity. All the provincial statistical societies disappeared except for the Manchester Society, and even there membership fell while financial problems loomed large as it was discovered that surveys were expensive. There was a shift away from original surveys after 1841 and although there was a renewal of activity in the 1850s, it was not of empirical research. The trend was towards historical essays and discussions of more general questions of political economy. Even the London Society shifted its interest away from social surveys of working-class conditions and turned instead to questions of public health, vital statistics, health of the troops, morality in the colonies, and the duration of life in different occupations, for all of which secondary data sufficed.

The state of the working classes

The period in which the statistical societies had flourished was one of rapid industrialisation and urbanisation, of working-class protest and collective activity, of government intervention in the factories, mines, in the towns and in education. Above all there was the problem of urban poverty. The government's attempts at legislation in the early 1830s were not notably successful and tended to create more disillusion and anger than hope. The 1832 Reform Act extended the vote only to the middle classes in the borough constituencies. Disappointment amongst those active in working-class political organisations (who had given strong support to the Whig government in passing the Act) resulted in Chartist demands for further political reform from 1836 onwards. The 1833 Factory Act caused more protest from reformers than it did praise, while the Poor Law Amendment Act of 1834 turned out to be exceedingly harsh in its application. The workers turned to collective action and 1834 saw both an attempt at a national formation of trade unions and the transportation of the 'Tolpuddle Martyrs'.

In the 1840s Chartism was a potent political force that the middle classes feared, while trade unionism continued to make progress, and the Rochdale Pioneers began their retailers' co-operative movement in 1844. There were unsuccessful attempts to pass further factory legislation in Parliament in 1838, 1839 and 1841. The Mines Act of 1842, however, stopped the employment of women below ground and no boy under 10 years of age was to be employed. The Factory Act of 1844 put further limitations on the hours of work of women and children, while the Ten Hours Bill of 1847 finally limited the hours of all children to 10 a day. Progress in public health measures was much slower, and only one Act had been passed by 1850, even though Chadwick's famous Report which established the connection between dirt and disease had been published in 1842. Standards and conditions in the schools were for the most part very unsatisfactory and education was neither free nor compulsory. Although, largely as a result of the activity of Kay-Shuttleworth, there was by the late 1840s a fairly wide acceptance of the idea that it was right and proper for the government to encourage the development of schools for the working classes, such education was seen to consist of the minimum amount of instruction necessary to keep the working classes contented and reconciled to their lowly station in life.

Members of the various statistical societies were mostly middle-class men who were professionals, industrialists or members of the establishment, and they espoused policies of free trade and economic laissez-faire.[51] They were suspicious of the factory reformers and

31

preferred to see the towns rather than the factories as the major source of social ills. To them it was urbanisation and the physical environment that it produced that determined the habits and character of the people; making surveys of their actual condition was the obvious first step to be taken towards its improvement. The goal, however, was not the formation of a welfare state, but the creation of an environment that would foster a thrifty and virtuous working class. Improvements in public health and education were to be the main planks of this enterprise and these topics formed the hard core of the statistical movement.[52] The moral stance taken by the early empirical sociologists towards the lifestyles of the poor was clear from the questions included in their schedules. Their calculations of the numbers of persons per bed were taken not only as proof of destitution and discomfort, but also of a 'fruitful source of evil'.[53] The first report of the Bristol Statistical Society tabulated the possession of books, deposits in friendly societies, the number of prints on the walls and the command of skills of 'domestic economy' by men and women.[54] Indices of this type were taken to illustrate the 'wretched and barbarous condition' of the workers in the towns. Notes were frequently made of the physical condition of the people in which 'clean', 'healthy' and 'respectable' were the clearly desired characteristics to be compared with 'dirty', 'disreputable' and 'drinks a lot'. The quest for indices of degradation sometimes reached extraordinary limits. A committee of the Statistical Society of London reporting on 'the state of the working classes in the Parishes of St. Margaret and St. John, Westminster'[55] found that the number of 'theatrical and amatory pictures' exceeded the 'serious' ones. At the same time there was no attempt to assess the effects of low wages or unemployment, or to look at income and expenditure. The last house-to-house survey reported in the *Journal of the Statistical Society of London* in 1848 listed individual dwellings in Church Lane, St Giles, in terse detail based on personal observation. Morally and ideologically the authors of the report were very explicit; they clearly ascribed degeneracy to the physical environment, claiming that it was 'physically impossible to preserve the ordinary decencies of life in such circumstances'. The solution was the provision of model dwellings for 'that large class of our labouring population which is prepared to adopt habits of cleanliness and decency'.[56]

The political and social ferment of the times, which saw its most vociferous expression in the form of Chartism, gave rise to fears among the middle classes of violence arising out of industrial unrest. No doubt such fears were mixed with genuine feelings of sympathy with, if not guilt about, the conditions under which the working classes lived. Yet views about the direction reform should take were numerous and inquiry failed to provide any clearest guidance on the matter.

Parliament seemed best able to promote factory legislation. The statistical societies focused their attention on the urban environment, but their sucess in promoting legislation, or even the idea of such legislation, in that area is questionable.

Yet another direction was advocated by a group of novelists who wrote about the relationships between workers and their employers. These 'industrial' novels began with Harriet Martineau's *A Manchester Strike* (1832), but the apotheosis of the tradition was seen in Disraeli's *Conningsby* (1844) and *Sybil* (1845), in Mrs Gaskell's *Mary Barton* (1848) and *North and South* (1855), and in Dickens's *Hard Times* (1854). Dickens was harsh in his judgement of industrialism. Behind the relationships between workers and employers lay the utilitarian philosophy, epitomised by Thomas Gradgrind. The work of the social statisticians was all 'Gradgrindery' in the world of *Hard Times*. Disraeli himself implied similar criticisms when he once quoted, presumably with approval, Mark Twain's well known comment about there being three kinds of lies: 'lies, damn lies, and statistics'.

Like the social accountants the industrial novelists had sympathy for the plight of the workers, but saw the solution in terms of enlightened and benevolent employers rather than in terms of ameliorating the debasing conditions of the urban environment. Like the social accountants they never really faced up to the possibility of collective industrial action on the part of the workers, but instead of just ignoring such action they scorned any expression of working-class solidarity. Trade unionists were presented in their novels as the treacherous workers' delegates in *Sybil* or as the incompetent and untrustworthy Slackbridge in *Hard Times*. Strikes and mass demonstrations always degenerated into chaotic and bloody riots.[57] Although the industrial novelists saw themselves as describing working-class life in a realistic and vivid manner, and although the characters in the novels were intended to be in some sense 'representative', scenes of physical violence between employers and workers abounded in dramatic fashion.[58] This was probably more the imaginative working out of underlying fears than a description of the commonplace.

Society was seen in terms of a two-class model of the rich and the poor — or 'two nations' as Disraeli called them — in which the workers and the employers, although economically interdependent, were in conflict, not because there was anything seriously wrong with the social fabric as it was, but because of the human failings, ignorance and lack of understanding of individuals on both sides. It was curious that in order to observe the working classes the urban novelists felt they had to travel north to the very heart of industrial England, symbolised in its greatness and its shame by Manchester.[59] There they explored for themselves parts of the towns where the industrial workers lived, and they presented the results through their middle-class characters who went on similar expeditions. Such expeditions had parallels with another form of empirical sociology which is the subject of the next chapter.

Notes

1   For details of the making of Domesday, see Galbraith, 1961.
2   Ibid., p.168.
3   Various of the questionnaires that Sinclair sent are given in volume XX, pp xxvii—xlii of *The Statistical Account of Scotland*. The questionnaire is also summarised in Lecuyer and Oberschall, 1968, p.41.
4   Catherine Sinclair, 1853, pp 17—19.
5   Sinclair, 1791—1799, vol.XX, p.xiv.
6   Sinclair, 1831.
7   For a recent study of Sinclair, see Mitchison, 1962.
8   Eden, 1797, Preface.
9   Clark, 1972, p.22, explains that the Bills were prepared by the Parish Clerk's Company, one of the city livery companies, and the first published specimen goes back to 1592. From 1603 they were published uninterruptedly once a week, and the number of parishes included in them was from time to time increased. The only plausible reason for their existence, says Clark, is that they were meant to give warning, or to allay false fears, of outbreaks of the plague.
10   The various arguments are summarised in Cullen, 1975.
11   See Strauss, 1954, p.203, who gives a biography of Petty.
12   See Glass, 1965, for a detailed account of King's work.
13   See Glass, 1952, for an account of this controversy.
14   See 'Report on the Best mode of taking the Census of the U.K. in 1841', *JSSL*, vol.III, 1840.
15   Quoted from Hilts, 1978, p.27.
16   Ashton, 1934, p.13 who gives a detailed account of the activities of the Manchester Statistical Society.
17   The report was never published. An abstract appears in the transactions of the Statistical Section of the British Association of 1834.
18   Ashton, 1934, p.21. The report itself did not actually refer to 'sampling' and there is no evidence that members of the Society used the term.
19   Loc. cit.
20   Elesh, 1972, p.52, gives a full list of these questions.
21   Quoted from Elesh, 1972, p.51.
22   The article was entitled 'On the Condition of the Working Classes in an Extensive Manufacturing District in 1834, 1835, and 1836'. It was published in London by James Ridgeway and R.H. Moore, and in Manchester by Bancks in 1838.

34

23 Published in the *JSSL*, vol.II, 1839, p.65.

24 Ibid., p.69.

25 Abrams, 1968, p.15.

26 'Prospectus' in *Annals of the Royal Statistical Society*, pp 22-8.

27 *JSSL*, vol.I, 1838, p.3.

28 Ibid., p.6.

29 Abrams, 1968, p.19.

30 *JSSL*, vol.18, 1855, p.101.

31 *JSSL*, vol.I, 1838, p.22.

32 Clay, 1839.

33 The relationship between crime and education had been hotly disputed since 1833 when the French statistician, Guerry, argued, against the conventional wisdom of the day, that education did not reduce crime. An account of this dispute is given in Cullen, 1975, pp 139-44.

34 *JSSL*, 1843, vol.VI, p.233.

35 Fletcher, 1848, p.346.

36 Guy, 1843, p.197.

37 See Cullen, 1975, pp 119-33 for details of the reports and some of the individuals involved in these societies.

38 Vol.I, 1845, p.i.

39 Glazer, 1964, p.7. It is unlikely that such people were trained in any way. They probably learned on-the-job.

40 *Children's Employment Commission. First Report of the Commissioners. Mines.* HMSO, 1842, pp 2, 3 and 5. Quoted from Glazer, 1964, p.8.

41 Glazer, 1964, p.8.

42 Cullen, 1975, p.24.

43 In Cullen's view, 1975, p.25, this entitled Farr to a wider recognition of a place among a small band of truly excellent practising social scientists in the nineteenth century.

44 Cole, 1972, p.106.

45 Symons, 1849.

46 Plint, 1851, p.19.

47 Ibid., p.44.

48 Ibid., p.100.

49 Cole, 1972, p.94.

50 Ibid., p.91.

51 See Cullen, 1975, p.135.

52 Loc. cit.

53 *JSSL*, vol.V, 1842, pp 213-5.

54 'An Account of an Enquiry into the State of 275 Poor Families in the City of Bristol', *JSSL*, vol.1, 1838.

55 *JSSL*, vol.III, 1840, pp 14-24.

56   'Report of the Committee of the Council of the Statistical Society of London to investigate the State of the Inhabitants and their Dwellings in Church Lane, St. Giles', *JSSL*, vol.XI, 1848, pp 1-16.

57   See Keating, 1971, p.229.

58   Ibid., p.227.

59   Ibid., p.3.

2 The social explorers

The idea of social exploration is one that pervaded both fictional and non-fictional literature in the nineteenth century[1] and from it emerged in the 1840s and 1850s a form of social inquiry that provided a distinct alternative to the somewhat dry social accounting of statistical aggregates. Social exploration is more than just a travelogue, an account of a journey during which the range and variety of human life is displayed in the manner of Daniel Defoe's *Tour thro' the Whole Island of Great Britain* (1724–26), or William Cobbett's *Rural Rides* (1830). It is more purposive, more geared to the discovery of the unknown and presupposes a rigid class structure in which a representative of one social class consciously sets out to explore, analyse and report upon the life of another class lower on the social scale. It tells the story of one person's journey into an alien culture and offers the detailed results of his findings. The most spectacular aspect of the explorer's role is not simply examining and writing about the lives of the poor, but temporarily becoming one of them. He must be prepared to confront and endure dangers and hardships similar to those of his more exotic anthropological counterparts.

The data that emerge from social exploration are typically qualitative, often emotive, frequently narrative and utilise the imagery of exploration primarily to draw attention to the inequalities in society and to force upon the reader an awareness of his social blindness. The urban poor are seen as strange 'tribes' or 'wandering hordes' who inhabit a separate 'territory' or 'dark continent' that remains to be 'penetrated' like the darkest forests of Africa and yet can be 'discovered' by the middle class and the wealthy in the very heart of Britain's industrial cities.

Engels and the Manchester slums

The earliest social explorer was almost certainly Frederick Engels, who came from a very wealthy family of cotton manufacturers in Barmen in Germany. There he was surrounded and impressed by the horrors of early industrial capitalism, in particular by the misery of the labouring classes, demoralised by poverty and drunkenness. He reacted against what he saw as the narrow and self-righteous moral sentiment of his family and became, like many other progressive German intellectuals in the late 1830s, a 'left Hegelian'.[2] In 1842, in his early twenties, Engels left for England, supposedly to train as a businessman in Manchester, where his family had been astute enough to establish a branch in the very cradle of industrial capitalism and where he was to remain for nearly two years. He spent part of his time working at the family mills just outside Manchester and at the city offices of Erman and Engels; but the remainder he devoted to reading literature, reports, parliamentary papers, books and pamphlets, newspapers and periodicals, as well as getting to know industrial England from personal experience. At the same time he was formulating his ideas that were to form the basis of his classic study *The Condition of the Working Class in England in 1844*.[3] In Manchester itself Engels went into action along several fronts. He made himself known to the Chartists and the Owenites; he attended their meetings, read their literature and became friendly with one of the Chartist leaders, James Leach. Additionally, he immersed himself into the turbulent political life of the period — the agitation against the New Poor Law, the factory reform movement, the Anti Corn Law League, trade unionism and sanitary reform. Quite what his connections were with the Manchester Statistical Society remains obscure. He certainly knew many of its members, but apart from Kay-Shuttleworth, whom he held in high regard, Engels's references to other members of the Society were all disparaging.

The study concentrated on 'The Great Towns' of London, Dublin, Edinburgh, Glasgow, Liverpool, Bristol, and the industrial towns of Yorkshire and Lancashire. It was only in these towns that, according to Engels, commerce and manufacture had attained their most complete development, that the concentration of property had reached its highest point and that the influence of these on the working classes was most clearly observable.[4] In his dedication 'To the Working-Classes of Great Britain' Engels told his readers:

> I wanted more than mere *abstract* knowledge of my subject, I
> wanted to see you in your own homes, to observe you in your
> every-day life, to chat with you on your condition and grievances,
> to witness your struggles against the social and political power of
> your oppressors. I have done so: I forsook the company of the
> dinner-parties, the port-wine and champagne of the middle classes,
> and devoted my leisure hours almost exclusively to the intercourse
> with plain Working-Men; I am both glad and proud of having done
> so.[5]

Certainly in Engels's descriptions there is a sense of regular and
prolonged walking of the streets. Of London he said that after 'roaming
the streets of the capital a day or two, making headway with difficulty
through the human turmoil and the endless lines of vehicles, after
visiting the slums of the metropolis, one realises that . . . '.[6] Of Bolton
he observed that it had, 'so far as I have been able to observe in my
repeated visits, but one main street, a very dirty one, Deansgate . . . '.[7]
However, it was Manchester that was the focus of Engels's attention. He
came to know its streets and houses more intimately than most of its
inhabitants (so he claimed) by walking them at all hours of the day and
night, on weekends and holidays. He was accompanied on many
expeditions by an illiterate Irish factory girl who introduced him into
working-class circles and into the domestic lives of the Manchester
proletariat.[8]

Engels discovered the social ecology of the city with its spatial
arrangements reflecting the social class structure. The town, he said,
was:

> peculiarly built, so that a person may live in it for years, and go in
> and out daily without coming into contact with the working-
> people's quarter or even with the workers, that is, so long as he
> confines himself to his business or to pleasure walks . . . .
> Manchester contains, at its heart, a rather extended commercial
> district, perhaps half a mile long and about as broad, and con-
> sisting almost solely of offices and warehouses . . . . This district
> is cut through by certain main thoroughfares upon which the
> vast traffic concentrates, and in which the ground level is lined
> with brilliant shops . . . unmixed working-people's quarters
> [stretch] like a girdle, averaging a mile and a half in breadth,
> around the commercial district. Outside, beyond this girdle,
> lives the upper and middle bourgeoisie . . . . And the finest part
> of this arrangement is this, that the members of this money
> aristocracy can take the shortest road through the middle of all

the labouring districts to their places of business, without ever seeing that they are in the midst of the grimy misery that lurks to the right and to the left.[9]

It was possible, Engels admitted, for anyone who knew Manchester to infer from changes in the character of the buildings that front the main streets the social characteristics of what was to be found behind them, but one was 'seldom in a position to catch from the street a glimpse of the real labouring districts'.[10] Engels then proceeded to a systematic area by area description of these districts that lay behind and hidden from the main streets. He began in the old town of Manchester in the north. There, even the better streets were narrow and winding, the houses 'dirty, old, and tumble-down, and the construction of the side streets utterly horrible'.[11] Here, one was 'in an almost undisguised working-men's quarter, for even the shops and beerhouses hardly take the trouble to exhibit a trifling degree of cleanliness'.[12] But all this was nothing compared with the horrors of the courts and lanes that lay behind. It was 'impossible to convey the idea' of the irregular cramming together of dwellings, crowded 'literally one upon the other', and of the 'filth and disgusting grime'. The words 'filth', 'excrement', 'refuse', '*débris*' and 'offal' Engels used many times in his descriptions; yet such rhetoric seemed inadequate to convey his impressions, so he specified in detail, for example: 'In one of these courts there stands directly at the entrance, at the end of a covered passage, a privy without a door, so dirty that the inhabitants can pass into and out of the court only by passing through foul pools of stagnant urine and excrement'.[13]

Engels described the view from Ducie Bridge at the bottom of which 'flows, or rather, stagnates, the Irk, a narrow, coal-black, foul-smelling stream, full of *débris* and refuse . . . . In dry weather, a long string of the most disgusting blackish-green, slime pools are left standing on the bank, from the depths of which bubbles of miasmatic gas constantly arise and give forth a stench unendurable even on the bridge 40 or 50 feet above the surface of the stream'.[14] Even this apparently failed to describe what 'surpassed all description', and on re-reading his account Engels felt that it was 'far from black enough to convey a true impression of the filth, ruin, and uninhabitableness, the defiance of all considerations of cleanliness, ventilation, and health, which characterise the construction of this single district, containing at least twenty to thirty thousand inhabitants'.[15] Engels's description moved in clockwise fashion round the belt of working-class districts, but the worst his language was able to convey was his description of an old man in Salford who was 'apparently about sixty years old, living in a cow-stable. He had constructed a sort of chimney for his square pen, which had neither windows, floor, nor ceiling, had obtained a bedstead and lived there, though the rain dripped in through his rotten roof. This man was too old and weak for regular work, and supported himself by removing manure with a hand-cart; the dung-heaps lay next door to his palace!'[16]

The focus of Engels's attention was largely the housing of the poor, which he took as an indicator of other conditions. As he put it: 'The manner in which the need for shelter is satisfied furnishes a standard for the manner in which all other necessities are supplied', although he did round off his account of the great towns by describing the tatty clothing of the people and the rotten food they consumed. However, the old man in his cow-shed was the nearest Engels came to describing the people. There is no feeling in Engels's account that he actually did chat to anybody, that he did ascertain their views, their habits, or how they saw themselves coping with their privations. It was not so much a description of a culture of poverty such as that so vividly portrayed by Henry Mayhew just five years later, as of the physical environment of poverty. Still, it was the first systematic use of personal experience as evidence to make a case. The imagery of exploration was not far below the surface when, for example, he commented that 'true, poverty often dwells in hidden alleys close to the palaces of the rich; but, in general, a separate territory has been assigned to it, where, removed from the sight of the happier classes, it may struggle along as it can'.[17] In several places he spoke of himself, or a road, or a railway as 'penetrating' these slum areas. His was the first account of the social ecology of a city; but he did more than just describe the spatial arrangements of the social classes. He interpreted the city as an interrelated social structure; as a living organism of mutually interdependent parts. While the separation of the classes was built into the very structure of the city, there was unity in the separation. The hidden suffering and squalor was connected with the riches and the lives of the bourgeoisie; the chaos of alleys, the little courts piled high in human excrement, were all inversely and inevitably related to the life of the middle classes, to the work performed in the factories, but above all to the structure of capitalist society as a whole.

In his preface to the first German edition Engels wrote that England was the only place where a project such as his could be undertaken. This was so because of the advanced character of its industrial and social development and because of the unique richness of documents and official reports and inquiries. These Engels used to the full.[18] The text of his book demonstrates that he had done considerable homework in parliamentary papers, books and pamphlets prepared by private investigators, and in current newspapers and periodicals. He clearly had consulted the *Journal of the Statistical Society of London*, for he reported results of some of the house-to-house inquiries made by members of the Society. He had read Edwin Chadwick's *Sanitary Conditions of the Labouring Classes in Great Britain* (1842) and based a great deal of his material on Kay-Shuttleworth's *The Moral and Physical Condition of the Working Class in the Cotton Manufacture in Manchester* (1832), for example to make comparisons between Manchester in 1832 and 1844. Paradoxically, such sources showed that there was nothing new or revelatory about Engels's descriptions of the physical environment in the big cities. He quoted *The Times* of 12 October 1843 as saying of London that 'within the most courtly precincts of the richest city on God's earth, there may be found, night after night, winter after winter, women − young in years and old in sin and suffering − outcasts of society − ROTTING FROM FAMINE, FILTH, AND DISEASE'.[19] Of Edinburgh, he quoted from Chadwick's Report of 1842 to the effect that in the dwellings of the poor, 'on the bed-posts chickens roost at night, dogs and horses share the dwellings of human beings, and the natural consequence is a shocking stench, with filth and swarms of vermin'.[20]

Engels's approach was an historic break with the German cultural tradition of philosophical−critical−social theorising; it was also something new to British empirical social research. Producing 'statistical accounts' of the condition of the working classes by sending round agents to collect quantitative information on wages, number of rooms, number of children, religious persuasion and so on was one thing. Interacting in a casual and informal manner with people whose life and culture were largely unknown to the researcher and observing over a period of time their living and working conditions was another. What was also new in Engels's study was not only the fact that his was the first that attempted to deal with *all* the workers of Britain and that the evidence was presented in a systematic fashion, but also that he tried to explain the conditions in theoretical terms. It had been competition on the land that had created the urban proletariat at the beginning of the industrial revolution, and it was competition both between and among classes that was responsible for the continued dehumanisation of the labouring classes. Under the free market economy of the capitalist system, labour was treated like any other commodity. The minimum wage was determined by what it took to keep a man alive, and the maximum by the competition between manufacturers and from other workers, particularly immigrants who were often willing to work for even lower wages. The workers produced by their labours more than the value of the wages they were paid; there was a 'surplus value' that constituted the capitalists' profit and was a measure of the degree of exploitation. The major results of industrialisation were disease, depression, drunkenness, crime, vice and prostitution. These were social phenomena, the inevitable result of the logical development of capitalist society, and were not to be explained by the weaknesses of individuals. 'Drunkenness', he claimed, 'has here ceased to be a vice, for which the vicious can be held responsible; it becomes a phenomenon, the necessary, inevitable effect of certain conditions upon an object possessed of no volition in relation to those conditions.'[21] Capitalism threw the new proletariat into a social hell in which they were underpaid, left to starve and to rot in slums, neglected, despised and coerced by the harsh factory discipline that was supported by bourgeois law. In this situation, Engels saw hope, however, that conditions would deteriorate still further to a point where revolution would become inevitable and the capitalist system would be overthrown.

Ideas that were to form the basis of Marx's theories were thus already apparent in Engels's study; furthermore, they were clearly related to an empirical base. In its conceptual and theoretical insights, in its use of concrete evidence and in its treatment of social phenomena like crime, child labour and drunkenness, the study remains a classic, but one that as a piece of empirical social research has been vastly underrated. To understand why, account would have to be taken of two main factors. First, it was half a century before Engels's book was translated into English and published in England where the study was carried out, and any impact of immediacy was totally lost. The subsequent history of its translators and translations has been uninspiring and in many ways unfortunate,[22] but just as Engels's book did appear in 1892, Charles Booth was already making an impact with his studies of the life and work of the people of London; the very people who might have recognised the import and significance of his study for empirical social research were busily engaged elsewhere. Second, Engels's subsequent lifelong association with Marx led critics and supporters alike to focus on Engels's (and Marx's) philosphical and political ideas, rather than on their attempts at empirical verification.[23] It was clear that Marx thought very highly of Engels's book and said so in many places, but from the point of view of empirical sociology in Britain he perhaps failed to stress the appropriate qualities.

Mayhew's accounts of the London poor

Just a few years after Engels had been exploring the slums of Manchester, a journalist, Henry Mayhew, was doing much the same in London. However, Mayhew's focus was on the people rather than on the conditions of their physical environment. He wanted to study the London poor, but in an industrial context, occupation by occupation, and then trade by trade. His idea was to investigate conditions of employment, particularly wage levels, and to relate these to the lifestyles of the poor. His implicit hypothesis was that low wages were the prime cause of poverty, and he wanted to find out what were the causes of low wages. He had no intention of conducting a house-to-house survey; that would be of little practical value in studying a trade. He did, however, want to be able to describe London life in the people's own language, and he felt that the opinions of the poor, particularly their own evaluations of their privations, were just as important as gathering facts about wage levels. Accordingly, he gathered thousands of pages of testimony from tailors, costermongers, needlewomen and so on by interviewing them in their own homes. His accounts were first published as a series of 82 'letters' in the *Morning Chronicle* in 1849 and 1850.[24] These letters averaged over 10,000 words each and 'seized public interest in a way that has scarcely ever been paralleled in British journalism'.[25]

Mayhew began by defining the poor as 'all those persons whose incomings are insufficient for the satisfaction of their wants — a want being, according to my idea, contra-distinguished from a mere desire by a positive physical pain, instead of a mental unease, accompanying it'.[26] This may well have been, as Yeo claims,[27] the first attempt to define a poverty line in the history of English social investigation, but it also gives more than a hint of Rowntree's definition of poverty half a century later, which was based on the notion of the amount of food necessary to maintain physical efficiency. Mayhew himself even spoke of those 'unable to obtain sufficient for their bodily necessities'.[28] He was an inveterate classifier, and he built up gigantic taxonomies by endlessly sub-dividing categories into yet more categories. He began by dividing the poor into 'two distinct classes, viz., the *honest* and *dishonest* poor'; the former he sub-divided into the 'striving' and the 'disabled'. In short, he proposed to consider 'the whole of the metropolitan poor under three separate phases, according as they *will* work, they *can't* work, and they *won't* work', a classification that became the basis of organisation for the remainder of the studies of the London poor.

Beginning with those who will work, Mayhew focused his attention on those who received no relief from the parish, and these included the poorly paid, the unfortunate and the improvident. Taking first the poorly paid, Mayhew wished to lay before his readers 'a catalogue of such occupations in London as yield a bare subsistence to the parties engaged in them', giving 'the weekly amount of income derived from each, together with the cause — if discoverable — for the inadequate return'. Following this, it was his intention

> to visit the dwellings of the unrelieved poor — to ascertain, by positive inspection, the condition of their homes — to learn, by

close communication with them, the real or fancied wrongs of their lot — to discover, not only on how little they subsist, but how large a rate of profit they have to pay for the little upon which they do subsist — to ascertain what weekly rent they are charged for their waterless, drainless, floorless, and almost roofless tenements; to calculate the interest that the petty capitalist reaps from their necessities.[29]

This done, he then proposed to treat of the poor receiving parish relief, after which 'the habits, haunts, and tricks of the beggars of London' would be duly set forth followed by a consideration of thieves and prostitutes.

The first visit Mayhew made was to Bethnal Green with a view to inquiring into the rate of wages received by the Spitalfields weavers who had 'always been notorious for their privations' and were, further-more, grouped together in a limited geographical area.[30] Mayhew wished his readers to understand that the sentiments he had recorded were those 'wholly and solely of the weavers themselves' and that his vocation was 'to collect facts, and to register opinions'.[31] He also wanted to acquaint the reader 'with the precautions adopted to arrive at a fair and unbiased estimate as to the feelings and conditions of the workmen in the trade'. Having put himself in touch with the surgeon of the district and with one of the 'more intelligent' of the operatives, 'it was agreed among us that we should go into a particular street, and visit the first six weavers' houses we came to'.[32] Having interviewed the six operatives, he wanted to see different classes of the same trade, for example those 'known to entertain violent political opinions'. He was accordingly 'conducted to a tavern' where Chartists were known to congregate and 'immediately proceeded to explain to them the object of my visit, telling them that I intended to take notes of whatever they might communicate to me, with a view to publication in the *Morning Chronicle*.[33] He next went to see 'some average case of destitution in the trade' and was conducted to such an individual that very evening.

This technique of investigation became characteristic of Mayhew's approach and he used it to study slopworkers and needlewomen, tailors, boot and shoemakers, toymakers, merchant seamen, the wood-workers, dressmakers, tanners and curriers. He usually interviewed a representative cross-section of workers, selected in consultation with a 'gentleman' acquainted with the trade and with knowledgeable operatives. He evolved a system of cross-checking individual testimonies and he presented any information from government reports or other statistical sources that might bear upon the problem of the causes of low wages. He collected what information he could from employers, tradesmen, merchants, local authorities, voluntary societies and the police. He sometimes even called meetings of operatives in order to obtain a larger number of informants.

The investigations became the work of a small team — Mayhew himself, his younger brother, Gus, and two assistants. Whenever possible, informants and respondents were interviewed in their own homes. Mayhew did most of the key interviewing and one of the assistants would act as stenographer. A fairly standard pattern developed which Yeo[34] reconstructed as follows. The interviews nearly always began with questions about wages and conditions of employment, after which respondents were asked to contrast wages and conditions at present with the past, and to account for the changes that had taken place in the trade, or to discuss what pleased or disturbed them about the work situation. Very often there were questions about household expenditures and consumption patterns. The results were compressed and edited rather than paraphrased to produce a cogent monologue more or less in the respondent's own words. By his emphasis on the actor's meanings, interpretations and understandings, Mayhew may fairly be regarded as a pioneer of what would nowadays be called 'interpretative' sociology.

Although he had to supply material that was good to read, Mayhew seldom allowed that task to take precedence over the correct presentation of the facts. His letters were packed with large quantities of statistics, some of them in tables, some in the text, and there were laborious calculations of wages that were double-checked wherever possible. Great care was always taken to establish the range of wages and different terms of hire within particular occupations, often after conducting supplementary interviews with knowledgeable informants. More surprising, however, was the extent to which Mayhew always went into great detail about how he pursued his inquiries, giving a kind of 'natural history' of the study as it went along. Of the slopworkers and needlewomen, for example, he says:

> My first step was to introduce myself to one of the largest 'slop-sellers' at the East end of the town; and having informed the firm that I was about to examine into the conditions and incomings of the slopworkers of London, I requested to know whether they would have any objection to furnish me with a list of prices they were in the habit of paying to their workpeople, so that on my visiting the parties themselves — as I frankly gave them to understand I proposed doing — I might be able to compare the operatives' statements as to the prices with theirs, and thus be able to check the one with the other.[35]

The firm did not co-operate, so Mayhew made his way to the workmen in the neighbourhood and interviewed them directly — on this occasion in their place of work. There he found that 'they one and all expressed themselves ready to answer any questions I might put to them'.[36] Mayhew found, perhaps not surprisingly, a general reluctance on the part of employers to divulge information on the wages they paid. Nor were there any government statistics on wages, so he had to rely very largely on the workers for evidence.

Throughout his study Mayhew was concerned with low pay and its causes. He looked at the effects of competition from the 'slop' branches of each trade — the cheap traders at the fringe of the market who employed 'dishonourable' (non-unionised) labour and paid wages so low that a man could not feed himself upon them. His innovation, however, was his concern with wage rates rather than the level of wages. It was the remuneration received from a given quantity of labour that was important. Like some of the criminologists of his time, he was aware that it was the rate of pay (as with the rate of crime) that had to be compared across trades. When the rate was pushed down by force of competition, particularly from the 'slop' trade, men worked harder and longer to maintain their wages. This created an artificial surplus of labour, and a further depressing effect upon wages ensued. In short, a vicious circle existed whereby 'over-work makes under-pay' and in turn 'under-pay makes over-work'.[37] This idea was at variance with the current wisdom of the economists who argued that wage rates were determined purely by the demand for and supply of labour.

Mayhew's studies were far from a descriptive sociography. He built up a series of insightful inductive generalisations from his data that today would have been regarded as important sociological theoretical innovations. From a study of unskilled labour in the docks he noted how irregular work and fluctuating wages tended to result in 'improvident' habits, thereby standing on its head the popular Victorian wisdom that it was weak morals and improvident habits that caused poverty.[38] He realised that different groups of workers reacted in different ways to the fact or threat of casual work or of changed circumstances. Those, like the tailors, the shoemakers and the costermongers, who had seen their status deteriorate rapidly, joined various protest movements like Chartism or Owenism. Others, like the coal-whippers, who averaged even lower wages, but who nevertheless felt their condition to be improving were, politically, more conservative.[39] The idea of 'relative deprivation' was there, even if Mayhew did not coin the phrase or consciously try to conceptualise it in some other terms. He was clearly aware of varying cultural patterns and that the cultures of some groups like the costermongers (those who carried goods from the London markets and sold them in the streets) was distinctive. They had even developed a particular form of language that made it difficult for others to follow their conversations. The idea of 'sub-cultures' was there, but once again not in any explicit conceptual sense.

Following a series of disputes with the editor, Mayhew left the *Morning Chronicle* in 1850. He set up his own office to continue the survey and began issuing *London Labour and the London Poor* in two-penny weekly parts. Much of this, says Thompson,[40] was a reworking, expansion and rearrangement of material on the street traders that had already appeared in the *Chronicle*. The parts were bound together in volume form before the end of 1851. At the same time Mayhew began an inquiry into prostitution. He envisaged that the end product would be a complete 'cyclopedia' of all those who will work, those who cannot work, and those who won't work. Beginning with the street folk, he planned to consider the producers, the carriers, the protectors and the servants. He proposed to sub-classify the producers according to the material they worked on, beginning with the workers in silk and continuing with workers in cotton, workers in wool and so on.[41] However, his examination of the street folk, scheduled to take six months and to occupy one volume, spilled over into another. Adding material on prostitution, he produced a third volume of the 1851 edition only 192 pages long.[42] Early in 1852 the weekly numbers of *London Labour* ended abruptly following a legal dispute with the printer.

Mayhew had increasingly been using the weekly publications to develop his political and economic theories and to criticise the political economists. He came to see the London trades as an integral part of the capitalist industrial system. The question of low wages he linked with the determination of wages in general. He was outraged by the economists' theories about the demand for and supply of labour. He even used the economists' own abstract and mathematical reasoning to develop his argument.[43] He saw the capitalists' behaviour as exploitative, not only because it led to the impoverishment of the workers, but because it robbed the worker of the value his labour had created. There is no evidence that Mayhew had read Marx, but the theory of surplus value was clearly there. Unlike Marx, however, he did not see the solution in terms of the overthrow of the capitalist system, but wished instead for wages to reflect the actual value created by the labourer, and he suggested a radical version of profit sharing.[44] His arguments eventually burst into a separate publication, beginning in 1851, entitled *Low Wages: their Causes, Consequences and Remedies*, but this, too, got entangled in the legal dispute with the printer and only a few numbers were published.

Mayhew, the systematic empirical sociologist, was in danger of becoming bankrupt, so he turned to writing novels to make money. He seems to have been beset with financial, legal and domestic worries.[45] However, in 1856 he showed a hint of his old energies and intellectual command. Not only did he take up and complete some of his work on the street traders, but he began an even more ambitious adventure in *The Great World of London*, running in monthly part-publication from March to November 1856. The prospectus for this envisaged a life's work in which the massive (and only partly completed) examination of labour and the poor was to take its place as only one part of a total survey of London life, commencing with professional London, which he divided into legal London, medical London, religious London, literary London and so on. After some pages of introduction dealing with London as a whole, Mayhew began with legal London which, naturally, he further sub-divided into the metropolitan institutions and people connected with the administration of firstly civil and then criminal law. These he sub-divided into the various courts and prisons. Mayhew then simply proposed to begin by dealing with the criminal prisons of the metropolis and 'plunged into a systematic, fully-documented and at times brilliantly-observed survey of the prisons of London, ending abruptly in mid-sentence with Part IX. Evidently, shortly after the publication folded, Mayhew left the country, and his publishers later commissioned John Binny to complete the volume under the title *The Criminal Prisons of London and Scenes of Prison Life* (1862)'.[46]

Based on direct observation and much interviewing, Mayhew and Binny presented case histories of each prison and described their penal regimes, giving a detailed account of a typical day, very much in narrative form, as Mayhew and others (who, he does not say, but he uses 'we' throughout) experienced it. There were verbatim reports of exchanges between warders and other prison officials and the prisoners as they were escorted around. From an examination of the distribution of delinquents in London the authors discovered that in the years 1841 to 1850 two of the seven metropolitan police divisions, which included the districts of Hoxton and Westminster, produced 65 per cent of all alleged criminals of the metropolis. They concluded, as did Plint in 1851, that the incidence of crime was in some degree a function of the opportunities afforded by the area. They rejected notions popular amongst their contemporaries that crime was due to ignorance, urbanism, industrialisation, or poverty. They say: 'the great mass of crime in this country is committed by those who have been bred and born in the business . . . living as systematically by robbing and cheating as others do by commerce or the exercise of intellectual or manual labour'.[47] It was professional crime that was the root of the problem. Crime was essentially a social phenomenon which was perpetuated by anti-social attitudes and the transmission of social behaviour from one generation to the next in a social setting characterised by poverty, drunkenness, poor housing and economic insecurity.

Besides not completing his study of the criminal prisons of London, Mayhew never returned to continue, still less to fulfil, his ambition of a complete study of the great world of London. He never went on to consider the rest of legal London, let alone other aspects of professional London. He did, however, manage to persuade his publishers to produce a new edition of *London Labour and the London Poor*, the first two volumes of which were concerned solely with London's 'street-folk'. There were the street sellers, street buyers, street finders, street performers, artists and showmen, and street labourers. Each of these he further sub-divided in minute fashion and considered each in turn. Thus there were the street sellers of fish, of vegetables, of eatables and drinkables, of stationery and literature, of manufacturing articles, of second-hand articles and so on. However, Mayhew the systematic social investigator had given way to Mayhew the journalist with an eye for 'character'. His style was less severe and at once more readable than his earlier letters. What emerged was a picturesque account of the street-folk of London which gave little hint of the extensive interviewing and cross-checking of data and information that had been so readily apparent in the *Morning Chronicle* letters. Rosenberg, in an introduction to a reprint of the 1861 edition, writes:

> The image of London that emerges is that of a vast, ingeniously balanced mechanism in which each class subsists on the droppings of the stratum above, all the way from the rich, whom we scarcely glimpse, down to the deformed and starving, whom we see groping for salvageable bone or decaying vegetables in the markets. Such extreme conditions bred weird extremities of adaption, a remarkably diverse yet cohesive subculture of poverty. Ragged, fantastic armies each with its distinctive jargon and implements, roamed the streets: 'pare-finders' with bucket and glove, picking up dog-dung and selling it to tanners; rag gatherers, themselves dressed in the rotted cloth they salvage, armed with pointed sticks; bent, slime-soiled 'mud-larks', groping at the low tide in the ooze of the Thames for bits of coal, chips of wood, or copper nails dropped from the sheathing of barges, a regiment of 300 who subsisted on average earnings of three pence a day.[48]

A third volume was created, with new material on exterminators of rodents and vermin, expanded work on street performers and a 'sample' of letters from the *Morning Chronicle*, including those on the slop cabinet-makers, dock labourers, transit workers and vagrancy. In 1862 a fourth volume was added, dealing with those who will not work. His earlier work on prostitution was supplemented by new material on thieves, swindlers and beggars that had been collected by other investigators.

The 1861 edition was, in Yeo's view, 'the most unsatisfactory remnant of an unfinished venture'[49] and it contained only a fraction of the material from the *Morning Chronicle* letters. Unfortunately, this has become all of Mayhew that historians and sociologists read, and for that reason he has never received serious consideration as a systematic empirical investigator, but has been regarded as no more than a gifted journalist 'with an undisciplined zest for collecting facts about the poor and picturesque characters among the poor'.[50] The worth of Mayhew's reportage has been hotly disputed. His supporters praise his intentions and assumptions as a social investigator and defend the accuracy of his work. Thompson[51] described it as 'rigorous' and 'meticulous', while Humpheries claimed that Mayhew was 'precise and articulate about what he saw' and that he left 'little to explain'.[52] Rosenberg found him 'searingly accurate . . . . He does not distort, but he edits, shapes, and intensifies',[53] while Yeo remarks that in the journalistic studies that followed Mayhew's, there was little of 'Mayhew's scrupulous attention to making clear what methods of investigation were to be followed or how the credibility of the evidence was to be established'.[54] Critics on the other hand have focused their attention on the 1861 edition and have argued that Mayhew's sampling was poor, that his statistics were insubstantial and his presentation selective and exaggerated. In a review of the 1861 edition Harrison called it 'a very ill-constructed work whose defects amply justify Ruth Glass's complaints that "there is no theme; by and large there is description without selection or analysis" '.[55] There was, says Harrison, no attempt to define the problem he was seeking to solve and the questions he asked were not standardised. Dyos dismissed Mayhew's work as 'essentially a form of higher journalism, not of social analysis'.[56] Like Harrison, however, Dyos was mistakenly equating the 1861 edition with the whole of Mayhew's work for the *Morning Chronicle*. From what he wrote for the latter it is clear that Mayhew deserves far greater consideration as a pioneer of empirical sociology than he has as yet been given. The fact that these remarkable inquiries were produced 130 years ago cannot be ignored, and cannot be properly judged by the standards and from the perspectives of the 1980s.

The imagery of social exploration, which could be seen in embryo in Engels, was more explicit in Mayhew. In his preface to the first volume of the 1861 edition he had written that his book was 'curious', as supplying information 'concerning a large body of persons, of whom the public had less knowledge than of the most distant tribes on earth'. Following the common anthropological practice of distinguishing the 'savage' on the basis of physical and biological characteristics, Mayhew had claimed that there were two distinct races of men:

> the wandering and the civilised tribes, the vagabonds and the citizens. . . . We, like the Kafirs, Fellahs, and Finns, are surrounded by wandering hordes — paupers, beggars, and outcasts, possessing nothing but what they acquire by depredation from the industrious, provident, and civilised portion of the community; that the heads of these nomads are remarkable for the greater development of the jaws and cheekbones rather than those of the head; — and that they have a secret language of their own — an English 'cuz-cat' or 'slang' as it is called — for the concealment of their designs.[57]

The metaphor of the social explorer was developed and exploited by people like George Sims, who in his *How the Poor Live* (1883) spoke of a 'voyage of discovery' that was 'into a dark continent that was within easy walking distance of the General Post Office'. William Booth's *In Darkest England and the Way Out* was built almost entirely on the analogy of exploration. After 'brooding over the awful presentation of life in the African rain forrests' by Stanley, Booth asked: 'As there is a darkest Africa, is there not also a darkest England?' The language of exploration was almost inexhaustible in its adaptability, making it very attractive to those writers who never 'walked' or 'rode' into a slum, but who instead 'penetrated' it.[58] The vogue for disguise in order temporarily to become a slum dweller probably began with James Greenwood's *A Night in a Workhouse* (1866). The reports of his experiences of one night in a London workhouse disguised as a 'casual' were published in the *Pall Mall Gazette* and caused a sensation. Jack London in his *The People of the Abyss* (1903) told how he posed as 'the-seafaring-man-who-had-lost-his-clothes-and-money', and he noted how class status often came from simply wearing the right clothes. The idea of the working class and the poor inhabiting an 'abyss' on the edge of society became popular, perhaps reflecting a feeling of despair at worsening social conditions. An 'abyss' was something one fell into or climbed out of and, furthermore, may be very 'deep'; it was metaphorically more stark even than a 'dark continent' or an 'African rain forest'.

Booth's inquiries into the life and labour of the people of London

The house-to-house survey, the first-hand observer's account, the use of informants and the utilisation of statistics collected by government officials, were by now all elements that had been used by social investigators — the accountants and the explorers — to gather information about people and social conditions in a systematic manner. It was the unique contribution of Charles Booth to combine all these elements into one large study. Booth was a successful businessman owning his own shipping line based in Liverpool.[59] His experience led him to appreciate the value of obtaining all the facts before taking a decision. In 1885 he became a member of the London Statistical Society and in 1886 produced for them an analysis of the 1881 Census returns. This gave him valuable experience in handling data, a realisation of their limitations, and also contacts in the office of the Registrar General. Booth was aware of the poverty that existed in the midst of plenty — to him it was 'the problem of problems'. He had developed the habit of exploring the East End of London, mingling with the people and becoming familiar with their lifestyles, and he conceived the idea of undertaking a complete survey of the facts of poverty throughout London.[60]

Booth chose to begin his researches in the East End, which was 'supposed to contain the most destitute population in England and to be, as it were, the focus of the problem of poverty in the midst of wealth'.[61] The East End inquiry in fact became a kind of 'pilot' study which formed the basis for a survey of the people of the rest of London. His major source of information was extensive cross-examination of school board visitors, who performed house-to-house visitations in the normal course of their duties. Every house in every street was on their books, where there were details of every family who had children who were about to go to school, were at school, or who had recently left. Most of the visitors had been working in the same district for several years and had extensive knowledge of the parents of the schoolchildren, especially of the poorest of them, and of the conditions under which they lived. In the East End inquiry they submitted to 20 or more hours of individual cross-examination on the information recorded in their routine notebooks. Booth and his assistants discussed with them every inhabitant of every house in every street in the district, verifying the facts by reference to the visitor's daily records. As the interviews proceeded, the information secured was entered into small notebooks, prepared on an identical plan so that any one of the entries could be compared with any other. The name of the street was given at the head of each page on which every house was noted and the occupants of each room were enumerated. Particulars were recorded of the occupation and probable income of every inhabitant, together with the number of children in each family. Booth also used other officials to give him data: the school divisional committees, the relieving officers, the district superintendents, the police and the clergy.

Each family was assigned to one of eight 'classes' on the basis of a combination of occupation, living conditions and income levels estimated from the visitors' reports. The result was a rather confused set of categories as can be seen in table 2.1.

Table 2.1
Booth's social classes

A	The lowest class of occasional labourers, loafers, and semi-criminals
B	Casual earners
C	Intermittent earners
D	Small regular earnings
E	Regular standard earnings
F	High-class labour
G	Lower middle class
H	Upper middle class

Class A thus referred to moral circumstances; classes B, C and D combined levels of income with their regularity, while classes G and H referred to more 'social' classes in the modern sense. It was class B — the 'very poor' — that was at all times more or less 'in want', and was ill nourished and poorly clad. Of the East End families, just over 11 per cent were in this condition. Only some of these, thought Booth, would be 'in distress'. Classes C and D, whose earnings were small or intermittent, constituted 'the poor'; they were not 'in want', but they had no surplus and their lives 'lacked comfort'. For illustrative purposes Booth gave rough income equivalents of his classes. Thus classes C and D had a 'sufficiently regular though bare income, such as 18/- to 21/- a week for a moderate family', while incomes in classes A and B fell 'much below this standard'. Booth discovered that 23 per cent of his families fell into classes C and D, giving a total of 35 per cent in classes A to D.

Booth felt that the figures for London as a whole would be considerably lower than in the East End, and he forecast that the poor would probably account for 25 per cent of the population of the metropolis. He used the same techniques to obtain his data on the rest of London, but while his earlier study had taken the family as the unit of analysis, this was producing too much data to cope with in the full survey, so he changed his unit to the street. Although he still classified each family into one of his eight classes, he was no longer able to relate income, occupation and poverty for each family. The change did, however, enable him to complete his celebrated 'poverty map' of

London, whereby each street was classified according to the general conditions of the inhabitants and given a colour accordingly.[62]

For London as a whole the results were as shown in table 2.2.

Table 2.2
The findings for London as a whole

		N	%	
A		37,610	0.9	⎫
B	'very poor'	316,834	7.5	⎬ 30.7 per cent in poverty or in want
C D }	'poor'	938,293	22.3	⎭
E F }	comfortable working class	2,166,503	51.5	⎫ 69.3 per cent in comfort or in affluence
G H }	middle class	749,930	17.8	⎭

Booth was surprised that poverty in the rest of London was nearly as high as in the East End, but he felt that it was, overall, not as bad as some of the sensationalists had made out. After all, only 8 per cent were on the verge of distress, not the 25 per cent that had been claimed by some writers. Conditions, claimed, Booth, were 'not so appalling as sensational writers would have us believe' and 'better than was commonly imagined previous to the publication of the figures for East London'.[63] Booth saw his results as grounds for optimism. The hordes of barbarians from the slums who were going to overthrow civilisation according to some of the more populist writers like George Sims, simply did not exist. By distinguishing between classes A and B, Booth was able to show that such people constituted less than 1 per cent of the population. They were 'a disgrace, but not a danger'.[64]

Turning to the causes of poverty, Booth took a subset of the main study and looked at the 'immediate' causes of poverty amongst 4,000 cases of the poor known to selected school board visitors in each district.[65] The results he presented are shown in table 2.3.

The table, however, is a little misleading. Booth has usually been credited with having discovered that poverty was not the result of individual failings, but was due to conditions of employment. The poverty of 55 per cent in classes A and B and 68 per cent in classes C and D was due to this cause. Hennock has argued that a close reading of the text shows that 'questions of employment' included both economic circumstances and personal failings that resulted in lack of an adequate income, while 'questions of habit' – drink and thriftlessness – resulted in mismanagement of income. It was thus not a

Table 2.3
The causes of poverty

		%		%	
	Analysis of causes of 'great poverty' (classes A and B)				
1	Loafers	–	–	60	4	
2	Casual work	697	43 ⎫			
3	Irregular work, low pay	141	9 ⎬	878	55	questions of
4	Small profits	40	3 ⎭			employment
5	Drink (husband, or both husband and wife)	152	9 ⎫	231	14	questions of
6	Drunken or thriftless wife	79	5 ⎭			habit
7	Illness or infirmity	170	10 ⎫			
8	Large family	124	8 ⎬	441	27	questions of
9	Illness or large family, combined with irregular work	147	9 ⎭			circumstances
		–	–	1,610	100	
	Analysis of causes of 'poverty' (classes C and D)				
1	Loafers	–	–	–	–	
2	Low pay (regular earnings)	503	20 ⎫			
3	Irregular earnings	1,052	43 ⎬	1,668	68	questions of
4	Small profits	113	5 ⎭			employment
5	Drink (husband, or both husband and wife)	167	7 ⎫	322	13	questions of
6	Drunken or thriftless wife	155	6 ⎭			habit
7	Illness or infirmity	123	5 ⎫			
8	Large family	223	9 ⎬	476	19	questions of
9	Illness or large family, combined with irregular work	130	5 ⎭			circumstances
		–	–	2,466	100	

distinction between poverty caused by the economic system and poverty caused by individual failings; in fact he explicitly refused to separate out these two causes, since the displacement was 'so frequently due to the conjunction of some form of personal disqualification and the presence of disadvantageous economic conditions that it may perhaps be assumed that only in a minority of cases is one set of influences alone sufficient to determine the question of employment for any one individual man'.[66] 'Questions of circumstance' related to those causes over which nobody could be expected to have any control and include illness and a large family, two factors that had little in common except that there was, for the moment, little that could be done about them. The debate about the causes of poverty was in essence a debate over the alternative strategies for its cure. By separating out illness, large family and mismanagement of income,

Booth produced a table in which questions of employment were of prime importance and it lent weight to his proposed cure: the removal of classes A and B from the London labour market.

Booth's original goal had been to discover 'the numerical relations which poverty, misery, and depravity bear to regular earnings and comparative comfort',[67] and even before the results of the 'first' or 'poverty' series had come off the press, he began a new line of investigation: an inquiry into the trades of London. He hoped that such an investigation would shed light upon the connection between poverty and conditions of employment. The unit of analysis became once more the family, more especially the family head, defined as anyone claiming to fill in an independent Census return. The major source of data for this 'industry' series was the 1891 Census,[68] complemented by materials from the London Board of Trade. In addition, there were innumerable interviews with workers, employers and trade union officials, questionnaires were sent to a wide range of firms, and special studies were completed by members of Booth's staff. Booth developed a new classification of social conditions using 'crowding' as an index. Taking two or more persons per room as 'crowded', he found 31.5 per cent in this condition, a finding that supported his previous investigations. As he put it: 'the total percentages "crowded" and "not crowded" agree very nearly with the totals of the previous classification "in poverty" and "in comfort" '.[69] The results were presented trade by trade. For the 'building trades', for example, Booth began by presenting the objective facts concerning the entire group — age and sex, size of family, social condition (degree of crowding), followed by comparative data on the constituent sections (architects, builders, masons, bricklayers and so on) in terms of poverty, crowding and numbers employed. Booth then turned to the particular sections and presented a more detailed but similarly objective analysis.

At the end of the industry series, Booth was still unwilling to come to a conclusion on the causes of poverty. His 'conclusion' was simply to point to the next task: to look at the various influences, particularly religious, on the existing state of things, and at the various efforts to deal with the problem of the urban poor. His plan of action was rather different from his earlier investigations:

> We have moved our camp from centre to centre all over London, remaining for weeks or even months in each spot in order to see as well as to hear all we could. Spiritual influences do not lend themselves readily to statistical treatment, and we have not attempted it . . . . Our object, rather, has been to obtain truthful and trustworthy impressions. . . . We have endeavoured to see, and with comparatively few exceptions have seen, all the responsible heads

of Churches of whatever denomination. An account of their work, its success and failures, forming the basis and material of this work, is contained in written reports of nearly 1800 personal interviews, of which 1450 were with the direct representatives of religious work and nearly 350 with other authorities.[70]

Booth also wished to revise completely the poverty map of 1899. This task involved him in systematically revisiting, 'every street, court and alley'. Booth ended up very sceptical of the efficacy of the efforts of organised religious communities to help the poor (or even to provide for their specifically religious needs). He had hoped that religion would act as a powerful influence on the moral and spiritual lives of the people. He sadly came to the conclusion that its influence was either negligible or pernicious. His maps showed that the Anglican churches were to be found in the more well-to-do areas. Booth seemed to sympathise with, or at least understand, the tendency of workers to reject the Church of England and to think religion in general irrelevant if not hypocritical. The worst bosses were often the most devout Christians. The moral forces shaping the lives of the workers were socialism and trade unionism, not religion. 'Taken as a whole', Booth declared, 'the effects of religious bodies to improve the condition of life . . . fail'. The upper classes observed the merest formalities, while the workers were indifferent or hostile. Large segments of the middle class and the poor were susceptible to meaningless evangelism, while the very poor, sunk in sloth, were beyond reach except as charity cases. Despite the statistics on church attendance and the number of missions and conversions, London, he found, was 'a heathen city'.

The Simeys calculated that the completed inquiry had involved Booth in an expenditure of some £33,000 (or a quarter of a million pounds at 1972 prices) all paid for by himself from the profits of his shipping business. The 17 volumes that finally emerged had taken him as many years to finish;[71] one might have anticipated that the final volume would contain a distillation of the kinds of policies and remedies necessary to alleviate the sum of human misery that he had so carefully documented. In the event, much of the volume was devoted to a lengthy and cryptic 'abstract' of the total inquiry, volume by volume, page by page, prepared by one of Booth's assistants. His own conclusions amounted to no more than 16 pages. In these he says:

> We see life cursed by drink, brutality and vice, and loaded down with ignorance and poverty, while industry is choked with its own blind struggles, and education is still mounting, and too often slipping back from, the first rungs of its ladder. We see religion paralysed by its own inconsistencies, and administration wrapped

up in the swaddling clothes of indecision and mutual distrust. Improvement there certainly has been, but in regarding the conditions of life at their worst, and in seeking to improve them, there are two distinct tasks: to raise the general level of existence, but especially the bottom level, is one: to increase the proportion of those who know how to use aright the means they have is another and even greater. But each effort should aid the other.[72]

As to how these tasks should be achieved, Booth felt that minimal government intervention was all that was needed. The very poor, classes A and B, constituted a burden to the community; their lives were 'in every way wasteful'.[73] Those most threatened by their existence were 'those who were themselves only a little removed from the same condition'. He suggested the establishment of 'industrial communities which, lying midway between pauperism and independence, should realise the intention expressed by the word "workhouse" '. To them the very poor would be banished, sealed off from the rest of society, where they would be taught skills and work discipline while their children were raised under strict supervision. If the poor failed in their special camps, they would be sent to poorhouses and their children taken from them. If they succeeded, they would be allowed to re-enter civilisation. Booth reconciled these policies with his staunch defence of *laissez-faire* individualism by arguing that individualism would be strengthened by this extension of 'state socialism', as he called it. Socialism, in his view, was the exercise of state power over those who could not help themselves, or who constituted a danger to the community. Jails, asylums, workhouses and so on were all examples of socialism.

Booth's survey had been a gigantic undertaking, unparalleled in its time and unsurpassed by modern empirical sociologists. Yet his work has generally been dismissed as mere fact gathering and unrelated to sociology proper. Such views are mistaken, for though Booth was unconcerned with sociological theory as such, there was more than enough theory implied in his work to give it form and significance as a sociological text. He never formally addressed himself to the task of formulating in general terms the relationship between social structure and the physical environment in urban areas. Nor did he attempt in a self-conscious fashion to deal abstractly and systematically with concepts like 'class' and 'institution', yet much of his inquiry was concerned with these matters. Booth probably never heard the term 'ecology', yet his genuine innovation over previous investigators was to consider the spatial—distributive aspects of a wide range of related social phenomena, and to focus on a single community.[74] In Booth's hands the notion of urban areas as units of analysis underwent significant development at both theoretical and technical levels. Pfautz[75] identifies four different types of area used in the course of the inquiry: administrative, for example, school board divisions, the Registrar General's registration districts and the ecclesiastical parishes; presentational areal constructs, notably the compass areas of the city like 'East London'; natural areas like 'the City', 'trades areas' and the 'poverty area'; finally, analytic areal constructs, self-consciously conceived and constructed with specific analytic purposes in mind, for example the 'compound blocks' used in the poverty map.

In a practical and naturalistic way Booth made generalisations *from* his data; generalisations which, if they had been put with less of Booth's characteristic humility and as a result of deductive processes, would perhaps have been regarded as imaginative and impressive 'insights' by more academically minded sociologists. Thus in a special inquiry into the 'Influx of the Population' in the poverty series, after considering the sources by region and distance from the City of migrants, their distribution by residence, and the causes in terms of 'push' and 'pull' factors, Booth noted: 'As a general rule (provincial migrants) settle most in the newer and more sparsely peopled outlying parts, especially those which have been built over'.[76] Indeed, Booth formulated what he called a 'general law of successive migration', which noted the 'centrifugal tendency' of the classes to move outwards from the centre of the city.[77] He says: 'The dominant social fact observable is the steady movement northward of the people. Throughout London movement from the centre outwards is noticeable'. He then went on to consider the forces underlying such patterns and processes, for example the natural increase of population, the excess of migration from rural areas and abroad, the demand for space for other than residential purposes and the requirements of higher standards of living. The available means of transportation was a primary factor in determining the direction of movement; another was the 'lie of the land' — as a general rule, the higher the ground, the greater the value. In Booth's words: 'As the land rises toward Putney Heath, so the inhabitants rise in social scale'.[78] Another factor was the family cycle. Booth says: 'The father of young children finds it best to establish their home as far from the crowded parts of London as he can afford to travel to and from his work . . . '.[79] In the industry series Booth carefully documented the 'localisation' of various trades, and numerous hypotheses were presented concerning the factors determining this process. In his inquiries into the City as a spatial order Booth was led to a very modern insight into the problematic separation between place of residence and place of work.[80] Here, in the 1890s, was Booth anticipating the very basis of a thoroughly modern and highly sociological urban ecology.

That Booth had ever read Marx is doubtful,[81] yet implicit in his analysis of the social structure of London is the pervasive conception of class as a 'style of life' involving a multiplicity of criteria and as a force in the community having considerable impact on various types of social institution. The concept of class served a pragmatic rather than a theoretical function, and was used primarily to make operational distinctions among different degrees of poverty and well-being. According to Pfautz,[82] two completely different types of class hierarchy figured in the inquiry: the 'letter' classes that generally informed the poverty and the industry series and which involved economic class position in the market, and the specifically 'social' classes that received greatest attention in the religious influence series, and primarily involved a position in a system of status-honour. In short, the Weberian distinction between 'class' and 'status' was implicit in Booth's work. Booth was concerned with the implications of class for educational and economic opportunities, and he found evidence of distinctive and significant class differences in this respect. He notes that 'the great majority of boys attending the secondary schools of London are of the middle and lower middle classes, with a fringe of sons of professional men, and in endowed schools (where no fees were paid) a sprinkling of the children of the working man'.[83] Even the scholarship children tended to be middle class. Booth also observed the different attitudes of the different classes toward the education of their children:

> At the very bottom education is disregarded, and every effort made to avoid or abbreviate school life; in the next class the children are hurried through their 'standards' in order to go to work as soon as possible; above this, the period is voluntarily extended from 13 to 14 . . . and so on till, with those who go to the university, the educational period lasts till 23 or 24 years of age.[84]

Booth further recognised the tendency of sons to follow their fathers' occupation as well as the existence of certain 'traditional' occupations for girls, especially in the lower classes. Upper working-class children were inclined to be more mobile both occupationally and socially.

Besides education, Booth also studied class-related aspects of living habits, family budgeting, clothes and leisure pursuits. He noted the different ways in which the factory girl and the working girl of middle-class social background would spend their money, and he observed class differences in attitudes and customs governing sex and marriage. Lower working-class girls, for example, were meant to follow 'very definite codes of rules'.[85] The idea of social norms was there, even if Booth did not coin the phrase. In terms of religion he focused on class differences in church attendance and on attitudes towards religion and its functions.

While he never employed the concept 'institution' in any sociological sense, it was clear that Booth was aware of what modern sociologists would call 'manifest' and 'latent' functions of organisations, associations and groups. His observations of ecological shifts emphasised the dynamic quality of such institutions. The postulate that each religious institution had its particular milieu, the change of which necessitated adaptation for survival, was explicit: 'The natural congregation of Protestant Nonconformist bodies consists mainly of middle class people . . . but . . . they have left, necessitating orientation to the people now living in the district'.[86] Even Booth's approach to the institution of prostitution was surprisingly objective for the 1890s, and allowed sociological insight into the problem of its control. He observed: 'The professional part played by women is very much against rescue work. If, however, the professional character . . . militates against successful rescue work . . . it may perhaps facilitate regulation'.[87] On the relationship between institutions and class differences, Booth saw that social conditions often led to the development of unique, class-specific and adaptive institutional arrangements such as the pawnshop, the moneylender, the provident and loan clubs, and the friendly societies for the working classes whose expenditures on the bare necessities of life exhausted their incomes.

Nobody who examined Booth's work in any detail could come to the conclusion that his was merely a 'fact-finding' exercise. There was no shortage of sociological insight and much of what he said was suggestive of what would now be regarded as in the best tradition of sociological research. In many ways he laid the foundations for later sociological work not only on poverty, but also on urban ecology, industrial sociology, social stratification, and on the sociologies of religion, education and leisure. Pfautz concludes that the materials in the 17 volumes strike a very modern note because Booth focused on the problems of an urban community in an industrial society, because of his use of statistical data and techniques of research to describe, to compare and to chart the course of change of the social structure and functioning of the world's largest city; because he rationally organised and pursued a collective research effort, and despite his abiding concern to bring about reforms, he developed a very sophisticated sociological eye and a scientific attitude towards social facts.[88]

Even while Booth was conducting his inquiries into the labour and life of the people of London he had been working on a cognate problem, scarcely mentioned in his volumes on poverty, industry and religion. In the late 1880s he discovered that an astonishingly high percentage of old people ended up in the workhouse, that in certain London districts old age was the primary cause of pauperism. Accordingly, in 1892 in his *Pauperism, a Picture and the Endowment of Old Age, an Argument*, he proposed that the state provide weekly pensions of five shillings for men and women reaching the age of 65. This, too, was socialism, but one that promised to grant people more, not less, independence. Responsibility for the old rested on society at large. Year after year Booth promoted his pension scheme in articles and books, notably his *The Aged Poor in England and Wales* (1899), always citing the volumes of statistics he had collected on the relation between old age and poverty. However, the swelling power of the trade unions, the emergence of the Independent Labour Party, the increasing radicalism of the Liberals — all these were disturbing events to Booth whose conservatism began to harden into dogma. In a series of pamphlets written in 1910 and 1911 he called for the expansion of the Poor Law and for its strict enforcement against 'those whose unrestrained lives cause injury to others as well as to themselves'. In his last work, *Industrial Unrest and Trade Union Policy* (1913), he deplored the new militancy of the trade unions and feared for the future of British industry unless the country adopted more restrictive labour policies. After 1914 Booth's thoughts turned to some of the industrial and social problems that he regarded as inevitable in the post-war period. However, his health was declining rapidly and in 1916 he died in his lifetime home in Gracedieu, just outside London.

Victorian boom — and depression

The decades of the 1850s and 1860s were ones of general prosperity. This was the time of the Victorian boom, symbolised by the Great Exhibition of 1851. It was a period of limited reforms apart from the Workshop Act and the second Reform Bill of 1867, the Royal Sanitary Commission of 1869 and the Education Act of 1870. 'Work', 'industry', 'thrift' and 'progress' were the key thoughts of the period, replacing those of 'crisis', 'conflict' and 'revolution' of the 1840s. The general rise in real wages, the reduction on taxes on foods and the shortening of the working day permitted unparalleled working-class improvement. The general prosperity, however, did not save large sections of the population from distress, as Mayhew's inquiries had revealed. But in their smugness, condescension, fear, guilt, humanitarianism or pity — whatever the motives — many wealthy Victorians saw philanthropy as a solution. That would at least be under their control, they could use it for purposes of control, and it meant that the social fabric that appeared to be working so well in Britain's best interests was not disturbed. Consequently, charitable institutions proliferated, but in a rather haphazard and disorganised fashion until the Charity Organisation Society was established in 1869. This was aimed at promoting a key plank of Victorian ideology: self help, an ideology which was reflected and popularised in Samuel Smiles's advice on the subject contained in the stories, examples and anecdotes of his immensely successful book *Self Help with Illustrations of Character and Conduct* (1859).[89]

The principal purpose of charitable work was, according to the Charity Organisation Society, to assist the poor to help themselves so that they could meet all the ordinary contingencies and crises of life — sickness, unemployment, bereavement and so on — by their own industry and thrift. Furthermore, such assistance was to be available only after the investigation of each individual case so that only the worthy and deserving would be helped — those who will work and who cannot work as opposed to those who will not in Mayhew's terminology.

From about 1873 onwards prices began to fall and continued to do so until the middle of the 1890s. The period was described at the time as the 'Great Depression', even though production was maintained and there was only a fairly limited increase in unemployment — it was prices and profits that were depressed. The interests of the capitalists and the workers diverged, and the problem of poverty in the midst of plenty was heightening the social divide. There was considerable social unrest. In London the clearances to make way for the railways, government offices and warehouses created increased pressure on housing and there was an increase in overcrowding. The problem was highlighted in dramatic fashion by a pamphlet published by a congregationalist Minister, Arthur Mearns, in 1883 entitled *The Bitter Cry of Outcast London*. In the winter of 1885—86 there were demonstrations and riots in central London, which more than ever made the poor look like a social menace. The prospect of hordes of vagabonds, thieves and paupers overthrowing 'civilised' society loomed before middle-class imaginations. There were the famous strikes by the East End match girls and the dockers in 1888 and 1889, which established the new and more militant trade unions as a potent force in the relationships between workers and their employers, while in 1889 Jack the Ripper savagely murdered five Whitehall prostitutes and the world's press temporarily turned its attention to the East End of London.

If it had been Chartism that lay behind the fears of the middle classes in the 1840s, in the 1880s and 1890s it was socialism fostered by the spread of education and the extension of the franchise. Beliefs in the need for a socialist organisation of society had a powerful effect on middle-class political thinking and it found expression in new political bodies such as the Social Democratic Federation and the Fabian Society. The former body was founded in 1884 by Hyndman (who Booth, so it was reputed, went to see to complain of his 'exaggerated' claims about the extent of poverty in London), who was a declared Marxist. William Morris, the wealthy poet and art designer, was a prominent member for a short time until he broke away to form another group — the Socialist League — later in 1884. The Fabian Society was also founded in 1884. Among its members were George Bernard Shaw, Sidney and Beatrice Webb and Annie Besant (who had led the match girls' strike in 1888). The Fabians believed in achieving socialism by gradually converting the major political parties to it by rational argument, not by revolution. Such rational argument was provided in a deluge of pamphlets. In 1893 the Independent Labour Party was formed and it included, albeit unenthusiastically, both the Social Democratic Federation and the Fabians. Its first few years were ones of strife as the employers hit back by forming their own associations which organised lockouts and the use of blackleg labour.

Strikes, riots, trade unionism and socialism were thus all active in the 1880s and 1890s. Yet none of the social explorers concerned themselves with these elements. Empirical sociologists, like journalists and the novelists of the period focused on the slum dwellers of an 'outcast London'. The idea of two nations in conflict was replaced by the variety and mystery of the working-class characters in the London streets, highlighting individual types, particularly the bizarre and the grotesque. Such a concern had had a long literary tradition that had been dominated since the 1830s by Charles Dickens, for example in his *Sketches by Boz* (1836), *Pickwick Papers* (1836) and *Oliver Twist* (1838), which also satirised both the workings of the old Poor Laws and the semi-starvation methods of the new Act of 1834.

The parallels between Dickens and Mayhew are very close. Dickens had worked as a journalist for the *Morning Chronicle* some 15 years before Mayhew did, although as a Parliamentary reporter, making his name under the pen-name 'Boz'. Like Mayhew, Dickens was concerned to expose the exploitation of the working classes by harsh employers and the filthy and debased circumstances under which they were forced to live. Like Mayhew he spent a lot of time talking to, interviewing and observing working-class characters on social explorations into parts of London not frequented by the middle classes. They shared many views, for example on education, philanthropy, sanitary reform and the corruption and hypocrisy of officials and bureaucrats.[90] Mayhew was apparently even considered as a collaborator on the project which eventually became *Pickwick Papers*. The two were certainly friendly before Mayhew became metropolitan correspondent for the *Morning Chronicle* in 1849, and in 1845 Mayhew even played a part in Dickens's amateur theatrical, *Every Man in His Humour*. In the work of the two men the distinction between fact and fiction was never absolute. Mayhew's sociological journalism partook of the selectivity and rhetorical organisation of fiction, while Dickens's novels frequently had a journalistic base in contemporary events and he insisted on the factual nature of his novels.[91] For both, London was essentially a city of streets teeming with people and both limited their views to that of the lower middle and lower classes. For both, the recognisable and familiar became unusual and romantic and the variety of life seemed inexhaustible.[92]

It is tempting to suggest that the distinction between literature and empirical sociology is a difficult one to make when comparing the products of the empirical sociologists as social explorers and the phenomenon of the urban novels. Certainly Mayhew himself also wrote novels and he alternated between his literary, journalistic and sociological activities. Too much can be made of this, however. Dickens was no empirical sociologist and Mayhew was nowhere in Dickens's league when it came to successful fiction. Empirical sociology and literature were very different media for the communication of ideas and it is always possible to distinguish between Mayhew the systematic investigator of the causes of low wages, Mayhew the metropolitan correspondent and Mayhew the pot-boiler novelist. Exactly the same scenes may be reported by the empirical sociologist and by the novelist through the eyes of his characters; but one is still part of a story while the other is part of the unfolding of evidence in relation to a theory about society or sections of it. Literary critics have often compared Dickens and Mayhew; and there is some evidence to suggest that Dickens even drew on Mayhew's *Morning Chronicle* letters as a source of material for his characters.[93] They were, however, very different kinds of reporters. Mayhew's declared intention was 'to collect facts and register opinions'. This meant minimising his own role and giving emphasis to the views of the poor and establishing these as the norm. Dickens interpreted and illuminated social facts rather than collected them with the result that he always projected himself onto the scene, commenting freely as he went along and very much from his own middle-class perspective. Mayhew clearly believed in the scientific method (or, rather, his version of it) and he had a respect for statistics, while Dickens felt that quantitative approaches were 'dreary'. Mayhew seldom used either personification or metaphor in his descriptions; but to Dickens these were standard literary practices.[94]

The distinction between the affluent West End of London and the outcast East End was not one that Dickens consciously made in his lifetime, but by the mid-1880s the East End had become as potent a symbol of late Victorian poverty as Manchester had been of industrial conditions in the 1840s. Keating[95] argues that it was Walter Besant who 'discovered' the East End in the early 1880s. Besant's aim was similar to that of the empirical sociologists — social reform — and he evaluated his working-class novels (*All Sorts and Conditions of Men*, 1882 and *Children of Gibeon*, 1886) according to the political interest they aroused in social problems. For him the distinction between a work of fiction and a sociological inquiry was of little significance — his world was still a carefully documented reality. Booth's early inquiries in the East End marked the culminating point of this discovery. His findings showed in the strongest possible manner the extent to which the novelists of the period were being highly selective in choosing the suffering poor and debased as representative of working-class life. After all, some 60 per cent of the East End population led decent, respectable, even comfortable, lives; only 11 per cent were 'in want' or 'in distress' and only 1.2 per cent could be classified as 'debased'.

Notes

1   See Keating, 1976, who treats social exploration as a characteristic type of nineteenth and twentieth-century literature.
2   See Mayer, 1936, for a full account of Engels's career.
3   The study was, in fact, not limited to England, but included material on Edinburgh, Glasgow, and Dublin. There has also been some controversy over whether Engels included the 'in 1844' in the original draft of the book (see note 22 below).
4   Engels, p.56. All page references are to the 1976 edition published by Panther Books, St Albans. This edition was first published with an introduction by Eric Hobsbawm in 1969. See note 22 for an account of the various translations of Engels's book.
5   Ibid., p.323.
6   Ibid., p.57.
7   Ibid., p.76.
8   Engels and Mary Burns lived together and she became his constant companion until her death in 1863. Quite what role she played and who exactly Engels came to know as a result of his relationship with her is not clear from anything that Engels wrote. Marcus, 1974, p.99, comments that very little about her has come to light.
9   Engels, p.79.
10   Ibid., p.80.
11   Ibid., p.81.
12   Loc. cit.
13   Ibid., p.82.

14   Ibid., p.83.
15   Ibid., p.86.
16   Ibid., p.96.
17   Ibid., p.60.
18   A complete list of all sources quoted by Engels may be found in the 1958 translation of Engels by W.O. Henderson and W.H. Chaloner, Oxford, Basil Blackwell, pp 372-4. It includes some 24 books and pamphlets, 17 newspapers and journals, and nine parliamentary papers.
19   Engels, p.66.
20   Ibid., p.68.
21   Ibid., pp 133-4.
22   Although first published in German in 1845, it was not translated into English until 1886 when an American socialist and reformer, Florence Wischnewetzky, undertook the task. Engels entered into correspondence with her and undertook to prepare a new preface to the English translation in which he would comment on the change in the condition of the British working classes in the intervening 40 years. It seems clear that Engels was not pleased with the translation and he was prepared to revise some passages, a process that took him some four weeks. A somewhat acrimonious and protracted correspondence ensued during which Engels, for example, refused to allow Mrs Wischnewetzky's plan to 'universalise' the book by dropping the 'in 1844' from the title. A year later Engels was snorting to a third party that Mrs Wischnewetzky 'translates like a factory' and that she had left 'all the real work to me'. In the view of Marcus, 1974, p.xiii, the translation, finally published in 1887, was 'generally lame and graceless and preserves few of the characteristic vigours and earthiness of Engels's prose'. Engels's disapproval, however, cannot have been too deep, for he was prepared to write another preface for the edition that was published in Britain in 1892, and made no reservations or comments on the translation, but simply remarked that 'the present English copyright edition is brought out with the full consent of all parties interested'.

Some 70 years later in 1958 Henderson and Chaloner published another translation, which in Marcus's view, 1974, p.28, 'though vigorous and pithy — and thus does capture certain qualities of Engels's prose — is extremely loose, frequently inaccurate, and on occasion it garbles or reverses Engels's meaning'. The new translators, although they checked all Engels's references, seemed to have a wish to discredit the work, concluding, 1958, p.15, that 'historians may no longer regard Engels's book as an authentic work which gives a valuable picture of social conditions in England in the 1840s'. Henderson and Chaloner, for example, accuse Engels of basing his historical introduction 'almost entirely upon the book called *The Manufacturing Population of England* (1833), and written by an obscure surgeon named

Peter Gaskell', 1958, p.xiii, and of naively accepting the myth of idyllic social conditions of an earlier age with which the 'horrors of working in the dark satanic mills of the factory towns' were compared. This, though partly true, was unfair, given that Engels did acknowledge his sources and admits in a footnote (to which Henderson and Chaloner do not refer): 'The history of the development of the proletariat contained in the introduction to the present work is chiefly taken from this work of Gaskell's', p.98. Henderson and Chaloner further accuse Engels of mistakes and inconsistencies, and of deliberately misleading his readers, all of which make it difficult to avoid the conclusion that 'Engels can hardly be taken seriously as an historian', 1958, p.xv.

The most recent translation was the work of the Institute of Marxism and Leninism in Moscow, and was according to an editor's note 'verified by the Institute against the text of the Second German Edition' (which had appeared in 1892, the very year Mrs Wischnewetzky's 'authorised' translation appeared in Britain). It was published in 1969 with an introduction by Eric Hobsbawm who earlier (1962) had already dismissed Henderson and Chaloner's criticisms as either 'trivial or wrong'. Interestingly, these translators left off the 'in 1844' from the title, claiming that this was how Engels originally had it. Furthermore, a close inspection of the text reveals that there is virtually no difference in the translation from that of Mrs Wischnewetzky's apart from a few additional footnotes that had been missing from the 1886 translation. Lastly, quite why Engels himself never translated his own work, given his fluency in English, remains a mystery. Perhaps after all, in spite of his protestations to the contrary, he was largely satisfied with the efforts of Mrs Wischnewetzky.

23   Marx himself never engaged in primary empirical social research in Britain (although he did in France. See note 6 to the Introduction). However, in the first volume of his *Capital* (1867) he uses a variety of secondary material, collected in his period of exile in London from 1849 onwards, to describe social conditions in Britain. While he remained in Britain, Marx lived in virtual isolation. He relied for evidence for his ideas almost entirely on English authors and experience. Berlin, 1963, p.182, says:

> Those pieces of detailed social and historical research, which form the best and most original chapters in *Das Capital*, are chiefly occupied with periods in which most of the evidence could be obtained from the financial columns of the Economist newspaper, from economic histories, from statistical material to be found in government Blue Books . . . and other sources to which access could be had without leaving the confines of London, or indeed of the Reading Room of the British Museum.

Marx was probably the first to use the Blue Books for scientific purposes, and in a way made pioneering use of official statistical information. In his chapter on 'The Working Day' Marx shows in detail the 'physical and mental degradation' forced on men, women and children by working long hours in unhealthy conditions. He tells of the bitter struggle to give some relief by way of legal limits on the number of hours worked and the passing of the factory acts. In a chapter on 'Machinery and Modern Industry' Marx, describing the crippling effect of machinery on workers and the environmental effects of capitalist exploitation of agriculture, uses a number of sources that Engels had quoted in 1844, for example, Andrew Ure's *The Philosophy of Manufacturers* (1835) and Peter Gaskell's *The Manufacturing Population of England* (1833). It is also clear from footnotes that Marx had studied the works of Petty, Arbuthnott and Eden. There are extracts from the *Morning Chronicle*, but curiously, no mention of Mayhew's studies, even though the latter's letters to the *Morning Chronicle* and the 1851 and 1861 editions of *London Life and the London Poor* appeared while Marx was in London. Lastly, it appears that Marx never came across the studies of poverty and the working classes in the *Journal of the Statistical Society of London*.

24   These letters have been collected together and a selection of them published by Thompson and Yeo, 1971, together with a commentary by Thompson on Mayhew and his relationship with the *Morning Chronicle*, and Yeo on Mayhew as a social investigator. All Mayhew's letters have recently been published in six volumes as *The Morning Chronicle Survey of Labour and the Poor: The Metropolitan Districts*, 1980.

25   Thompson, 1971, p.11.

26   Letter I, 19 October 1849, reproduced in Thompson and Yeo, 1971, p.102.

27   Yeo, 1971, p.54.

28   Mayhew never, in fact, actually used his definition to make any estimates of the numbers involved. He probably intended it only as an indication of the kind of people with whom he was concerned. Yeo points out, 1971, p.55n, that he later toyed with a dietary criterion and discussed the 'point of sufficiency' of wages.

29   Letter I, 1849, Thompson and Yeo, 1971, p.103.

30   Letter II, 1849, Thompson and Yeo, 1971, p.104.

31   Ibid., p.105.

32   Ibid., p.108.

33   Ibid., p.111.

34   Yeo, 1971, p.64.

35   Letter VI, 1849, Thompson and Yeo, p.117.

36   Ibid., p.118.

37 Letter LXVI, 1850, Thompson and Yeo, 1971, pp 384-8.
38 Yeo, 1971, p.82.
39 Ibid., p.85.
40 Thompson, 1971, p.41.
41 Yeo, 1971, p.476.
42 Ibid., p.477.
43 Ibid., p.77.
44 Ibid., p.81.
45 Thompson, 1971, p.47.
46 Thompson notes that the publishers (Griffin, Bohn and Co.) may have commissioned Binny without Mayhew's permission. Their note at the front of the book reads: 'The publishers think it right to state that, in consequence of Mr. Mayhew's absence from England, they placed the completion of the volume in the hands of Mr. Binny, who has supplied all after page 498'.
47 Mayhew and Binny, 1862, p.383.
48 Rosenberg, 1968, p.vi.
49 Yeo, 1971, p.477.
50 Ibid., p.51.
51 Thompson, 1967, p.58.
52 Humpheries, 1971, p.xix.
53 Rosenberg, 1968, p.vii.
54 Yeo, 1971, pp 65-66.
55 Harrison, 1967.
56 Dyos, 1967, p.13.
57 Mayhew, 1861, vol.I, p.2.
58 See Keating, 1976, who in his introduction describes both the literary and the investigatory aspects of social exploration between 1866 and 1913, connecting social research with the novelists of the period.
59 See Fried and Elman, 1971, for a brief but informative account of Booth's early experiences. A more detailed version may be found in Simey and Simey, 1960.
60 It is usually claimed that Booth was prompted in this by a comment made by the founder of the Social Democratic Federation, Henry Hyndman, to the effect that a survey conducted by them had shown that 25 per cent of the population of London lived in distress, and that Booth had visited Hyndman to tell him that the figure was exaggerated and that he would undertake an elaborate survey to show that this was the case. Hennock, 1976, has shown, however, that no such SDF survey existed and that Hyndman was probably confusing a survey of unemployment made by them with a survey undertaken by the *Pall Mall Gazette*, the results of which appeared after Booth had already formulated his ideas. Booth's study, argues Hennock, was more

likely a reaction to the general confusion on the extent of poverty being generated at the time.

61   Booth, 1887, p.374.

62   The 'Descriptive Map of London Poverty 1889' was scaled at 25 inches to the mile and measured 16 ft by 30 ft. Every street was coloured according to the apparent means of the inhabitants in terms of a seven-point colour scheme. A second map 'Showing degrees of Poverty in London in areas with about 30,000 inhabitants in each', was coloured according to a seven-point scale of percentage poverty, Pfautz, 1967, p.30n.

63   Booth, 1889, p.165 and 1891, p.23. Quoted from Hennock, 1976, p.72.

64   Booth, 1889, p.39. Quoted from Hennock, 1976, p.75.

65   He does not say how he selected his school board visitors. Presumably, the 4,000 cases were *all* those known to those he selected; it seems there were nine. It is doubtful, therefore, whether his subset constituted a random sample in any sense. He does say that 'it would not be safe to generalise very confidently from an analysis of this sort unless it can be supported by other evidence. The figures have, however, statistically one great element of value. They are representative of *all* the poor in the districts from which they are drawn and not only of those who apply for relief'. By 'representative' Booth clearly meant a complete enumeration.

66   Quoted from Hennock, 1976, p.82.

67   Booth, 1889, p.6.

68   In this connection, Booth served as consultant to the Registrar General on the preparation of the schedules for the 1891 Census. Indeed, he was able to prevail on the authorities to include a special set of questions on the number of persons per room and the number of servants employed, which became the basis for a new social classification of the people. Moreover, he personally instructed the 3,000 enumerators in order to maximise the validity and reliability of the results of these queries (Pfautz, 1967, p.32).

69   Industry series, I, p.10.

70   Religious influences, I, p.7.

71   Booth had published his early studies on Tower Hamlets in the *Journal of the Royal Statistical Society*. It first appeared as a monograph in 1889 entitled *Life and Labour of the People*. Though embracing only East London, the volume was a vast compendium of charts, maps, statistics, harrowing descriptions of families, homes, streets, conditions of work, all brought together under the general subject of poverty. Two years later a second volume appeared, this time entitled *Labour and Life of the People*. The title had been turned round because another author laid claim to the original title. This volume took

in all the districts omitted from the first, covering a total population of three million. It was here that the street was first used as the unit of analysis. In 1892 Booth began work on his industry series and by 1897 five volumes had been published. These Booth added to a four-volume re-issue of his previous study of poverty, the whole now constituting a nine-volume second edition of *Life and Labour of the People of London*. After he had completed his investigations of religious influences, the whole was added together in a third edition with the same title as the second, amounting to 17 volumes in all.

72 Final volume, p.200.
73 Ibid., p.207.
74 See Pfautz, 1967, p.86.
75 Ibid., p.108.
76 Poverty series, III, p.12.
77 Religious influences, I, p.15.
78 Ibid., p.207.
79 Final volume, p.205.
80 See Pfautz, 1967, p.106.
81 Simey and Simey, 1960, p.58, cite a letter written to his wife in 1876 in which Booth wrote that he shared with one of his employees, a German, a keen interest in working-class movements, 'though not in Karl Marks (— is that the name? —)'.
82 Pfautz, p.128.
83 Poverty series, III, p.261.
84 Industry series, V, p.332.
85 See Pfautz, 1967, pp 149-50.
86 Religious influences, I, p.30.
87 Final volume, pp 126-7.
88 Pfautz, 1967, p.170.
89 *Self Help* in fact sold a quarter of a million copies by the end of the century, sales far exceeding those of the late nineteenth-century novels. For an account of Smiles and his work, see Briggs, 1965, chapter 5, 'Samuel Smiles and the Gospel of Work'.
90 See Humpheries, 1980, p.179.
91 Ibid., p.184.
92 Ibid., p.183.
93 See Nelson, 1965, who found parallels between some of the characters in *Our Mutual Friend* (1864) and those in Mayhew's *Morning Chronicle* letters. See Humpheries, 1980, p.223.
94 For a detailed comparison of the styles of the two writers, see Humpheries, 1980, chapter 6, 'Mayhew and the Literature of His Time'.
95 Keating, 1971, chapter 4, 'Walter Besant and the "discovery" of the East End'.

3 Empirical sociology in the early twentieth century

The early twentieth century was an extraordinary period in the history of British empirical sociology. The basis of a fully modern, analytic and theoretically founded empirical sociology looked as though it would emerge from several quarters all at once. Yet each promise proved in the end to be a false dawn. One might for example have expected that Booth's studies would have become the basis of an active school of empirical sociology in Britain, even of a new era in which empirical evidence was linked at the very least to insightful empirical generalisations, if not ultimately to general sociological theory. Booth had taken the strengths of both social accounting and social exploration and had welded them into a social survey that in many respects remains unparalleled today in terms of coverage, depth and wealth of sociological insight. Yet he had little time for explicit and deliberate theorising and the social theorists of the day saw his work only as mundane fact gathering. Even his followers like Rowntree and Bowley, who made many improvements in Booth's techniques of research, failed to perceive the wider implications for sociological inquiry. Instead they reverted to social accounting and perpetuated the separation of empirical research from social theorising.

Rowntree's surveys of York

Rowntree, like Booth, was the son of a wealthy businessman, this time with an expanding cocoa business in York. Like Booth, he successfully continued the business aspect of his life and used the profits to finance empirical social research. Like Booth, he had become aware of poverty in the midst of plenty, and was acquainted personally with the conditions under which the working classes lived. By 1897, at the age of 26, Rowntree was fully established in the world as a director of the family business, he was an active social worker in York and, of that year, a married man.[1] He became fascinated by Booth's London surveys and wondered if a similar degree of poverty existed in provincial cities. Accordingly, he decided in 1899 to undertake a detailed investigation into the social and economic conditions of the wage-earning classes in the City of York.

Rowntree improved on Booth's methods of inquiry in a number of respects. First, whereas Booth had relied largely on school board visitors for his information, Rowntree revived the idea of going directly to the working-class families about whom he wished to know. York was small enough, with its 15,000 houses and its population of 75,812, to make possible, if laborious, a house-to-house visit of every working-class household. In all, 11,560 families living in 388 streets and accounting for 46,754 people were studied. These included all working-class households, not just those with schoolchildren as had been the case with Booth. The bulk of the information was obtained by a paid investigator aided by a small team of part-time helpers who went systematically from house to house, as indeed many had done in the 1830s for the statistical societies (although Rowntree seemed unaware of this tradition of statistical investigation). Rowntree comments that the work of the investigator 'involved the paying of many thousands of visits, and required no small amount of discernment and tact. He found that the people, with few exceptions, were willing to supply the information sought'.[2] Most of the information was collected from housewives and included particulars of housing (the number of residents, rooms, houses sharing taps and toilets, and whether back-to-back), age and occupation of householder, the rent paid, details of other wage earners in the house, and the sex and age of children. The investigator also made informal notes like 'Mother very poorly, daughter's husband out of work' and 'One child, respectable, wife and house dirty and untidy. Very little furniture' much as members of the statistical societies had done 70 years before.

Direct information on wages, however, was frequently not obtained. Rowntree commented later in a letter dated 1952: 'Many of the women would not know what their husbands were earning, and even if they had known, they would not have told me'.[3] Instead Rowntree estimated wages. In the case of skilled workers it was assumed to be the average wage that obtained in the district for the particular trade, but for unskilled workers he relied on information supplied by employers. His own position as a large-scale employer undoubtedly helped him enormously at this stage of the survey. The London and North-Eastern Railway for example gave him exact details of the wage of every worker on their payroll. Rowntree made allowances for short-time and overtime, and the cost of tools based on information supplied by trade union secretaries, masters and the workers themselves.

Another fundamental improvement on Booth's method was Rowntree's definition of a poverty line. This was based on evidence from developments in nutritional science concerning the amount of calories, protein and fat necessary to maintain persons in a state of physical efficiency. 'Primary' poverty existed where incomes were insufficient to provide the bare necessities of physical efficiency, no matter how wisely and carefully those incomes were spent. 'Secondary' poverty existed where incomes, though sufficient if wisely and carefully spent, were nevertheless spent in such a way that the family did not maintain the necessities of physical efficiency. Furthermore, it was *family* income that Rowntree took into account, not just the wages of the chief wage earner. He divided the population into seven classes, where classes A to D were based on family incomes of under 18s, 18s and under 21s, 21s and under 30s, and over 30s for a 'moderate' family consisting of parents and two to four children, while classes E, F and G related to domestic servants, the servant-keeping class, and persons in public institutions. The latter three classes were excluded from the investigation, either because they were not working class or were living away from their homes. Working-class families were reclassified up or down if they had fewer or more children than the number specified for a moderate family. Family income included wages of father, mother and children, and payments made for board and lodging by older children or lodgers.

To obtain the number of people living 'in poverty', Rowntree did not, as Booth had done, simply select a level of income as a poverty line. Instead he calculated what income was required by families of different sizes to provide a minimum of food, clothing and shelter necessary for the maintenance of merely physical efficiency. To do this he had to calculate the average price paid for various foods and fuel and take the actual cost of rent paid for houses. The income of each family was then compared with these standards to ascertain how many were living in primary poverty. Rowntree found 1,465 families, comprising 7,230 persons, were living in this condition. This represented 15.46 per cent of the wage-earning class in York and 9.9 per cent of the whole population of the city. This assumed, however, that every penny earned by every member of the family went into the family purse, and did not allow anything for travel, recreation, or luxuries of any kind, or for sick or funeral clubs.

To obtain the number in secondary poverty, Rowntree took the total number of households where the investigator saw 'evidence' of poverty, and subtracted from these the number shown to be in primary poverty. On this basis 43.4 per cent of the wage-earning class (27.8 per cent of the total population) were living in poverty, of which 27.9 per cent (17.9 per cent of the total population) were in secondary poverty. Booth, who naturally enough viewed Rowntree's study with great interest, saw the comparison of the figures for London and York as 'very close'. He thought that Rowntree's study was the answer to those critics who believed that he had uncovered a special 'metropolitan' problem of a quite exceptional character. Yet the strict comparability of the figures was doubtful. The figure Rowntree compared with Booth's for London was his 'overall' proportion of those in poverty, obtained by combining primary and secondary figures. This was 27.8 per cent compared with Booth's 30.7 per cent. Both sets of figures were in some degree subjective in that they depended on the individual judgements of observers, in the case of Rowntree on his investigators, and in the case of Booth on the school board visitors.

Rowntree's analysis of the causes of poverty was altogether more sophisticated than Booth's had been. He distinguished six 'immediate' causes of primary poverty — death of chief wage earner, incapacity of chief wage earner, chief wage earner out of work, chronic irregularity of work, largeness of family and lowness of wages. He found that in over half of the cases of primary poverty, it was due to insufficiency of wages where the chief wage earner had regular work. In only 2.3 per cent of the cases was it a result of the chief wage earner being out of work, and in 2.8 per cent of the cases it was due to irregularity of work. Most of the rest was a result of largeness of family or death of chief wage earner. Rowntree concluded that the wages paid for un-skilled labour in York were, on the whole, insufficient to provide food, shelter and clothing adequate to maintain a family of moderate size in a state of bare physical efficiency. This much was just an elaboration of what Booth had already shown to be the case in London, but Rowntree went on to put the idea of poverty into a dynamic context of the life-cycle. He argued that the life of a labourer was marked by five alternating periods of want and comparative plenty. As a child he would probably have been in poverty until he grew up and was able to supplement the family income by earning money. When he married and had children himself, he probably sank back into poverty until *his* children grew up. Finally, when his children left home he would, in old age, sink once again back into poverty. Rowntree realised that his study was only a static snapshot, whereas in reality people were moving out of and falling into poverty all the time. This meant that probably nearly *all* the working classes suffered from poverty at some time in their lives. The causes of secondary poverty, Rowntree argued, were largely drink and gambling, but he clearly recognised that these were as often symptoms of other circumstances as direct causes of poverty.

Another major innovation Rowntree made in terms of research methods was the use of family budgets to obtain detailed records of diets and patterns of expenditure. For this purpose notebooks were prepared and given to 35 families. On what basis they were selected, Rowntree does not say, but, in the event, only 18 of the budgets were used. In the notebooks the housewife was asked to record the total of income from all sources on a weekly basis, to give an account of all monies spent, showing the kind and quantity of goods bought each day and the prices paid, and to record what the family ate and drank each day. These budgets provided evidence of the serious nutritional deficiencies suffered by the poorer sections of the labouring classes. He calculated that the labouring classes received on average about 25 per cent less food than had been proven by scientific experts to be necessary for the maintenance of physical efficiency.

Rowntree went on to consider a number of topics the investigation of which required no small amount of methodological sophistication. He used the data from his main study to detail housing conditions with a mixture of quantitative and quasi-statistical information; he looked at rent levels, overcrowding both by persons per room and persons per acre, and standards of health. However, in subsidiary investigations he examined the physical condition of a 'sample' of 1,919 schoolchildren, and he collected information on public houses, counting the number of persons present in the singing rooms attached to six public houses in the central parts of York at 9 p.m. on two nights in 1901, a procedure that anticipated similar attempts by Mass Observation in the 1930s. He also made a detailed case study of three public houses.

Rowntree visited every elementary school in York in order to determine the provision of education, and he conducted a 'Church Census' on two Sundays in 1901 that recorded the number of persons attending public worship on these two days. He tried to ascertain the working-class attendance by asking the enumerators at each church to discriminate as far as possible between the 'working' and the 'upper' classes. He attempted to gather information on trade unionism in York, but he found them 'exceedingly averse to imparting information'. He also presented information on the operation of the poor relief system in York and considered the probable effect of universal old age pensions on poverty.

The results of Rowntree's investigations were published in 1901 as *Poverty, a Study of Town Life*. 'The appeal of the book', writes Briggs, 'did not depend on its style, which was workmanlike rather than dramatic — the strength of the text rested on its economy of treatment and the steady accumulation and unfolding of evidence'.[4] The findings were offered in a cooler, more detached manner than Booth's; yet although the techniques of research were rather more sophisticated than those Booth had used, in the process the sheer humanity and the contact with the reader detectable in much of Booth's writings was lost. Rowntree never engaged in social exploration as Booth had done, while the wandering hordes of Mayhew and the distant tribes and the darkest African rain forests of William Booth had been replaced by 'poverty cycles' and levels of 'physical efficiency'. The graphic vignette made way for the statistical table; the individual became part of the statistical aggregate. It was not the poor, but poverty itself — its extent, its depths and its causes — that was studied. But more important was the loss of sociological insight that had been so apparent in Booth's work. Rowntree's book was descriptive and followed very much in the tradition of the social accountants. His aim had been 'to state facts rather than suggest remedies'. He apparently never perceived in Booth's work its major innovation which was to combine the two traditions of social accounting and social exploration as a basis for making insightful empirical generalisations. Rowntree had clearly come across Engels's *The Condition of the Working Classes in 1844*, for he refers to it in a footnote, but only in the context of Engels's estimates of the number of Irish that had come over to England in the early 1840s. He apparently never saw the relevance of Engels's ideas and theories about the development of capitalism to his own study of poverty in York.

Although Rowntree had not set out to propound remedies, his book nevertheless contained an implicit demand for state action and pointed to a need for a future welfare policy. Rowntree became a vigorous advocate of state-sponsored social security. He travelled to several parts of the country giving lectures on his book. Having discovered, or rather confirmed Booth in his discovery, that poverty was related to questions of employment, Rowntree turned his attention to the problem of un-employment in York. In collaboration with Lasker he made a detailed investigation. Over a three-day period in June 1910 he sent 60 investi-gators to call on every working-class house in York to ascertain whether any person there was out of work on 7 June and desirous of finding it. Once the unemployed were located, detailed investigation of each case followed. For this purpose he used a smaller number of investigators and the information they supplied was strictly checked. Each investi-gator was given an 'inquiry schedule' listing questions to be asked. An 'unemployed' person was carefully defined as one 'who is seeking work for wages, but unable to find any suited to his capacities and under conditions which are reasonable, judged by local standards'. The infor-mation was produced in great detail in the book which emerged in 1911 as *Unemployment: A Social Study*. There were tables listing the condition of every worker, detailed descriptions of selected families, and separate treatments for youths under 19, regular workers, casual workers, builders, the work-shy, and women and girls.

At the time York had 82,000 inhabitants of whom 1,278 fitted the definition of 'unemployed'. One-third of these were simply casual workers who suffered from under-employment and irregularity of work rather than from unemployment proper. Over one half of the unemployed were described as 'men of character and physique'. The authors say: 'Our figures show it is quite mistaken to regard the unemployed problem as purely one of the efficiency and character of the workers'. Rowntree and Lasker did not refrain on this occasion from suggesting a number of reforms, for example, training for youths, regulation of work by public bodies and decasualisation.

Bowley and the sample survey

Further major advances in the techniques of survey research were made by Arthur Bowley who had graduated from Cambridge in 1891 with a degree in mathematics. However, he developed an interest in economics and social problems, especially the problem of social reform in Britain at the turn of the century. His first book was an account of England's foreign trade in the nineteenth century, and he went on to consider the relationship between movements of wages and prices — the subject of his first paper to the Royal Statistical Society in 1895 and the first of many on that topic. In the same year he went to join the small and mainly part-time staff of the newly established London School of Economics when its first session began. When the Chair of Statistics was created in 1919 he became its first occupant and he continued to teach statistics to successive generations of students until his retirement in 1936.

It was Bowley who pioneered sampling techniques in survey investigation and the first account of the use of such techniques was the one he gave to the Royal Statistical Society in 1912. He reported on working-class households in Reading based on a random sample of one in 20 households, amounting to 840 out of a total of 18,000. Three years later, with Burnett-Hurst, he published his *Livelihood and Poverty* which was based on a systematic random sample of about one in 20 working-class households in each of the four towns. For Northampton the method of inquiry was described as follows. From a local directory listing all residents in the borough, every twentieth house or building was noted. These were then classified according to whether they were dwelling houses, shops, factories and so on. A list of 'principal residents' was used to exclude from the list households who were assumed to be not working class. The remainder 'practically coincided with the wage-earning class'.[5] Each house (743 in all) was then visited and information sought on occupation, earnings, household composition, rent, rooms and kind of house. Those who were found to be not members of the wage-earning class were excluded. Similar methods of sampling were used in the other three towns. In all, 2,139 houses were sampled covering 9,720 persons.

Bowley found that 13.5 per cent of working-class households were on or below the poverty line as defined by Rowntree. Bowley himself used a slightly modified version of Rowntree's food scale. Rowntree's standard had been mainly vegetarian, it did not distinguish between the needs of children of different ages, and it assumed scientific expenditure at minimum cost. Bowley's standard was rather less rigid and considered that a workman would sacrifice other necessities in favour of additional meat and he allowed greater elasticity in the diet of children by differentiating according to age. However, Bowley adopted Rowntree's standards for clothing, cleaning and lighting without any change except that due to a rise in prices. On Bowley's new standard the proportion of working-class households in poverty was only slightly less — 13 per cent compared with 13.5 per cent. These figures were in close agreement with the proportion of working-class families that Rowntree had found to be in primary poverty in York at the beginning of the century, when he estimated that 1,465 families out of a total of 11,560 or 12.7 per cent were below the poverty line. However, Bowley's figures masked a wide disparity between the results for individual towns, which varied from under 7 per cent to over 20 per cent.

Jones[6] has argued that the figures gave too rosy a picture of conditions in the towns investigated, because the household or family was used as the unit of analysis. The families which contained the largest number of dependants fared worst. Some 27 per cent of the children were living in families which failed to reach the low standard taken as necessary for healthy existence. In Reading nearly half of the school-children and 45 per cent of the infants were living 'in primary poverty irrespective of exceptional distress caused by bad trade or short-time'.[7] The principal cause for this state of affairs was, as Booth and Rowntree had found, low wages. The authors say: 'Actually one-half of the households below the poverty line at Warrington and Reading, nearly half at Stanley, and one-third at Northampton, were living in poverty because the wages of the head of the household were so low that he could not support a family of three children or less'.[8]

A final chapter in the book was devoted to a 'Criticism of the

Accuracy of the Results' by Bowley himself in which he considered the possible sources of error from inaccuracies, unsuitable definitions of 'working class' and 'poverty', from unrepresentativeness of the sample, and from sampling error. He even calculated probable errors and confidence intervals. Of major significance, however, was that Bowley was able to demonstrate that very little error resulted from such sampling procedures by comparing his results with those from Census enumerations at several points, and that an inquiry adequate for many purposes could be rapidly and inexpensively made by a proper system of sampling.

Bowley was now Professor of Statistics at the University of London. One of his earliest courses was devoted to the interpretation of government publications, and a major objective of a great deal of his work was to demonstrate that the intensive survey was simply not necessary. In 1915 he published a book, which contained the substance of five public lectures given in 1914, entitled *The Nature and the Purpose of the Measurement of Social Phenomena*. In this he was, once again, far ahead of his time, this time in laying the foundations of what contemporary sociologists would call 'measurement theory'. He says: 'The general problem of social statistics is to define or delimitate and enumerate classes, to specify attributes or characteristics of the members of those classes, to measure these attributes and describe their variation, and to discover relationships and causal connections'.[9] A clearer statement of modern empirical research would be difficult to find. Bowley goes on: 'Like other investigators, the statistician has to invent his own units of measure . . . . The possibilities of description are not exhausted even when no unit can be devised, for objects can be placed in order without any measured scale'.[10] This is probably the first statement about 'levels of measurement' by any sociologist.

Bowley then turned to the issue of what categories of classification one could or should use. What we need, he says, is a working definition of 'society' which will at once involve us in its relationship to territory and territorial sub-division. The relationship of persons to areas is quite complex, especially where many people do not reside and work in the same places. Measurements of density of population can, as a result, be very misleading. Finally, he looks at the various ways of measuring family income, national production and consumption, standard of living, and economic progress.

Bowley continued by looking at 'The Problems of Social Classes'. Booth and Rowntree, it was true, had used categories of social class that were largely economic in nature, but Bowley's treatment was remarkably modern in that it took occupation as well as income and habits as determinants of social class. A social class, suggests Bowley,

> consists of a group of persons and their dependants who have intercourse on equal terms so far as sex and age allow. The determinants will then be occupation, income, and habits. It is at once clear that there can be no hard and fast line separating one class from another, and perhaps the most hopeful way of identifying classes will be to try to find a few distinct types and suppose people grouped in classes about those types which they most resemble.

Bowley made rough distinctions between the 'upper', 'professional', 'middle' and 'manual' classes, but concluded: 'It is doubtful whether it is possible to divide a society into such well defined social classes that a useful measurement could be made of the number in any class'. He proposed a multi-dimensional classification by using an analytical grid derived from the combination of occupational or economic attributes on the one hand and of cultural or behavioural indicators of social interaction on the other.

Bowley was of the opinion that the analytically informed use of official statistics was for most purposes all one needed to achieve an adequate understanding of social organisation and social problems. At the same time the sheer cost of extensive inquiries was on its own sufficient to discourage private inquiry. Government-financed research was not only likely to be more comprehensive than anything the individual investigator could mobilise, but would be more impartial and more authoritative. Private surveys Bowley regarded as problem-exposing pilot studies which, it was hoped, would result in definitive government investigation.

Between them Rowntree and Bowley had made considerable technical advances on the conduct of surveys from the time of Booth, yet they had moved further away from an analytical empirical sociology, back to the notion of social accounting, a trend that may be even more clearly seen in a study published in 1907 as *West Ham* by Howarth and Wilson. This was sponsored by a committee that included Bowley, Hobhouse and Beatrice Webb among other eminent people. The organising secretary, G.E. Arkell, had worked with Booth. The collection of data on rents, rates and wages was meticulous and exhaustive. Yet, says, Abrams,

> the end product is strangely emasculated. Apart from enormous statistical tables, the sense of evidence is weak. The central object of study, to show that the system of casual labour was the mainspring of a spiral of economic dependence paralysing a whole neighbourhood is simply not achieved . . . . There is something

desperately inconclusive, even mindless, about the whole work. Its intention is descriptive. Its perspective is administrative. . . . What is most striking is the lack of any sense of sociological argument; in the end, the study makes no claim to persuasiveness beyond the traditional one, 'great pains have been taken to get exact facts'.[11]

The main recommendation to emerge was that the amount of casual labour in the area should be reduced with the help of government legislation setting up a trust that would act as sole employer for the area.

The Webbs

What has been called 'the tradition of Booth' in the end amounted to very little, although there were a few inquiries that were inspired by it.[12]

Another promising source, however, lay in the kind of empirical inquiry undertaken by Beatrice and Sidney Webb. Beatrice Potter (as she then was) had been one of Booth's assistants in his early inquiry into Tower Hamlets. She began in 1887 to assist 'Cousin Charlie' by making an inquiry into dock labour. At first simply one of the interviewers, Beatrice soon established herself as an independent authority. In the same year an article of hers appeared in the highly respectable pages of *The Nineteenth Century*.[13] Other articles soon followed. Booth prescribed for her the job of investigating 'sweated' labour in the East End tailoring trade. In the courses of the inquiry she acquired a job as a 'plain trouser hand' and 'learned how to sweat'. The investigation brought her into the public eye by producing a command to give evidence before the 1888 Select Committee of the House of Lords on the Sweating System.

Beatrice had become highly skilled as an interviewer and social investigator, but she became convinced that the complexity of the problems she had encountered meant that they were beyond solution by individual effort and could be dealt with only by collective action. This meant a departure from the principle of individualism adhered to by Booth. It also meant a departure from the territorial exploration of urban poverty. Beatrice had earlier visited some of her relatives who had not risen in the world and who lived in Bacup, Lancashire. There she discovered the 'respectable' working class and its organisations, especially the co-operative societies. These excited her imagination. They were living, growing things, ignored by the classical economists but, thought Beatrice, full of hope and promise. Instead of following Booth's suggestion that she should follow up what she had begun by an intensive study of women's labour in general, she decided to examine the co-operative movement as providing a possible alternative to the capitalist system. Early in 1889 she began work on a book which subsequently appeared as *The Co-operative Movement* and which was to hold the field as the only impartial study of its subject for many years to come.

In 1890 Beatrice met Sidney Webb, a socialist, whom she married in 1892. According to Cole, the Webbs subsequently formed a partnership that was unique in British history. 'There had never been' she wrote, 'a married partnership which was so complete and so equal in its achievements'.[14] The first fruits of this partnership were the Webbs's classic studies of trade unionism, *The History of Trade Unionism* (1894) and *Industrial Democracy* (1897). Both were characterised by a thorough and painstaking research for the facts, a feature that became characteristic of all their work. In the second of her autobiographies (published in 1948 as *Our Partnership*) Beatrice comments that after their marriage their honeymoon 'was spent investigating on the spot the ramshackle trade societies of Dublin . . . . Thence to Belfast, interviewing hard-fisted employers and groups of closely organised skilled craftsmen. . . . The honeymoon holiday ended at Glasgow, attending the Trade Union Congress, collecting trade union documents and interviewing trade union secretaries'.

The History of Trade Unionism traced the origin and growth of the trade union movement as a whole, industrially and politically, and concluded with a statistical account of the distribution of trade unionism according to trade and localities. This work, however, the Webbs regarded as 'little more than an historical introduction to the task we had set before us: the scientific analysis of the structure and function of British Trade Unions'.[15] This is what they attempted in their *Industrial Democracy*. They saw trade unions as small democracies that had changed from a 'primitive' to a 'representative' form. Policy making had passed from the hands of the direct membership to representative bodies and organisations. This change was occasioned by the 'exigencies of their warfare with the employers' and was largely piecemeal, pragmatic and unconscious. They went on to discuss the resulting relations between elector, representative, and civil servant, between central and local government, and between taxation and representation, the difficulties associated with federation, the devolution of authority to sub-groups, the use of referenda, and inter-union relations.

The second part of the book consisted of a descriptive analysis of trade union functions – the methods used (mutual insurance, collective bargaining and legal enactment), the regulations imposed in terms of standard rates, sanitation and safety, entrance into a trade and so on, and the policies actually followed. Their analysis, they believed, covered every existing type and variety of trade union action and every trade in every part of the kingdom. As far as possible they made their descriptions quantitative, reporting statistics wherever they could be obtained. In the third part the Webbs 'ventured into the domain of theory'.[16] They traced the 'remarkable change of opinion among English economists as to the effect of trade unionism on the production and distribution of wealth'. They then presented a new analysis of the working of competition in the industrial field, and gave their own interpretation or theory of the way in which the methods and regulations used by trade unions actually affected the production and distribution of wealth. This theory led the Webbs to conclude that some forms of emerging democracy were infinitely more effective than others.

It was clear from the Preface to their book that the Webbs saw their task as a sociological one and they offered 'practical help' to the student contemplating 'scientific work in any department of Sociology'. He must begin by looking at the structure and function of the organisation in which he is interested. His primary task is to observe and dissect facts, and to use these to test as many hypotheses as possible. He must adopt a definite principle in his note taking, he must read what has previously been written about the subject. The Webbs suggest that the proceedings of Royal Commissions and Select Committees are useful here. The actual investigation can use 'three good instruments of discovery' — documents, personal observation, and interviews. Significantly, they feel the need to 'add a few words as to the practical value of sociological investigation'. They argue that nobody can avoid being a 'practical sociologist'; we all need to make social decisions, and these clearly are all the better for being informed. They note that social investigation is expensive, yet 'practically no provision exists in this country for the endowment of support from public funds or any kind of sociological investigation'. They suggest that something of the order of £1,000 (at 1897 prices!) may be necessary to meet just the expenses of carrying out any worthwhile investigation, yet in London, 'the wealthiest city in the world, and the best of all for sociological investigation, the sum total of the endowment for this purpose does not reach £100 a year'.[17]

A close reading of the text of the Webbs's monumental work suggests that, like Booth's studies on poverty, it is replete with sociological insight built up inductively from the evidence, but left implicit rather than explicitly stated as an aspect of sociological theory. Their work was concerned with social institutions, their structure and their operation. Much of what they were looking at concerned the development and operation of bureaucratic structures, and although they did not present explicitly any theory of bureaucracy, and there is no evidence that they had come across any of Weber's work on the subject, they were clearly aware that certain forms of democratic organisation had a tendency to result in oligarchy, or self-perpetuating leadership. This anticipated much of Michels's work and even his celebrated 'iron law of oligarchy' which appeared in his book *Political Parties: A Sociological Study of the Oligarchical Tendencies of Modern Democracy*, first published in German in 1911 and translated into English in 1915. Thus the Webbs say:

> We see, therefore, that almost every influence in the trade union organisation has tended to magnify and consolidate the power of the general secretary. If democracy could furnish no other expedient of popular control than the mass meeting, the annual election of public officers, the Initiative, and the Referendum, trade union history makes it quite clear that the mere pressure of administrative needs would inevitably result in the general body of citizens losing all effective control over the government.

On the other hand, some emerging forms of modern democracy resulted in an elected representative assembly, appointing and controlling an executive committee under whose direction the permanent official staff perform its work. This form of democracy was much more effective.

The Webbs looked at trade union doctrine and tried to explain the conflicting policies of the trade union world in terms of three assumptions that they called the Doctrine of Vested Interests, the Doctrine of Supply and Demand, and the Doctrine of the Living Wage. While their work was not explicitly functionalist, and no reference was made to Spencer's treatises on sociology, the Webbs were clearly aware of the distinction between 'manifest' and 'latent' functions. The Doctrine of Vested Interests had the unintended consequence of promoting resistance to inventions and the obstruction of improvements, while the Doctrine of Supply and Demand resulted in a policy of restriction of numbers which had the unintended consequence of distributing 'the capital, brains, and labour of the nation less productively than would otherwise be the case'.[18] The Webbs saw trade unions in a dynamic context, losing some of their present functions and gaining others, for example supervising the instruction and education of new members. Further, trade union structures were themselves integrated into a wider set of interrelated social institutions to which they must respond and adapt.

In short, *Industrial Democracy* was for its time an amazing piece of sociological analysis, combining detailed empirical evidence with conceptual analysis and a concern to explain the facts discovered by way of theoretical interpretation. The notion of looking at the structure and function of social institutions was one that Beatrice had learned from her childhood mentor, Herbert Spencer. His books inspired in her the ambition to become a social investigator, and she resolved to develop Spencer's highly theoretical sociology into a more practical human science by grounding it in a firmer foundation of fact.[19] However, although the idea of institutional analysis persisted throughout much of the Webbs's later work, after their *Industrial Democracy* they never again attempted consciously to develop a general sociological theory.

Sidney was interested in socialism, not sociology, in promoting reform, not in developing sociological theory, and it was these political interests that increasingly began to dominate the lives of the Webbs. Sidney and Beatrice had realised that in the provision of social utilities such as public health, education, provision for the destitute, the sick and the aged, neither the co-operatives and the trade unions, nor profit-making enterprises could be expected to cope. Such provisions could be made only by the local authorities on the basis of need. Accordingly, comments Beatrice,

> it was important to discover by what means the various parishes and counties and municipalities were, in fact, governed: how their several administrations had arisen from the past and how they were now developing, and by what extensions and improvements these social institutions could be best fitted for the additional tasks that they would find themselves undertaking. Thus it was decided in 1898 to investigate the structure and functions of English local government.[20]

The Webbs acquired two research assistants who 'settled down, together or separately, in town after town, taking elaborate notes of the minutes and reports of the local authorities, and making an equally detailed study of contemporary local newspapers and pamphlets, whilst attending the meetings of the local authorities concerned, and interviewing the representatives and officials'.[21]

A tremendous study of local authority structure emerged. Ten large volumes were published between 1906 and 1929 containing over 4,000 pages in all. However, these works, argues Hamilton, were rather less readable than those of the trade union books. She argues that it is a question of language — the sentences get longer and longer, and 'have the tired fall of something submitted to repeated drafting, amended and extended, with a qualifying adjective here, an adverb there'. In fact, she argues that one is 'reminded of that curiously blunted language in which the Reports of the Commissioners and Committees, and of Government Departments, are composed'.[22] The sheer amassment of detail, while for the most part not quantitative like the work of the statistical societies and always placed in developmental and historical context, is in a strange way increasingly reminiscent of the social accounting tradition whereby the facts — admittedly in different guise — are intended to speak for themselves, without the aid of an interpretative theory.

The Webbs's studies were partly concerned with the way the Poor Law was being operated by local authorities and in 1905 Beatrice was appointed to the Royal Commission on the Poor Laws. The result was a battle on the Commission itself, with Beatrice writing a *Minority Report* that eventually was to become more significant than the *Majority Report*, but which in the short run was ignored. The Webbs decided that their task was to convince the country of the need for a more radical approach than simply proposing the relief of the poor by a combination of voluntary bodies and statutory authorities as recommended in the *Majority Report*. For the first time the Webbs turned propagandist on a large scale.

The campaign failed and the Webbs turned as political activists to the Labour movement to secure their goals. In fact the Webbs's political role was a spectacular one. Sidney had already been elected to the London County Council back in 1892 where he laid the foundations for a system of secondary education; together they were responsible for setting up the London School of Economics and Political Science, for the reorganisation of the University of London, and for proposals to re-shape state education in England which, practically unaltered, formed the basis for the Education Acts of 1902 and 1903. They founded the *New Statesman* and the Fabian Research Department, which continued the tradition of practical fact finding, and which in 1917 became the Labour Research Department. Sidney was later to become President of the Board of Trade in the first ever Labour administration of 1924, and Colonial Secretary in the second Labour government of 1929. With all this political activity it was not surprising that the Webbs's commitment to sociology suffered.

The Sociological Society

Another development that looked promising for the future of empirical sociology in Britain was the foundation in 1903 of the Sociological Society by an assortment of historians, philosophers, biologists, journalists, politicans, clergymen, town planners, geographers and businessmen. The Society published a series of *Sociological Papers* between 1905 and 1907 and began its own journal, the *Sociological Review*, in 1908. One might have expected that the Society and its journal would have become a major outlet for those who, by the beginning of the twentieth century, would have described themselves as 'sociologists' whether of the empirical, philosophical, or administrative variety. Theory and research might at last meet up and discover mutual interests.

Fletcher in his *The Making of Sociology* (1971) argues that the formation of the Sociological Society was a significant point of arrival and departure for sociology as a whole, not just in Britain, but in America and Europe. There was a sense of the ending of the first long period of the making of sociology (symbolised by the death of Herbert Spencer in that year) and the beginning of something new, as expressed in Lester Ward's *Pure Sociology*, published also in 1903. One element of this newness it was generally agreed was that the subject should now be organised and institutionalised so that teaching and research could go forward on a secure basis. At its early meetings eminent men were gathered from all walks of life, from the eugenicists Galton and Pearson to literary men such as H.G. Wells and George Bernard Shaw. Elder scholars and younger men met in face-to-face discussion. There was continuity from old to new as Geddes delivered papers on civics while Charles Booth was in the chair and contributions to the discussion were made by W.I. Thomas from the newly flourishing sociology department at Chicago University. There were men who propounded the theories of Comte, Spencer and LePlay. A paper by Victor Branford 'On the Origins and Use of the Word Sociology' represented some kind of synthesis and conspectus for what sociology was about. Above all this awareness was international. There was agreement that Britain had been the slowest to develop academic sociology and there was much discussion about the possibility of introducing the subject into the universities, especially the University of London. The two men who were to fill the first two chairs of sociology in Britain — Edward Westermarck and Leonard Hobhouse — were active participants in the Society. Durkheim was a prominent contributor to the discussion on the nature of sociology as was Ferdinand Tonnies. In short, British, French, German and American sociologists were all engaged in face-to-face discussion about the problems of their emerging discipline. Empirical sociology was also represented. Harold Mann reported on 'Life in an Agricultural Village in England' and W.H. Beveridge on the problems of unemployment. Beatrice Webb gave a paper (chaired by Westermarck) on 'Methods of Investigation'. The empirical sociologists were thus able to deliberate side-by-side with social theorists, philosophers and anthropologists.

The enthusiasm with which the Society was begun was not maintained, however. Its founding had represented the alliance of three distinct and competing schools of thought — the town planners, the eugenicists and the social workers.[23] The town planners and the eugenicists looked as though they might themselves develop new modes of social inquiry that would prove beneficial to British empirical sociology, the former by promising to link the work of Comte, Spencer and LePlay to the empirical study of cities and other regional units, and the latter by developing a sophisticated statistical approach to the study of relationships between social variables. In the event, far from benefiting empirical sociology, both had unfortunate consequences.

The man generally regarded as the instigator of the Sociological Society, Victor Branford, saw the Society as a platform for the views of his friend and colleague, Patrick Geddes, who argued that the science of cities, or 'civics' as he called it, should be the major concern of sociologists. Geddes, whose early training had been in biology and zoology, had been introduced to LePlay's detailed occupational and regional studies of family, place and work while studying in Paris. After his marriage in 1886 Geddes settled in Edinburgh where he engaged in a series of activities that laid the basis for his later career as a town planner. He founded four university residence halls for students, and he initiated the rehabilitation of old tenements and the transformation by voluntary labour of neglected patches of land into garden and play spaces. He converted the Outlook Tower on Castle Hill into what was later described as 'the world's first sociological laboratory'. Actually it was a sociological exhibition centre, a library and a meeting place where he held a series of conferences in the 1890s.

In 1903 Geddes read a paper to the Sociological Society in London (Charles Booth was in the chair at the time) on 'Civics as Applied Sociology' in which he proposed that the evolutionism of Comte, the functionalism of Spencer, and the idea of family, place and work from LePlay, should be combined into empirical surveys of the city as the fundamental unit of analysis to reveal the distinctive features of urbanism. He saw the city as an adaptive organism, responding to an historical and structural environment, and to study it properly involved combining the several disciplines of geography, economics, anthropology, demography and eugenics, all of which would be united as 'civics'.

Also in 1903 Andrew Carnegie donated $2.5 million to the town of Dunfermline along with the large Pittencrieff estate. Geddes was one of two men engaged by the trustees of the money to study and report on the best means of making the Pittencrieff estate into a public park and providing it with recreational and cultural facilities. Here was a golden opportunity for Geddes to apply all his ideas to a practical venture, unfettered by constraints, monetary or otherwise. For about three months Geddes 'haunted the streets of Dunfermline, tramped up and down every square rod of the future park, studied from every angle the historic ruined abbey and palace that lay between park and town'.[24] He was accompanied by a local photographer who recorded everything that Geddes looked at. 'With this complete photographic survey of his subject and with a trunkful of notes, sketches, and reference material, Geddes then departed for London, there to write a major part of his *City Development: A Study of Parks, Gardens, and Culture Institutes'.*[25] When he read his manifesto on civics to the Sociological Society he was able to table a printed and generously illustrated advance copy of *City Development*. The volume was quarto size and its 230 pages were filled as much by photographs, artists' sketches and architects' drawings as by printed text.

Though limited by his commission to the study of Pittencrieff Park, he found a means of making the report touch on every aspect of city life, for example, the problem of pollution and sewage disposal in the town (and even beyond) had to be tackled in order to clean up the stream running through the park. The question of park entrances and boundaries could be solved, argued Geddes, only by the Trust acquiring all property adjacent to the park and becoming a model landlord and a pioneer of housing reform. There were plans for an open-air museum of native dwellings, a history palace, an art institute, an outdoor theatre and a large concert hall. 'Everything he planned had a purpose and was an expression of an ideal' wrote one of Geddes's biographers.[26]

This was Geddes at his best. Yet it was just as sociology that the study was defective. He argued that each city, if it was to improve itself, needed three volumes to itself. First, a general survey of the geographical and historical facts of a good guide book, well illustrated with photographs, along with an interpretation of the city as a concrete product of social evolution; second, a social survey of the condition of the people (along the lines of Booth and Rowntree); and third, plans for practical development, plans that would 'recover the best ideals of the past and reinstate them in the fresh light of evolution'.[27] Geddes's *City Development*, however, was really only concerned with the last of these. It was *not* a social survey, although he urged strongly for a survey of Dunfermline such as 'that of London by Charles Booth, or by Rowntree in York'. Although he mentioned the idea of the culture of the city and of people, place and work in his report, he did not himself undertake to investigate these empirically.

The 20 trustees were somewhat taken aback on learning what *City Development* had cost them for the charges of photographer, architects, surveyors, artists, engravers and printer, not to mention Geddes's honorarium, but they were flabbergasted at his estimate for carrying out the suggestions — £1 million. The trustees turned down the plan, although not in favour of the alternative one which also had been costed at a comparable figure, and despite Geddes's protestations that by spending the interest on the money donated by Carnegie, the project could be carried out gradually over 50 years leaving the capital sum intact.

Geddes, no doubt bitterly disappointed, came to the conclusion that what was needed was the education of the people into the need for city development based on comprehensive surveys, and he plunged as an active propagandist into the town planning movement. He mounted a travelling Cities Exhibition to stir up public interest in what he was now calling 'geotechnics'. He persuaded the Sociological Society to establish a Cities Committee whose prime task it was to stimulate local community surveys on a 'do-it-yourself' basis. Most of the ensuing surveys, however, were village surveys that gathered geographical and geological information, data on land use and institutional facilities, on economic demands and resources, on transportation and occupational patterns. Most of the data were not even 'social', still less were they 'sociological' in the sense that Geddes had earlier intended. The end result was, in the words of Abrams, that Geddes had

> created an opportunity for the rapid growth of a sociology peculiarly appropriate to the world's most highly urbanised nation . . . . But he threw the opportunity away. His failure to devise an adequate method for urban sociology and his premature diversion into planning propaganda and educational projects were crucial. They discredited urban sociology among urban sociologists and established an essentially nonsociological use of the social survey among planners.[28]

The other school of thought that became associated with the Sociological Society and which promised to further the cause of empirical sociology in Britain was initiated by Francis Galton and Karl Pearson. These men, followed by George Udny Yule, developed the science of statistics that radically changed the meaning of the word 'statistics'. Instead of referring to collections of data or 'state-istics', Galton and his followers used the word to refer to the mathematical manipulation of data in order to reveal their essential characteristics. It was Galton who pioneered correlation and regression techniques, and developed the use of frequency curves, particularly the 'normal' curve, while Pearson refined the techniques of correlation to invent the correlation coefficient 'r' or 'Pearson's r' as it became known. Pearson also invented chi-square, the most widely used statistic among British sociologists today, and he pioneered the calculation of probable errors of statistics as well as the publication of statistical tables. Yule took Pearson's theory of correlation and laid the foundations of partial correlation and of linear regression for any number of variables. His interest in the practical application of statistics to social problems led him to consider the relationship between sets of categorical data (or 'nominal' data as it would now be called), and he developed the analysis of contingency tables, inventing his famous statistic 'Q', still known as 'Yule's Q', for measuring association between attributes which he published in 1900. All these developments took place in the last decade of the nineteenth century and the techniques of correlation would clearly have been extremely useful to those who wished to analyse the results of social surveys undertaken before 1914. The development of sophisticated survey-analytic techniques seemed a real possibility at this time yet, once again, that promise was to be frustrated.

Galton was initially a mathematician who became an explorer and meteorologist. He was also cousin of Charles Darwin whose *Origin of the Species*, published in 1859, had had a profound influence on him. His ambition became to apply statistics to the laws of heredity, and in 1875 he was conducting experiments with sweet-pea seeds to develop the laws of the inheritance of size. The idea of a regression line to measure correlation between sizes of seeds of mother and daughter sweet-pea plants emerged from this work. At the same time he developed the use of frequency curves and had by 1889 even managed to invent a unit-free measure of association by using his ideas about the 'normal' curve and its properties. Galton became interested in the connection between heredity and human ability and he noted that able fathers tended to produce able children. He introduced the term 'eugenics' in 1883 in his book *Inquiries into Human Faculty* to describe the science that would utilise the principles of heredity to attempt to improve the ability of the human stock.

Galton read a number of papers to the Sociological Society in the first year of its existence that outlined the nature and aims of his new science. In 1904 he founded a research fellowship in national eugenics at the University of London from which developed the Galton Laboratory of National Eugenics. At the same time Pearson was developing the parallel science of 'biometrics' — the application of statistical techniques to genetics. Like Galton, Pearson had studied mathematics at Cambridge and in 1884 he became Professor of Mathematics and Mechanics at the University of London. By 1895 Pearson had established his Biometrics Laboratory, which in 1906 amalgamated with the Galton Laboratory to become the Eugenics Laboratory with Pearson himself as director.

Yule's correlational techniques

Yule had been a student of Pearson's and when in 1893 Yule returned from a period of study in Germany, where he had been working in a field of experimental physics, Pearson offered him a demonstratorship. While he was developing his ideas about correlation, Yule also became interested in the application of statistical techniques to social problems. In 1896 he published an article on 'Notes on the history of pauperism in England and Wales from 1850, treated by the method of frequency curves'. He had also come across Booth's empirical studies of London poverty and in particular his book *The Aged Poor in England and Wales* (1894).

In 1895 Yule published an article in the *Economic Journal* entitled 'On the Correlation of Total Pauperism with the Proportion of Out-relief' in which he drew attention to a statement made by Booth in his book to the effect that 'The proportion of relief given out of doors bears no general relation to the total percentage of pauperism'. This was one among many other conclusions 'to be drawn from the study and comparison of the official statistics' relating to all the poor law 'unions' in England and Wales. These Booth had divided in 20 groups according to industrial character. The unions in each group were then arranged in order of their total percentage of pauperism the highest at the top of the list. The percentage ratio of the cost of out-relief to total relief, the percentage of crowding, the type of administration and persons per acre were then listed for each union. The tables thus constituted an 'array' — a listing of cases with the values of several variables for each case. It was not a conventional two-variable table, which would have shown the relationships more clearly. Each group was treated by itself and Booth's main method of comparison was to compare the individual unions that happened to be at the top and the bottom of each list with the mean of the whole list. Even, says Booth, 'if we abandon the comparison of extremes, and study either group from top to bottom, neither policy of administration, nor proportion of out-relief, nor the percentage of crowding appears to have any definite relations to the degree of pauperism'.[29] Because there was clearly not a perfect correlation, Booth had concluded that there was no correlation at all — an approach which, according to Selvin, was well-founded in Mill's *A System of Logic* and his 'canon of concomitant variation'.[30]

Yule, however, drew a scatter plot or 'correlation surface' as he called it for the years 1871 and 1891 showing the numbers of unions combining a given percentage of population in receipt of relief (the rate of pauperism) with the number of out-paupers to one in-pauper (giving the ratio of out-relief to in-relief). Yule's figures differed from Booth's whose proportion of out-relief to total relief was by cost and not by numbers. Furthermore, Yule's data were derived, it seems, not directly from Booth's, but from returns made elsewhere, and the figures referred to one day, while Booth's referred to a whole year. These differences, claimed Yule, were not, however, what led to the difference in conclusion.

Yule's correlation surface clearly showed a marked degree of correlation, but one that was distinctly skewed. Although he realised that, as a result, it was not strictly legitimate to compute Pearson's coefficient of correlation, Yule had no alternative statistics at his disposal. Although, apparently, no great weight could be attached to the value of the coefficient, 'its magnitude may at least be suggestive'. For 1871, r turned out to be .26 and for 1891, r was .39. Yule concluded that the rate of total pauperism in the unions of England was positively correlated with the proportion of out-relief given, and that this correlation was distinctly greater in 1891 than it had been in 1871.

Yule's results could clearly be used by those who argued that giving more out-relief *caused* a higher level of pauperism; that to reduce the level of pauperism one needed to reduce the proportion of relief given as out-relief. In a later paper published in 1899 entitled 'An Investigation into the Causes of Changes in Pauperism in England, chiefly during the last two Intercensal Decades', Yule attempted to analyse what *were* the causes of changes in pauperism. However, far from concluding that the correlation between pauperism and level of out-relief could not legitimately be interpreted as one of direct causality, he found, using techniques of multiple regression and correlation, that five-eighths of the decrease in pauperism was accounted for simultaneously by changes in out-relief ratio, the proportion of people over 65 and changes in population density. The latter two accounted for relatively small proportions of the changes in pauperism and were themselves being held constant in the equation when the relationship between pauperism and out-relief was being investigated.

Unfortunately, as in 1895, Yule had taken the ratio of out-relief (to in-relief) as the only indicator of 'administrative policy'. This enabled Yule to conclude: 'Unless, and until, then, it can be shown that some other quantity whose changes are closely correlated with changes in out-relief ratio can account for this observed association, there is no alternative to considering the result as indicating a direct influence of change of policy on change of pauperism'.[31] Yule, clearly, was no radical, and apparently did not find these conclusions either surprising or unwelcome. If he had, he might have looked at the conditions under which out-relief was given as a prior factor which caused both proportion of out-relief given and levels of recorded pauperism.[32] Yule's values can clearly be seen when he discusses the manner in which out-relief appears to have been affected by changes in the proportion of old in the population. He says: 'I have not included changes in pauperism in these equations. Of course, in as much as changes in out-relief ratio helps to estimate changes in pauperism, change in pauperism would help to estimate change in out-relief ratio — it is difficult to imagine any causal relation between the two such that pauperism should influence out-relief ratio'.[33] It did not, apparently, even cross Yule's mind that out-relief *should* respond to the level of pauperism. Yule appeared to be more interested in the elegance of his statistical methods than in the humanitarian consequences of his conclusions.

Yule's correlational techniques would clearly have been very useful to Booth in his attempts to establish the causes of poverty, yet there is no evidence that Booth even acknowledged Yule's articles of 1895 and 1899. It was unlikely that Yule, 'a courteous, even courtly man'[34] did not at least inform Booth that he had used the latter's data in his 1895 paper, while the later paper appeared in the *Journal of the Royal Statistical Society*, a copy of which Booth would certainly have received as a member of the Society. Even more curious was that Booth's followers made no reference to the developments in statistical methods. Rowntree never made use of correlation in his highly statistical analysis of the causes of poverty even though he had consulted Pearson on several occasions.[35] while Bowley, who was Professor of Statistics at the London School of Economics, wrote a book published in 1909 called *An Elementary Manual of Statistics*, but it contained no reference to Yule, Galton or Pearson. In fact the word 'correlation' did not appear in the index and the topic was not covered anywhere in the book. In short the innovations in correlational statistics pioneered by Galton, Pearson and Yule failed completely to diffuse to Booth, Rowntree and Bowley. Why this should be so is a topic that will be taken up in the concluding chapter.

The first department of sociology

One last hope for the establishment of an institutionalised empirical sociology in Britain was the setting up in 1907 of the Department of Sociology at the London School of Economics. The first lectures in the subject dated back to the 1904—5 session when there was Edward Westermarck, a Scandinavian who held a chair in philosophy at Helsinki, lecturing on general sociology, Leonard Hobhouse, an Oxford classics graduate, on comparative ethics, and there were lectures on ethnology and Japanese civilisation. When the Department was founded the chair was shared jointly by Westermarck and Hobhouse, each on a part-time basis. The remit was clear enough: to help establish the academic status of sociology in the universities and to promote the application of scientific method to sociological studies. In appointing two philosophers it was clear that precedence was being given to establishing the academic status of sociology, and it turned out to be at the expense of empirical sociology. The first sociology syllabus in 1909 in effect offered an introduction to evolutionary philosophy and comparative anthropology. At the very heart of the sociological enterprise in the view of both Westermarck and Hobhouse was the sociology of morals. It was not that either of them was against empirical enterprises — far from it — but rather that 'empirical' meant comparative, and the focus was not on Britain. Most of Westermarck's empirical material was on Morocco, while Hobhouse's interest lay in comparing moral cultures and social institutions amongst societies 'simpler' than Britain. Hobhouse was also made editor of the *Sociological Review* when it began publication in 1908. It had been hoped that this would foster active co-operation between the new Department at the LSE and the Sociological Society. In the event Hobhouse's attempt to create a synthesis of moral philosophy and social analysis bore little relationship to the work active members of the Sociological Society were trying to promote in its committees. There were criticisms of Hobhouse's editoral policy in recognition of which he resigned as editor in 1911.

The divergent tendencies in sociology were emphasised again in 1912 when the LSE established a separate Department of Social Science and Administration under E.J. Urwick, an active member of the Sociological Society. This Department, like the School of Science that had been set up in Liverpool in 1909, was devoted to the training of social workers. It was just as inimical to the development of an empirical sociology as was the Department of Sociology under Hobhouse.

Considering the difficulties experienced by Hobhouse and Westermarck in setting up their department of sociology it is perhaps not surprising that other universities were apprehensive about following suit. In fact it was nearly 50 years before the next department of sociology was established. However, it must also be kept in mind that for 600 years there had been just two universities in England (Oxford and Cambridge) and the four ancient universities in Scotland. It was not until 1832 that Durham was founded, followed by London in 1836 and Manchester in 1880. So at the turn of the century there were just five universities in England and four in Scotland. Five more were founded in England between 1900 and 1909 (Birmingham, 1900; Liverpool, 1903; Leeds, 1904; Sheffield, 1905 and Bristol, 1909). The older universities were steeped in philosophy or moral philosophy and were inimical to new developments, while the new universities of the early twentieth century were probably apprehensive about including a discipline whose status was in doubt and appearing in any case to be degenerating into warring factions.

The period between 1900 and the outbreak of war was marked by the creation and initial growth of the Labour Party and the increasing political strength of the trade unions that went with it. In 1906 the Trades Disputes Act was passed, reversing the effect of the Taff Vale case of 1902, which had made the unions responsible for losses suffered by employers during a strike. Thereafter, however, the influence of the Labour Party in Parliament failed to progress any further and in some respects support for it fell. The trade unions, by contrast, made great strides forward. New beliefs in the form of syndicalism were spreading. The idea was that the unions should take over in each industry and run it for the benefit of the workers. Industrial strife from 1911 became more serious. There were strikes and troops were used on the docks and on the railways. There was a national miners' strike in 1912. By 1913 the number of strikes had reached its peak.

In 1906 the Liberals won a landslide victory in the General Election. They had not been elected on a platform of radical reform, but changing social attitudes and political events pushed them in that direction. The revelations of poverty by Booth and Rowntree, the discovery that a high proportion of the recruits for the Boer War (1899–1902) were unfit for military service, concern about unemployment and the growth of collectivist thinking had all contributed to pressures that resulted in the appointment of a Royal Commission on the Poor Laws in 1905. Twenty members were appointed including six from the Charity Organisation Society, Beatrice Webb and Charles Booth. Although the results of their inquiries were not published until 1909, the pressures that led to the creation of the Commission were still there in 1906. The Liberals passed some useful, although minor reforms, but in 1908 the Prime Minister, Campbell-Bannerman, was forced to retire through ill-health. He was replaced by Asquith. Lloyd George became Chancellor and Winston Churchill was appointed to the Board of Trade. The government's electoral support was flagging so a number of major reforms were introduced, beginning with the Pensions Act of 1908. Booth's inquiries in this area had undoubtedly been very influential. A number of Acts limited working hours for men for the first time, initially in the mines, but later in the 'sweated' trades. Labour exchanges were set up in 1909, and National Insurance was introduced in 1911. The cost was to be met through highly progressive taxation.

It was against this background that sociology in Britain had become fragmented, and interest in empirical sociology in particular, as one of the fragments, declined. Its long-established interest in social reform seemed to wilt whenever the need for reform seemed less urgent or when the government itself was busy legislating reform.

Notes

1   See Briggs, 1961, for a full account of Rowntree's life and works.
2   Rowntree, 1901, p.14.

3   Quoted from Briggs, 1961, p.28.

4   Ibid., p.31.

5   Bowley and Burnett-Hurst, 1915, p.52.

6   Jones, 1948, p.72.

7   Ibid., p.45.

8   Bowley and Burnett-Hurst, 1915, p.41.

9   Bowley, 1915, p.7.

10   Ibid., p.9.

11   Abrams, 1968, p.151.

12   Thus Davies made an investigation into the history and present conditions of the parish in which she was living — Corsley in Wiltshire. She conducted a house-to-house survey of the 220 households in the village, family budgets were collected, and information was sought on wages from employers and from the inhabitants themselves. She used Rowntree's definition of poverty, and found 12 per cent of the families were living in primary poverty. The results were published in 1909 as *Life in an English Village*. McKibbin (1978) looked at the writings of three women — Helen Bosanquet, M. Loane, and Lady Florence Bell — who attempted to go beyond the Booth-type survey, and instead of measuring the economic and material conditions of the families in a statistical manner, were more interested in how social classes could be revealed and understood through their codes, conventions, habits and mental horizons. Lady Bell's *At the Works*, published in 1907, became fairly well known. This was an account of the development and process of ironmaking in Middlesbrough towards the end of the nineteenth century, of the lives of the workmen, their wives and their children. The information was derived over a period of 30 years, during which time she and 'several female visitors' went to more than 1,000 working men's homes and conducted informal interviews.

13   See Cole, 1945, p.52.

14   Ibid., p.ix.

15   Beatrice Webb, 1948, p.43.

16   Beatrice and Sidney Webb, 1897, p.viii.

17   Ibid., p.xviii.

18   Ibid., p.810.

19   See Feaver, 1975, p.xiii.

20   Beatrice Webb, 1948, p.150.

21   Ibid., p.156.

22   Hamilton, 1933, p.183.

23   See Halliday, 1968.

24   Boardman, 1946, p.307.

25   Ibid., p.308.

26   Ibid., p.314.

27   Geddes, 1903, p.19.

28 Abrams, 1968, p.120.
29 Booth, 1894, p.63.
30 Selvin, 1976, p.41.
31 Yule, 1899, p.165.
32 Yule was aware of the possibility of spurious interpretations of data, and he had discovered the 'nonsense correlation', particularly those that emerged from time-series data. It is a pity, however, that he did not discover spurious correlation at this stage, because here appeared to be a classic example. Both the proportion of out-relief given and the percentage of the population in receipt of relief of some kind, were undoubtedly the result of differences in local policies for the administration of the Poor Law of 1834. 'In-relief' meant in effect assignment to the harsh conditions of the workhouse. 'Out-relief' was similar to modern supplementary benefits, being given while the person continued to live at home, but the application of the regulations relating to the giving of out-relief varied enormously from union to union. In some cases, over 80 per cent of all relief was given in the form of out-relief, and in others, under 20 per cent. There was no right of relief and in all cases was subject to 'good behaviour'. Additionally, it was often given only if there was clear evidence of actual destitution, and if there were no relatives who could assist without themselves becoming destitute. In some unions, there was a practical refusal of out-relief. Clearly, in those unions that were more liberal with the out-relief, there would be a higher recorded or 'identified' proportion of paupers.
33 Yule, 1899, p.275.
34 Selvin, 1976, p.45.
35 Briggs, 1961, p.42.

4 The inter-war period

Government sampling experiments

In 1923 a government department was tempted to dip, very tentatively, into the uncertain waters of sampling.[1] The Ministry of Labour wanted a fairly detailed picture of about a million and a quarter workers who were recorded from week to week as 'unemployed'. A trial run was made by recording certain characteristics of one in three 'live' claim forms for unemployment benefit. The first analysis related to 372,875 persons, but its value was limited because the particulars recorded were not full enough. Additional information could be obtained only by interviewing each claimant. The results of this preliminary experiment were shown to Bowley, who suggested that a sample of 1:1,000 claimants would be accurate enough for many purposes. The Director of Statistics at the Ministry of Labour, John Hilton, fortified by Bowley's assurance, decided to try a sample of about 10,000 cases throughout Britain. This was roughly 1 per cent of all claimants at employment exchanges.

Every hundredth claim in each box of live insured claims was tabbed and the person to whom it referred was to be invited into the manager's room for interview when he next called at the exchange. Each manager was given a different starting point so that selections were distributed evenly over all occupations (the files were classified by occupation). Local variations in the 1 in 100 ratio were allowed to avoid managers in large exchanges from being overburdened. No manager was to be asked to report on more than 30 cases. When 'tabbed' claimants did not appear at the exchange, then substitutes were allowed by taking persons either side of the tabbed one.

In addition to the 1 per cent sample, 10 per cent of all claims made during the period 2 November 1922 to 17 October 1923 were examined to investigate periodic claims. This made possible comparisons between the ages of persons whose claims were 'live' on 17 October, and the ages recorded in the 1:3 and the 1:100 samples. The comparison convinced Hilton that the 1 per cent sample was 'nowhere very wide of the mark' and that it 'answered most of its purposes quite as well as a 10 per cent or 33 per cent enquiry would have done'.[2] Four other investigations were made into the circumstances of persons insured against unemployment during the next few years. In 1926 the Statistical Department of the Ministry of Labour gave thought to the idea of extending the sampling principle to include the employed as well as the unemployed who were insured. This amounted to 17.5 million people. A sample of 1 in 218 was taken from the files kept at the Central Claims and Record Office in Kew. In a paper to the Royal Statistical Society in 1928, Hilton claimed that the value of the small sample was that it permitted 'much more detailed information upon the particular features of the individual case to be collected and analysed, and that there resulted a very considerable saving in the economy and time of prosecuting the inquiry and presenting its results'.[3] Thus 'it was possible to present, within a few months, a detailed account of all the immediately relevant circumstances of 17,500,000 persons'. Furthermore, the information furnished 'for the first time an age distribution of persons insured against unemployment, industry by industry, and from this distribution it was for the first time possible to tabulate the rate of unemployment among persons of varying ages, not only among the insured population as a whole, but among persons engaged in particular industries'.[4]

Replications of earlier work

Apart from these elaborations and extensions in the use of sampling procedures, the inter-war period saw very little development in sociological research methods or techniques. A number of pre-war surveys were replicated, more fact-finding surveys were carried out, although not by techniques any more sophisticated than those of Booth, Rowntree and Bowley, and finally a somewhat abortive attempt was made to apply anthropological techniques to the study of British society. The study by Bowley and Hogg (1925) *Has Poverty Diminished?* was probably the first time a social survey in Britain was repeated in the same areas and by 'as nearly as possible the same methods' as in an earlier study: in this case *Livelihood and Poverty* (1915) by Bowley and Burnett-Hurst. It became the first of a series of such replications. Bowley and Hogg aimed to produce a sample of 800–1,000 working-class households in each of the five towns by taking systematic samples from voting registers, or, in Northampton, from the Town Directory. The number and proportion of the families in poverty were estimated on two different assumptions: that all workers were fully employed, and that some worked more or less than normal full time, the actual income earned in a specific week being taken as the basis of measurement. On the question 'Has poverty diminished?', the authors concluded:

> The improvement since 1913 is very striking. Even on the assumption that all the families suffering from unemployment in a particular week had no adequate resources and that their unemployment was chronic, the proportion in poverty in 1924 was little more than half that in 1913. If there had been no unemployment, the proportion of families in poverty in the towns taken together would have fallen to one third, and of persons, to a quarter of the proportion in 1913.[5]

The number of families in poverty due to insufficient wages of the head of the household had dropped dramatically and was only one-fifth of the 1913 proportion. Part of this was explicable in terms of wage rates in relation to prices, but also partly in terms of a reduction in average family size. The authors, following the Booth tradition, made no policy recommendations; instead they claimed: 'It is not part of our plan to discuss remedies, but only to provide the detailed numerical setting-out of the problem'.[6]

The next replication was of Booth's monumental study under the chairmanship of Sir Hubert Llewellyn Smith, who had taken an active part in the original survey. Work began in 1928 centred at the London School of Economics and financed by the Rockefeller Foundation and various British trusts, city companies and charities. The first volume was published in 1930 as the *New Survey of London Life and Labour*. It presented a vivid picture of the changes in social and economic conditions that had taken place during the 40 or so years since Booth's inquiries. It was illustrated by statistical tables and diagrams and based mainly on the study of material already available in published form. Volumes II, V and VII, published in 1931, 1933 and 1934, gave a detailed account of each of London's chief industries, trades and services, paying more attention to the workers engaged in them than to industrial development. Volumes III and VI described social conditions in the Eastern and Western sections of the City and County of London. These appeared in 1932 and 1934. Associated with them were two series of coloured maps, comprising volumes IV and VII, showing the local distribution street by street of relative comfort and poverty. The final volume (IX) was published in 1935. It was divided into four parts, the first dealing with leisure, the next with workmen's clubs and social organisations for adolescents, and the third was concerned with drink, gambling, sex delinquency and crime. The last part gave some typical pictures of the worker's family life from the inside.

In order to measure the changes in conditions since Booth's day, it was essential to follow his methods as closely as possible. But, to make trustworthy comparison with later and contemporary surveys in other parts of the country, an independent survey of a random sample was necessary. This was directed by Bowley himself using the improved methods pioneered in the Five Towns surveys. The New London Survey was thus, in effect, two surveys in one.

In the replication of Booth or 'street survey' it was necessary to determine the boundaries between Booth's original economic classes A to G, paying particular attention to the poverty line. Booth had placed this at 21s a week for families of moderate size. Bowley estimated that in 1928–30 one would require £2 a week to buy the same as would 21s in 1890. Booth's classes B, C and D were combined, while class A was omitted altogether, because the criterion for identifying this class was more one of morals than of economics. Above the poverty line, classes G and H were also combined, since Booth's criterion of distinction had been the number of servants kept. The two remaining classes were regular standard earners (class B) and higher-class labour (class F). Booth had combined these when he extended his enquiries from East London to the rest of London, but Bowley thought it convenient to separate them. Bowley's classification thus amounted to four classes: the poor earning between £2 and £3 a week, the skilled earning between £3 and £5 a week, and the middle and upper classes earning over £5 a week. A coloured street map showed the predominant social and economic condition of its inhabitants.

The information on streets was, following Booth, obtained by questioning school attendance officers as to the social conditions of the families on their books. The officers usually knew the occupations of the chief earners in each household containing children of school age and from this average earnings could be estimated. The information was checked and supplemented from other sources such as officials connected with poor relief and employment exchanges.

In a closely reasoned chapter Bowley discussed the precise procedure followed to ascertain the proportion of the population to be assigned to each of his four classes, and how far it was fair to assume that conditions in that part of the population containing schoolchildren truly reflected conditions among the rest of the population. Booth had argued that, if anything, such families would be worse off than others, but he was unable to test this opinion. Bowley, however, could use his independent sample survey to check the assumptions. He concluded that a fair comparison could be drawn between the new and the old street survey, because virtually the same method was used in each. Furthermore, the proportion of working-class *families* in poverty was practically the same whether the calculation was based on families of all descriptions or on families with schoolchildren only. However, the experience of the latter tended to exaggerate the amount and proportion of poverty among working-class *individuals* in private families by about one-fifth over the London area as a whole.

In the sample survey Bowley used almost the same minimum standard of expenditure needed by any family to maintain health and efficiency as in his Five Towns survey, allowance having been made for changes in prices and conditions. The sample consisted of 30,000 working-class families chosen on a systematic basis from borough records or the voting register. The sampling fraction was about 1:50, but this varied from borough to borough. Small boroughs had a sampling fraction of up to 1:20 to make sure of full representation. 'Family' was defined as in the Census, while 'working-class' families were obtained by excluding families deemed to be 'middle class' on an occupational basis. In the week of investigation 11 per cent of the persons sampled in East London were found to be in poverty. This corresponded to 6.5 per cent for the Five Towns in 1923–24, 15.5 per cent in York in 1889, and 16 per cent in Merseyside in 1929–30.

The broad result of the street survey was to show that, in the enlarged area of London investigated in 1929 containing over 5.5 million people, there were nearly half a million persons in poverty according to Booth's definition of the term, amounting to 8.7 per cent. This figure was reached after careful allowance had been made for the fact that the street survey had been confined to families containing schoolchildren. Taking just these families, the sample survey showed the proportion in poverty in 1929 to be 10.7 per cent; according to the street survey it was 11.6 per cent, while the corresponding figure estimated by Booth in 1889–90 was 37.3 per cent. The closeness of the results obtained by the two independent methods in the new survey was striking, and both showed a decrease in poverty in the 40 years since Booth of about 70 per cent. If the number in poverty is related to the whole population, then Booth's figure in 1889–90 was 30.7 per cent compared with 9.6 per cent in the New Survey, again a decline of about 70 per cent. Another major difference between the Booth survey and the New Survey was that while the former attributed poverty mainly to low wages, in 1929 it was unemployment that was responsible for nearly half of the total cases of poverty, while inadequate wages in relation to size of family accounted for just under one-fifth.

The New Survey warned the reader against linking economic earnings with housing conditions. A separate map illustrated the distribution of overcrowding. Because the building and repair of houses had ceased during the war, many families were forced to share accommodation, making crowding much less associated with poverty than it once was. To the authors of the New Survey, overcrowding was now 'the dominant social question of London'.

In 1936 Rowntree, too, repeated the inquiry he had made at the beginning of the century. He wanted to discover what changes had occurred in the living conditions of the workers in the City of York. Much the same method of investigation was followed as before. There was a house-to-house visitation by a team of five women and two men who called on as nearly as possible every working-class household. The same particulars were sought as to number in the family by sex, age and occupation, and the rent, size and condition of the house. Rowntree had access to the wages books of some 60 per cent of the workers included in the inquiry through the friendly co-operation of several of the largest employers in the city. Trustworthy information on the rest could be had from employers and trade union leaders concerning normal rates of pay for different kinds of work.

The second York survey also included other sources of income such as pensions, unemployment and health benefits, public assistance and so on, all of which could be checked from a knowledge of the local scales. There was also a slight difference in the procedure dealing with the earnings of children. In the earlier inquiry family income meant total earnings, including those of grown-up children living at home. In the later inquiry family income included only estimated payments by older children for board and lodging. The sums allowed as pocket-money for children earning up to 15s a week were not included as earnings.

As his new 'poverty line' standard Rowntree adopted an expenditure of 43s 6d for man, wife and three children, or 53s with average rent added. The figure included allowances for food, clothing, fuel and light, and household and personal sundries. It had been reached as a result of an earlier investigation into what Rowntree called *The Human Needs of Labour*, an account of which was given in a book of that title published in 1937. In the allowance for food (just over £1 a week) Rowntree incorporated the latest developments in nutritional science, especially those relating to the discovery of vitamins.

Rowntree did not again attempt to measure the extent of 'secondary' poverty. He had come to the conclusion that it was impossible to estimate with any reliability the number of families who fell below the poverty line as a result of unwise spending on non-essentials. The new survey covered 16,362 families, comprising 55,206 persons (compared with 11,560 families and 46,760 persons in the earlier survey). In each case this represented just over 60 per cent of the estimated population of York. The average size of family had fallen from 4.0 to 3.4 persons per family. The 'working-class' proportion of the total population was again estimated at about 70 per cent, but his definition of 'working-class' had changed to all families whose chief wage earners were in receipt of not more than £250 a year.

In his book, which was published in 1941 as *Poverty and Progress*, Rowntree reported that 17.8 per cent of the total population of the City of York, or 31.1 per cent of the working-class population, fell below the poverty line. The corresponding figures for his earlier inquiry were 9.9 per cent and 15.5 per cent. This did not mean that poverty had increased, since there had been changes in his definitions of the 'poverty line', the 'available family income', and in the 'working-class' population. In particular, his earlier poverty line would have equalled 30s 7d at 1936 prices, not the 43s 6d after paying rent of his present investigation. Taking 30s 7d as the poverty line, the number of persons in primary poverty in 1936 was 6.8 per cent of the working-class population. This calculation, however, still failed to take account of the change in definition of 'available income' and 'working class'. Taking account of the latter by relating the number in poverty to the total population, the old proportion was 9.9 per cent and the new 4.2 per cent, an improvement in spite of an increase in unemployment from practically nil in 1899 to 10 per cent in 1936. Some 70 per cent of poverty was shown to be now related to questions of employment — either unemployment, inadequate employment, or inadequate earnings. Unemployment in particular accounted for only 2.3 per cent of primary poverty in 1899. In 1936 it accounted for 44.5 per cent.

The three main causes of poverty were, according to Rowntree, inadequate wages of workers in regular employment, unemployment and old age. Together these accounted for three-quarters of the poverty of the city. Inadequacy of wages accounted for 32.8 per cent; unemployment, 28.6 per cent; and old age, 14.7 per cent. The greatest *per capita* deficiencies, however, occurred amongst the old.

As with Booth's study the measurement of the extent and causes of poverty was only a small part of the total inquiry. The published account of the Second York Survey fell into three parts. Part One was concerned with the economic study of the population and gave illuminating analysis of families classified on the basis of income available for paying the weekly rent. The last chapter contained a very brief account of miscellaneous topics — thrift, co-operation, trade unions, friendly societies, life insurance, social services and poor relief. Part Two was devoted to improvements in housing, health and education, while Part Three was a study of leisure and religion.

Poverty and Progress was, in Briggs's view, an optimistic book, even though it was published in 1941 during one of the grimmest years of the Second World War.[7] Behind all the facts he obtained were certain discernible twentieth-century social trends to small families, more old people, higher real wages, more comprehensive social services, improved housing and better health. In spite of all these improvements Rowntree was by no means complacent, and his book was as much a call to action in new circumstances as his pioneer survey of 1901 had been.[8] His emphasis was on the inadequacy of the changes — for thousands of people life was still centred on the grim struggle with poverty and insecurity. His final words to his readers were:

> It is gratifying that so much progress has been achieved, but instead of looking backward we look forward, then we can see how far the standard of living of many workers falls short of any standard which could be regarded, even for the time being, as satisfactory. Great though the progress made during the last 40 years has been, there is no cause for satisfaction in the fact that in a country as rich as England, over 30 per cent of the workers in a typical provincial city should have incomes so small that it is beyond their means to live even at the stringently economical standard adopted as a minimum in this survey, nor in the fact that almost half of the children of working-class parents spend the first five years of their lives in poverty, and that almost a third of them live below the poverty line for ten years or more.[9]

Rowntree was hopeful that poverty could be eliminated. 'We have examined', he says, 'the causes of poverty. Every one is capable of remedy without dislocating industry or our financial resources. They can be removed just as the slums, once thought to be inevitable, are being removed today'.

In terms of techniques of research, one striking feature of the book was that while Rowntree remained suspicious of sampling, he wrote a supplementary chapter in which he tried to check the sampling methods by comparing the results of the full house-to-house inquiry with the results he would have obtained had he used a sample. It was, in his own words, a 'brainwave' which 'for the first time in the history of the world, I had the opportunity of testing the accuracy of sample surveys'.[10] He arranged the 16,362 schedules in street order and took every tenth one, just as he would have done had he called at every tenth house. The results were then compared with the complete survey. He concluded that 'so long as one is dealing with fairly large figures, the results obtained by the sampling method are for the most part (though not in every case) substantially accurate'. The complete survey of working-class families showed 31.1 per cent below the poverty line. The sampling method gave figures varying from 30.1 per cent to 33.1 per cent. Rowntree concluded that 'the difference between these figures and the accurate one is immaterial', but he added that when considering smaller figures, for example, the numbers of people who were 'poor' for particular reasons, the sample method produced unsatisfactory results which might involve 20 per cent or even 45 per cent inaccuracy. However, what he called errors of 20 per cent and 45 per cent would usually have been described by statisticians as errors of 1.7 per cent and 1.8 per cent. Thus Rowntree showed from his complete house-to-house survey that 4 per cent of the cases in primary poverty were due to illness. A sample gave him a figure of 5.8 per cent, but instead of describing this error as 1.8 per cent, he took 1.8 as a percentage of 4 giving a '45 per cent' error.

Other surveys

Apart from these replications of earlier work there were many surveys of new areas, mostly taking fairly large systematic samples of about 1:50, amounting in many cases to several thousand respondents. Very often the sample was combined with a complete enumeration of limited details, following the example of the New London Survey. Most were concerned with poverty, unemployment, housing and overcrowding, and the problem of old age. The most ambitious and perhaps well-known of these was the Merseyside Survey, directed by Caradog Jones. Shortly after the New London Survey began, a generous bequest to the Social Science Department of the University of Liverpool by the same Rockefeller Trust made possible a parallel investigation of Merseyside. This was a depressed area and presented at that time a remarkable contrast to other parts of the country and especially to London, the South East and the Midlands, which maintained their relative prosperity even during the economic depression of the early 1930s. Thus the depressed areas had 14.5 per cent of their insured population unemployed in 1929 when other areas had only 7.3 per cent. By 1933 the unemployed in the depressed areas had risen to 28.8 per cent while elsewhere it was 15.2 per cent.

The region defined as Merseyside for survey purposes took in the four boroughs of Liverpool, Bootle, Birkenhead, and Wallasey, plus the adjacent urban districts on both sides of the river. The survey began in 1929 and a full account of it was published in three volumes in 1934.

The first volume opened with a history of the development of the area and of the contribution of different nationalities to the population. Existing inhabitants were analysed by age, sex and marital status. Discussion centred chiefly on the problems of poverty and overcrowding, together with a study of working-class budgets. Volume II contained a detailed examination of Merseyside's industrial character, including special studies of the workers engaged in essential industries and of unemployment, occupational mobility and the surplus of labour. The third volume considered selected groups of the population — infants, schoolchildren, adolescents, pensioners and families without a male head, together with an examination of the use of leisure and church attendance.

Certain basic facts were first obtained concerning a large random sample of working-class households. This group then served as a control or standard with which any special groups could be compared. Thus the various characteristics of those 'in poverty' or 'overcrowded' could be compared with the existence of those characteristics in the entire working-class sample. The Voters' Register was used as a list from which to select every thirtieth house in which private families ordinarily slept. Families not regarded as working-class were excluded mainly on an occupational basis. The sample drew 6,906 families, comprising a population of 28,845. As in the original Booth inquiry, school attendance officers were used as informants who succeeded in obtaining the desired information from 93 per cent of the persons approached. Standards of overcrowding were adopted from the New London Survey. The results showed that families fell into poverty most frequently because the chief earner was out of work or failed to obtain regular work. However, among more than half the overcrowded families, the chief earner was in regular work. Thus inability to pay a higher rent was not by any means always the major factor responsible for overcrowding. Many families became overcrowded as the number of children increased and grew up.

One novel aspect of this survey was the special stress laid throughout on size of family and social class in different groups within the community. The Registrar General's categories of occupational class were used. The mean size of family in the large random sample of working-class households was taken as the norm, as was the proportion of male heads of families falling into each occupational grade. Against this 'normal' background a study was made of a variety of subnormal groups in the population — the deaf, the blind, the mentally deficient, the chonically sick, the epileptic and the physically handicapped. The data were collected from existing records of the authority or society interested in their welfare. The study showed that all these subnormalities were related predominantly to the lowest occupational group and in families which were larger than average. This finding supported the arguments of eugenicists who saw a decline in social efficiency if subnormal types maintained a higher fertility rate than the rest of the population. Abrams concluded that

> . . . the Merseyside Survey had, by the use of quantitative and sampling methods, opened up a new insight into a social problem which tended to be obscured by the standard social survey into poverty and overcrowding. For the first time one had to face the possibility not merely that the elimination of material poverty might leave untouched some forms of social ill-health, but that general economic prosperity might even increase the dimensions of these evils.[11]

Following the publication of the Merseyside Survey in 1934, Wells produced what was probably the first 'survey of surveys'. He defined a local survey as 'a fact-finding study, dealing chiefly with working-class poverty and with the nature and problems of the community'.[12] Characteristically, such surveys pursued many lines of inquiry simultaneously and this distinguished them from surveys of special topics like housing, education and so on. What they all had in common was a major interest in two topics: working-class poverty and the community in a restricted geographical area. Other topics were dealt with, but only to the extent in which they illuminated or constituted an aspect of the two main topics. The aim of the local social survey was, in Wells's view,

> the collection of facts relating to social problems and conditions in order to assist directly or indirectly the formulation of practical measures with reference to such problems. That is to say, it does not, as a rule, itself put forward any specific scheme of action, nor on the other hand, is it concerned with evolving any comprehensive sociological theory. It collects facts, which others may use as they please.[13]

In terms of scope Wells distinguished between the 'typical', the 'regional' and the 'community' survey. Typical surveys were interested not so much in the peculiarities of their regions as in the degree to which they typified social conditions. Thus Rowntree had said of his *Poverty* that 'the result of careful investigation shows that the proportion in poverty in London is practically equalled in what may be regarded as a typical provincial town'.[14] Regional surveys directed attention to environmental influences upon the social life of the community, while community surveys were concerned with the education of the locality under study. These aims were often fused, as in Mess's *Industrial Tyneside* (1928) and Jennings's *Brynmawr* (1934), which dealt wholly or mainly with the conditions of the distressed in these areas, but did so in full recognition of the natural and historical factors that had made the region.

The regional survey tradition initiated by Geddes had been reviewed earlier by Branford and Farquharson (1924), who defined a regional survey as 'a complete and scientific study from every point of view, all the departments of the study being viewed in relation to one another, and presented in vivid pictorial maps and diagram form, and all contributing to the spirit of the place and its potentialities, and providing a definite basis for definite plans for its future development'.[15] As such it included both rural and urban aspects and their interrelationships and, following LePlay and Geddes, it stressed people, place and work.

Wells made some interesting points about the way in which the various surveys had been organised. Out of the 32 cases of general surveys that he considered, 13 had been initiated by a local group, and 11 by an individual personally connected with the area. In 15 cases the investigation was organised by an individual who was not a professional social investigator. Wells concluded:

> In general terms it may be said that the typical contemporary survey on a large scale is initiated by a local body, that its organising unit is a temporary ad hoc body; that the working staff consists of a head executive officer with a small secretariate; and that the collection and tabulation of data is undertaken largely by voluntary workers, either students or members of local social groups, although paid assistance (for example school attendance officers) is sometimes employed.[16]

Not all surveys between 1930 and 1939 were concerned primarily with poverty, however. Hanham (1930) made an inquiry into casual labour in the Merseyside area based on information obtained from employers, trade unions and interviews with a sample of workers; Bakke (1933) had made a study of the environment and home life, the problems, behaviour, institutional affiliations and attitudes of unemployed men in Greenwich, a working-class London borough, while Springrice (1935) looked into the health and living conditions of working-class women. In 1937 a survey of working and living conditions in Birmingham carried out by the Bourneville Village Trust showed how surveys could be applied to the problem of urban sprawl. The effect of the policy of suburban development was narrowed to two topics: the effect of the journey to work and the effect on children's leisure activities. A sample of over 7,000 working-class households was drawn, and heads of households were interviewed using a questionnaire that had a surprisingly modern-looking format.[17] It was discovered that the effect of the building of suburbs was increasing the amount of travel necessary to get to work and was thus adding to the cost of living. The trust concluded that the city must cease its aimless, sprawling expansion of the past 20 years into ever new suburbs, and at a distance of some 20 to 30 miles, a new satellite town should be built with its own facilities and work people — both brought out from the central wards of the City.

In 1939 Ruth Durant published her book *Watling. A Survey of Social Life in a New Housing Estate*. She wanted to know whether the estate had grown into a community, and what role the new Community Centre had played in local social life. The study was not a formal survey, but was rather 'a summary of several intensive studies of local events, records, groups, and organisations'. There were reports of informal interviews with key informants, extracts from local newspapers, and descriptions of the estate itself, the nature of its local community and its institutions, and of the Community Centre. She concluded that the estate had begun as a community, but as it grew more and more into an ordinary town it looked less and less like a traditional community with a common mode of living and striving for common objectives.

The social survey during the inter-war years, then, had expanded into new substantive areas, and was no longer restricted to the study of working-class poverty. But it remained essentially a practical undertaking, geared to specific questions and problems. It was not, as Wells had stressed, concerned with evolving any comprehensive sociological theory, but it did not even attempt to generate, still less test, specific hypotheses.

A textbook on research techniques

Beatrice and Sidney Webb continued their political activities in the period between the wars, but somewhat less intensively. Beatrice had long cherished the idea of writing a book about her methods of investigation, and by 1921 she was preparing some draft chapters for it.[18] However, she decided to put her personal experiences of investigation in autobiographical form into her *My Apprenticeship*, which was published in 1926. The idea of writing a book specifically about methods of social study reappeared again in 1931, by which time Beatrice was 73 years of age. She gave Sidney the chapters she had written in the early 1920s for him to use in preparing the book; and their *Methods of Social Study* was published in 1932.

Their intention was not to write a treatise on methodology, but merely to 'explain our own approach to an understanding of the department of sociology dealing with the upgrowth, the modification and the dwindling, sometimes even to insignificance − of particular kinds of social institutions'.[19] However, in any contemporary sense it *was* a treatise on research methods and was almost certainly the first book on such a topic in Britain. They consider the subject matter of sociology and the nature of social facts, the necessary mental equipment of the social investigator − trained attention, objectivity and sympathetic understanding. They look at the role and use of classification and of hypotheses, and print in full the abortive questionnaire they had used to begin collecting facts for their trade union history. This was no doubt intended as a warning to future social investigators, but instead of using the experience to improve their use of questionnaires as a tool of investigation, they abandoned them altogether in their subsequent research. They suggest that the basic skill in social research is the art of note taking. Each fact and its source should be noted on a separate sheet of paper; sheets that can be rearranged and shuffled indefinitely. Facts never emerge in the order in which one wishes to present them; therefore to note them in chronological sequence is useless. The Webbs comment that

> . . . the main sources of our information were records, and persons located in the various towns and villages of England and Wales, sources which, for reasons of time and expense, had each to be exhausted in a single visit . . . . In our investigations, dealing as they did with the life-history of thousands of distinct organi-sations, the data for which were to be found in innumerable separate documents, pamphlets, or books, or were discovered in my observations and interviews, the conglomerate note-book system would have involved disentangling and rewriting, from all the separate note-books, every note relating to a particular year, a particular organisation, or a particular place, or indicating a particular relationship.[20]

The system of reshuffling sheets of paper enabled the Webbs to re-classify materials in different ways and according to different hypotheses. The result, they claim was also the discovery of new and slightly different interpretations of the facts. As an example, they say:

> When we had actually completed and published our *History of Trade Unionism* (1894) after three years' collection of facts from all industries in all parts of the kingdom, which we had arranged more or less chronologically, we found to our surprise that, apart from the vague generalities in common use, we had no systematic and definite theory or vision of how trade unionism actually operated, or what, exactly, is affected. It was not until we had

completely re-sorted all our innumerable sheets of paper according to subjects, thus bringing together all the facts relating to each subject, whatever the trade concerned, or the place, or the date, and had shuffled and re-shuffled the sheets according to various tentative hypotheses, that a clear, comprehensive, and verifiable theory of the working and results of trade unionism emerged in our minds, to be embodied, after further researches by way of verifications, in our *Industrial Democracy* (1897).

It may not be so far-fetched to suggest that here in this unusual insight into the mode of operation of two great empirical sociologists were the beginnings of what contemporary sociologists would call multivariate analysis, that is the rearrangement of data in many different ways so as to reveal patterns and relationships between phenomena which, at first sight, were not at all apparent. The Webbs always made extensive use of existing documents and literature, and in their commentary on 'the written word' they are careful to distinguish between original documents and contemporary literature. It seems that, where documents were too numerous to be each inspected, 'we had necessarily to proceed by the method of sampling'.[21] Beatrice was by now a skilled interviewer. In a chapter on 'the spoken word', she describes an interview as a 'conversation with a purpose' which has many uses. 'It may be a necessary passport to the inspection of documents, or to an opportunity of watching, from the inside, the constitution and activities of some piece of social organisation'.[22] The interview is designed to elicit 'facts from a competent informant by skilled interrogation'. The first and most essential quality for the interviewer is preparedness of mind. He must discover and understand as much of the situation beforehand, especially learning terminology and, 'not to have read and mastered what your client has himself published on the question is not easily forgiven!'[23] The Webbs suggest that no paper of questions should be apparent and no attempt should be made to take notes − these may arouse suspicion. The less formal the conditions of the interview the better. The interviewer must respect confidences, never argue, never 'show off', and must accept whatever is offered him with the utmost grace.

Personal observation was a technique that the Webbs used to great effect. They say: 'We have made a practice of visiting and watching every accessible meeting forming part of the particular institution that we were studying, from parish councils to parliaments'.[24] A day-by-day diary was kept of all proceedings and, although they admit that such notes are impressionistic, they claim:

In our own case we have found them of considerable value. In the first place, they indicate points into which inquiry should be made, and which might not otherwise have been thought of. They draw attention to omissions. They suggest hypotheses to be tested on other examples. Although they possess in themselves no more evidential value than the scandalous allegations of a sensational newspaper, they may show us the track. When supplemented by the more trustworthy methods of investigation that we have described . . . personal observation of the institution at work may be transformed into unimpeachable truth.[25]

The Webbs had taken the various methods of social investigation pioneered by Booth — the use of documents, personal observation and the interview — and turned them into self-consciously developed instruments of sociological research. Their empirical researches, although highly fused with value, speculation and propaganda, were systematic attempts at data gathering, and they used both induction and deduction to varying degrees in their work. Yet by 1932 their reversion to social accounting was virtually complete. They had become, in the words of Abrams, 'slaves to empirical purism. Much of their work reads like a parody of the worst features of the statistical tradition. Yet for a time it was orthodox doctrine in British social research'.[26] Thus the Webbs say:

The only right way in which to approach the subject-matter of sociology is not to focus the enquiry upon discovering the answer to some particular question in which you may be interested. On the contrary, you should choose a particular section of the social environment, or, more precisely, a particular social institution, and sit down patiently in front of it, exactly as if it were a form of energy or a kind of matter, the type-specimen of a plant or some species of animal, and go on working steadfastly to acquire all possible information about it, with the sole purpose of discovering every fact concerning its constitution and its activities, together with every ascertainable action and reaction between it and its environment.[27]

Mass Observation

One of the most interesting and curious episodes in the inter-war years was an organisation founded in 1937 by Tom Harrison and Charles Madge called 'Mass Observation'. Harrison was an anthropologist who had been struck by the fact that while anthropologists were being generously financed to go all over the world to study so-called 'primitive' peoples, no one at the time was making comparable studies of modern industrial societies like Britain. He had occasion during two years in the New Hebrides, Melanesia, to live among people who were still eating each other, and when the expedition was over he decided 'to return to study the cannibals of Britain'.[28]

Harrison was supported in this task by the poet Charles Madge, then a *Daily Mirror* reporter who later became Professor of Sociology at Birmingham University. Madge was concerned about the gap between ordinary people and the news media. Harrison and Madge joined forces to form a nationwide network of participant observers who kept diaries and observations which they sent to a central office for analysis. These observers were all volunteers recruited in answer to a request for help made in letters to the national newspapers. Originally, in February 1937, there were only 30 observers. By the end of the year there were hundreds, and by the end of 1938 there were thousands.[29] In addition to these volunteers there were also full-time observers looking in detail at a typical northern industrial town (which the Mass Observers called 'Worktown' — it was in fact Bolton) and at a metropolitan London borough.

The first study asked observers merely to note down everything that happened to them on 12 February 1937. On 12 May the same procedure was followed — the difference was that this was Coronation Day. The results were published in 1937 as a book entitled *May 12th*. The first study by the full-time observers concentrated on the major leisure activities of the working class — smoking, pub-going and football pools.[30] The function of Mass Observation was 'to get written down the unwritten laws and to make invisible forces (of custom and agreement) visible'.[31] These unwritten laws were to be viewed as in continual change and flux, and as varying from day to day and from house to house. 'Our aim should therefore be not so much to describe it exhaustively, as to find out the principles that govern its change, though this will involve an exact description and analysis of its workings on the widest practicable scale'.[32] The subject of study was social habit. The material on 'smoking as a social habit' was, in fact, derived from a fairly lengthy questionnaire from '336 reports from observers'. They recorded feelings of mutual hostility between smokers and non-smokers, when and why people began smoking, the rituals, mannerisms and paraphernalia that smoking entailed (like tapping the end). The numerical analysis was liberally sprinkled with extensive quotes. On pub-going Mass Observers made 'sample counts' in typical beer-houses on the peak night at peak hours on Friday and Saturday between 9.00 p.m. and 10.00 p.m. They made random counts on all nights and asked the barmen to supply a list of 'regulars'. Estimates of what proportion of the population were typically in a pub on any one occasion were checked against beer consumption in the town. In reviewing their first year's work Madge and Harrison considered and analysed various criticisms that had been made of them in the press and then analysed the personnel of Mass Observation in terms of occupation, class, age, sex and geographical location. That Mass Observers were shown to be untypical of the population at large was taken by Madge and Harrison to be an advantage, since these persons had shown themselves to be particularly observant, articulate and detached. They also presented an analysis of the reasons why Mass Observers joined the organisation and what they thought it was for. The book also included an essay by Malinowski on 'A Nation-wide Intelligence Service' which attempted to outline what Malinowski saw as the potential for this new organisation.

In 1938 Mass Observation studied the reactions of ordinary people to the international crisis,[33] and with the outbreak of war the focus turned to the 'home front'.[34] These studies used a variety of techniques. As well as participant observation of particular events and the reactions of people to them, there were accounts by observers of a full day, surveys of a more formal kind, with interviews and questionnaires, and content analyses of documents. The noting of overheard remarks and intro-spective autobiographical accounts were also used.

The war, however, stopped the continuing progress of the big project in Bolton. It had been intended to publish four volumes — on politics, religion, the pub and leisure. In the event only *The Pub and the People* (1943) appeared, and that was 'produced under many difficulties, when the unit had been disbanded'.[35] There were a few more publications after the war — *Puzzled People: A study in popular attitudes to religion, ethics, progress and politics in a London Borough* (1948); *The Voters' Choice: a special report* (1950) on the election of that year; *Britain Revisited* (1961), which attempted to update some of the earlier studies; and finally *The Pub and the People* which was reprinted in 1970.

Mass Observation had pioneered the study of areas rarely touched upon by earlier sociologists. Besides smoking, pub-going and football pools, there were studies of seaside humour, the Monarchy, religious beliefs, peace hopes, village life, industrial incentives, sex habits, capital punishment and newspaper reading. The reports apparently aroused much interest at the time, and some readers appreciated the fact that they contained extensive quotes of the actual words of people. How-ever, while the effort had been impressive, the results were rather less so. While remaining a useful source material for historians, they were of little interest to sociologists — except perhaps as an example of a lost opportunity. The studies lacked any theoretical grounding and tended to confuse the observation of events by participants with participant observation. There was no training of interviewers, yet the conduct of the largely unfocused interviews needed considerable skill. What tended to emerge was a series of unrelated quotations that were of doubtful scientific value. The difficulties of simply reporting overheard conversations, or of observing 'everything that happened' was not properly appreciated. Observation, too, was a skilled job, yet the bulk of panel members were middle class — and not typical ones at that. Abrams comments that it was strange, too, that in 13 years of prolific activity, Mass Observation made no contribution to the development of content analysis.[36]

Institutional progress

Institutionally sociology made very little progress in the period between the wars. The Sociological Society and its journal the *Sociological Review* languished. The quality of articles in the latter deteriorated to a point where in the 1920s it even published lengthy and uplifting free verse. In 1920 Victor Branford, who had played a key role in the founding of the Society in 1903, created LePlay House which became the focus of town planning and regional surveys carried out by Geddes and a few others. The activity was quite considerable, but little of the material was ever published. In 1930 the Society became by legal incorporation the Institute of Sociology and an editorial board was established for the *Review*, which improved greatly. The Institute also did some useful work, notably its conferences on the relationship between sociology and allied disciplines, reports of which were published in book form, for example *Class Conflict and Social Stratification* (1938) edited by Professor Marshall.

At the London School of Economics Hobhouse had died in 1929 and Westermarck retired in the same year. Morris Ginsberg was appointed Martin White Professor of Sociology. Like his predecessors Ginsberg was also a philosopher by training and had an interest in comparative studies. His staff included only a Reader and an assistant lecturer. Together they offered to some 30 students courses on comparative social institutions, comparative economic institutions, social psychology, ethics and social philosophy, comparative religion, the family, social developments in modern England and recent British contributions to sociology and social psychology. There was still very little place for empirical sociology or for any instruction on methods of social inquiry.

After a visit to England just before the Second World War, Ernest Harper, an American sociologist, was moved to write that he had found sociology in England to be in 'a rather undeveloped and even moribund condition'. It was to him 'a distinct shock' to learn that only a single chair of sociology existed in the universities of Great Britain. The Sociological Society was 'below par' and its journal 'certainly not up to the standard of the earlier *Sociological Papers*'. His conclusion was that although some work was being done along the lines of local studies, 'on the side of theory, research, and teaching, sociology in England appeared definitely weak. Perhaps it would be fairer to say that it appeared to be rare'.[37]

Compared with the United States, Britain was certainly far behind. In 1901 it had been found that sociology was being offered in 169 institutions.[38] The American Sociological Association was founded in 1905 and by 1908 it estimated that about 400 institutions then gave some attention to sociology and there were some 50 full-time professors. Between the wars there was a marked expansion of academic sociology, specialisation into substantive areas took shape, and there was a concentration of leadership in research and theory in the Department of Sociology at the University of Chicago. Dominant figures were W.I. Thomas, Robert Park, Charles Cooley and Edward Ross. All were concerned with making sociology more scientific and less speculative. The quest for respectability and academic legitimation, however, resulted in the building up of technical vocabularies and taxonomies, and a period of intensive fact gathering followed. Empiricism was rampant, but the Chicago school produced some of its classic studies of ghettos, hobos and delinquents.[39]

The period between the wars was, for Britain, one of marked industrial dislocation and transformation. Overall economic growth was as great as it had been in the period 1870—1914 and Britain's industrial performance was at least average when compared with her European rivals. Whether people prospered or not depended on their trade or occupation. The old-style industries declined, but others forged ahead. Prices fell for most of the inter-war period while money wages remained reasonably stable. Those who remained in jobs found their real wages rising. The effect was also uneven geographically. The North East, Lancashire and Yorkshire and South Wales suffered most, while the Midlands, London and the South East prospered. Instead of two nations of the rich and the poor of the 1840s, there were now two Englands of the prospering and the depressed working classes. Unemployment overall was high. It never dropped below one million and it reached nearly three million in 1932. In some areas unemployment rates were as high as 70 per cent. The first Labour Government of 1924 seemed no more successful at solving the country's problems than had been the Liberals. The sheer cost of saving the unemployed from starvation meant that social reforms of various kinds were just not possible. The general strike of 1926, the Wall Street crash of 1929 and the ensuing depression, and the collapse of the second Labour Government in 1932 were all crucial events as far as the working classes of Britain were concerned.

Notes

1   See Jones, 1948, chapter VII, 'Government Sampling Experiments' on which this account is based.
2   Hilton, 1924, p.552. Quoted from Jones, 1948, p.81.
3   Hilton, 1928, p.519. Quoted from Jones, 1948, p.82.
4   Hilton, 1928, p.528. Quoted from Jones, 1948, p.85.
5   Bowley and Hogg, 1925, p.16.
6   Ibid., p.25.
7   Briggs, 1971, p.282.
8   Ibid., p.286.
9   Rowntree, 1941, p.476.
10   Quoted from Briggs, 1961, p.293.
11   Abrams, 1951, p.52.
12   Wells, 1935, p.13.
13   Ibid., p.18.
14   Rowntree, 1901, p.356.
15   Branford and Farquharson, 1925, p.4.
16   Wells, 1935, p.58.
17   See Abrams, 1951, chapter II, 'Portrait of a Survey', who describes the survey in detail and reproduces the questionnaire in an appendix.
18   See Marshall, 1975, p.vii.
19   Sidney and Beatrice Webb, 1932, Preface.
20   Ibid., pp 89-90.
21   Ibid., p.108. While the Webbs describe the method of sampling and comment on its advantages, there is no evidence that they used it to select informants or respondents.
22   Ibid., p.135.
23   Ibid., p.136.
24   Ibid., p.160.
25   Ibid., p.199.
26   Abrams, 1968, p.150.
27   Sidney and Beatrice Webb, 1932, p.40.
28   Harrison, 1970.
29   Easthope, 1974, p.101.
30   See Madge and Harrison, 1938.
31   Ibid., p.8.
32   Ibid., p.9.
33   Published as *Britain, 1938*.

34 Published as *War Begins at Home*, 1940.
35 Harrison, 1970, p.5.
36 Abrams, 1951, p.112.
37 Harper, 1943.
38 Tolman, 1901/2.
39 See Oberschall, 1972, for a full account of the institutionalisation of American Sociology.

5 Post-war British empirical sociology

Well before the end of the Second World War there was a change in public opinion. A heightened sense of common danger and of national unity had emerged after Dunkirk in 1940, and from the beginning of the Churchill coalition government in the same year to the fall of the Attlee administration in 1951 there was a great social optimism. The extensive planning and implementation of new social services and the reform of the old seemed remarkable in a nation mobilised for war on a scale never seen before; but an emphasis on equality of sacrifice and hostility to the pre-war establishment of privilege and vested interests provided the atmosphere conducive to major reforms. While Churchill concentrated on gaining military victory, the Labour members of the coalition, together with progressive Conservatives like R.A. Butler and leading reformers like Keynes and Beveridge, produced a series of proposals for reform. The Board of Education proposed reform in 1941 and in 1942 the Medical Planning Commission advocated the setting up of a national health service. The Labour Party itself produced a new programme of reforms entitled *The Old World and the New Society*, stressing the need for full employment, wide-ranging social services, and full education for all.

The most well known of all the blueprints for the brave new world was the Beveridge Report of 1942. This proposed that existing national insurance schemes — excellent though they were in many ways — should be part of a comprehensive policy attacking want, disease, ignorance, squalor and illness. The novelty was that the plan was to cover all classes, and in return for insurance payments a comprehensive range of benefits could be provided, all organised by a Ministry of Social Security. The proposal amounted in effect to the setting up of a welfare state. The Report was very popular and 635,000 copies were sold. Although the plan was not put into immediate effect, the proposals had enormous influence over attitudes to reform in subsequent years. In 1944 the government issued a White Paper which contained most of the Beveridge ideas. The first major Act was the Education Act of 1944. Secondary education for all was to be provided on a tripartite scheme of grammar, technical and secondary modern schools. Local authorities were responsible for providing primary, secondary and further education and all education was to be free. The aim was to provide equality of opportunity for all and parity of esteem as between types of schools — themes that were to be taken up by empirical sociologists in the 1950s. Indeed much of the sociology in that decade flowed from the needs of a newly emerging welfare state.

The influence of the London School of Economics

Immediately after the war the London School of Economics still had the only Department of Sociology in Britain. Indeed in 1948 only the University of London could boast of having sociologists on its staff and the LSE itself continued to possess the only professorial chair in the discipline throughout the 1950s. Besides the Department of Sociology, which was chaired by Morris Ginsberg, who continued the tradition of comparative sociology, there was also the Social Science Department, led by T.H. Marshall, which taught social administration and social work, and the Population Investigation Committee directed by David Glass. It was this organisation (which had been set up in 1936) that proved to be the most significant of the three for the development of empirical sociology in Britain.

Glass had previously worked in the Department of Social Biology at the University of London under Hogben, who saw his population studies as being mainly in the tradition of political economy that had begun with Petty and Graunt in the 1660s. Furthermore, such work provided an alternative to eugenics by suggesting that social factors were at least as important as hereditary ones in the transmission of physical and intellectual skills from one generation to the next. Glass had been appointed as Reader in Demography at the London School of Economics in 1946, and in 1949 he became Martin White Professor of Sociology, a post he was to retain until his death in 1978.[1] Trends in fertility had always been one of his major concerns (a topic on which he had published earlier in Hogben's *Political Arithmetic*); but his interest in the idea of social and occupational selection was already evident in the same volume where with J.L. Gray from the Department of Social Biology he reported a study of educational opportunity and the Oxbridge scholarship system. Following a memorandum from Marshall calling for a long-term programme of research into social selection and differentiation in Britain, Glass embarked on a study which was to have a formative influence on the development of empirical sociology in Britain and which was to provide new momentum for the tradition of social accounting.

The inquiry itself was directed initially by Caradog Jones and later by John Hall who together published, in the first volume of the *British Journal of Sociology* which the London School of Economics had just launched in 1950, the results of a limited pilot study carried out amongst an assortment of adult education class members and other individuals in various organisations including trade unions. This showed that there was a considerable measure of subjective agreement as to the social grading of occupations. They developed what they called the 'standard classification' of occupations (subsequently more popularly known as the 'Hall-Jones' scale) which corresponded closely with the undirected judgements of independent samples of the public.[2]

The main inquiry, which was conducted in 1949, obtained the life histories — in respect of social origins, education, occupation, marriage and fertility — of a random sample of nearly 10,000 adults from the civilian population of Britain. Glass was able to obtain the services of the recently formed Government Social Survey in carrying out the interviews; indeed, the Survey also designed the sample and helped with the preparation of the final interview schedule.[3] Besides the main study six more specialised local inquiries were undertaken dealing with particular aspects of social status and social mobility. The results were written up independently by members of the research team and all were published in 1954 as *Social Mobility in Britain* edited by Glass.

The key article was written by Glass and Hall and it looked at changes in status between fathers and sons, and computed an 'index of association' from the ratio of observed to expected frequencies in a cross-tabulation of fathers' and sons' statuses so that an index of one would indicate 'perfect mobility'. The results revealed that throughout the status hierarchy, the association was significantly higher than would be expected on the basis of perfect mobility and that there were significant differences between the degree of association for the various strata into which the respondents were classified. Furthermore, on the basis of a cohort analysis there were no major differences between successive generations in the overall intensity of the status association, although the authors admitted that the seven-fold classification of status was perhaps too coarse to record such changes.

The main inquiry was used by other members of the team, for example to see whether there were consistent and significant differences between the levels of education attained by individuals whose fathers were at different levels of social status, and to study the relationship between the social origins of brides and grooms. The former study was by Jean Floud and it showed that, in spite of increases in grammar school and university places, the chances of sons of working-class parents getting to those institutions had not improved in comparison with those of sons of middle-class parents.

In the more specialised inquiries Martin explored the range of subjective attitudes to and determinants of social status based on a stratified sample of over 1,000 respondents drawn from the Electoral Registers of Greenwich and Hertford. Two studies were concerned with the problems of educational selection. Himmelweit, using data from a survey of 725 boys aged 13 and 14 in grammar and secondary modern schools in London, investigated how the 'education for all' principle embodied in the 1944 Education Act had worked out in practice. She found that while the upper working-class was more adequately represented in the grammar schools since 1944, the lower working-class continued to be under-represented. Martin looked at the attitudes of parents towards different types of post-primary education from a sample of 1,446 parents whose children were passing through the secondary school selection process in south-west Hertfordshire in 1952. There were other studies of self-recruitment in four professions by Kelsall, and of social stratification and leadership in voluntary organisations by Bottomore and by Chambers.

Glass was no theorist; there was no general sociological theory that underpinned the study and there were no hypotheses that were specifically tested. At the heart of the scientific enterprise in Glass's view was the business of exposing inequality — charting it, unravelling its complex patterns, and finding means to overcome it. He was a 'man of the radical left' according to Westergaard, and in his introduction to the book Glass stepped outside the frame of studies which it contained to put forward his personal views: that the continued existence of the public school system put an upper limit to the amount of mobility that could be achieved, that children could not be divided into three types, each requiring a different kind of secondary education, and that comprehensive schools were at least a step in the right direction.

The Population Investigation Committee was also involved in another inquiry that was to have a formative influence on the development of empirical sociology in Britain. This was a social survey into the social and economic aspects of pregnancy and childbirth organised by a joint committee of representatives from the PIC and from the Royal College of Obstetricians and Gynaecologists. The actual direction was undertaken by J.W.B. Douglas with Griselda Rowntree as research assistant and Glass as Secretary. The idea was to ascertain the availability of maternity services to the different social classes and in different parts of the country, the use made of these services, their effectiveness in educating mothers and in reducing mortality, the need for domestic help during pregnancy, and the nature and extent of expenditure on childbirth. In what was the first national cohort study in Britain nearly 14,000 mothers of all children born in the first week of March 1946 were interviewed by health visitors.

Strictly speaking it was not a 'sociological' survey in that there was no attempt to explain the findings in theoretical terms, but of note for present purposes was the sophistication of the techniques of inquiry that were used. The extent of the pilot work and the pre-testing of the questionnaire eventually used was itself an innovation. An exhaustive list of questions was tried out on a small sample of mothers by professional interviewers, and a remodelled questionnaire was then tested by some health visitors in selected areas. Verbatim answers were recorded and further modifications were made, while precoded items were developed for all factual questions. The resulting questionnaire took nearly an hour to complete in an interview. A new technique, however, was to devise two separate questionnaires that reduced the interviewing time to 25 minutes; these were then distributed to different authorities. Mothers who had left an authority were traced through birth notification lists, while omissions and discrepancies were referred to the health visitors who had actually carried out the interview. In all some 3,000 queries were made, there were sample checks for punching errors, while tabulations were checked against known marginals. Checks on the adequacy of the sample suggested that only unmarried mothers were under-represented. Probably for the first time on a large scale social survey tests of significance were calculated for many of the tables. The statistic used was for the most part chi-square, which had been formulated by Pearson almost half a century earlier. Tabulations were made with the assistance of Hollerith machines, again almost certainly the earliest use of them in Britain for processing the results of survey research.

Special area studies were made of five selected authorities on the quality of the services provided and the administrative problems associated with them. Douglas and Rowntree visited all five authorities personally, having discussions with those responsible for providing services, visiting clincis, looking at health visitors' records and consulting with local authorities. Douglas and Rowntree, who drafted the report which was published in 1948 as *Maternity in Great Britain*, were able to claim, probably with some justification, that there was 'every reason for confidence both in the quality of the original data and in the accuracy of the tabulations'.[4] Considerable inequalities in the provision of maternity welfare both between areas and between social classes were uncovered, and the authors concluded that 'in all aspects of maternity care well-to-do mothers get better attention than those who are poor'.[5]

It had not originally been intended to continue the research beyond 1948, but since the investigators realised that they were in possession of a fully representative sample of children from all types of homes and from all parts of Britain, it was decided to follow them through for at least part of their career. The study in fact became the first stage of a long-term series of follow-up inquiries that have become minor classics in their own right. The first was *Children Under Five* (1958) which concentrated on the major types of illnesses suffered by a sub-set of the children. The next stage followed them through to their primary schools and the results were published as *The Home and the School* (1964). Much of the information for this study was produced by the teachers themselves; the results revealed inequalities as between the social classes that closely paralleled the findings of Glass's 1949 study. *All Our Future. A Longitudinal Study of Secondary Education* (1968) reported the results of the next investigation. This described the educational progress of the same group of children during their first five years at secondary school. The techniques of inquiry used followed the earlier study: teachers supervised IQ tests and gave their own ratings, headmasters gave the results of public examinations, school doctors gave yet another medical examination, and school nurses and health visitors made further visits to pupils' homes. The findings suggested that the social class differences in educational opportunity which were significant at the primary school had increased at the secondary and had extended even to pupils of high ability.

The sample was visited again in 1972 by professional interviewers by which time the respondents were 26 years of age. Questions were asked about family and household, religious beliefs, training for work, type of employment and earnings. In 1976 the Population Investigation Committee was awarded a three-year grant from the Nuffield Foundation to continue the 1972 study by making a full analysis of the cohort's social mobility. Questionnaires were sent to the cohort in 1977 and analysis of the material is currently under way. The style of all these inquiries was very descriptive and very much in the social accounting tradition. It is interesting to note that, in looking back from the perspective of 1976, some 28 years since the beginning of the 1946 inquiry, Douglas justified longitudinal cohort studies not in terms of their scientific value, but in terms of providing 'the most efficient and also the cheapest opportunities to assess the effectiveness of new services and new policies'.[6]

The London School of Economics was the focus of another strand of influence on the development of early post-war empirical sociology in Britain: Fabianism. Ever since Sidney Webb wrote his *Facts for Socialists* in 1887 the Fabians had been attempting to promote socialism by laying a foundation of fact. However, collecting 'new' data by way of primary empirical research was not one of their traditions. Nor did they even re-analyse existing sources; rather they re-presented official and other data in a way that would convince others of the need for socialist reforms. This feature is well exemplified by the ongoing series of Fabian Research pamphlets. It is difficult, however, as Margaret Cole found when she wrote the *Story of Fabian Socialism*,[7] to assess their record since there are no 'principles' that could be said to have 'influenced' researchers. There have been only individuals who occasionally published through Fabian outlets, but it is always difficult to decide when an individual is acting as a Fabian and when acting in some other role. Hobsbawm has argued that the claims of the Fabians are, in any case, exaggerated, if not mythological. They were not inspirers and pioneers of the Labour Party, nor had they 'destroyed' the influence of Marxism in Britain, nor were they particularly influential in laying the foundations of the welfare state. Being neither liberal, nor working-class, neither Marxist nor Conservative, 'they had no place in the British political tradition'.[8] Certainly Fabian research leant more towards social administration than it did towards sociology.

The problem is exemplified in Richard Titmuss's connection with the Fabian Society. He wrote a number of Fabian Tracts, the most well known of which was *The Irresponsible Society* (1960) in which he accused the government of irresponsibility in making no attempt to discover the hard facts of poverty and dependency. Titmuss always believed that facts were a prerequisite for reasoned argument, yet at the same time he recognised that not all variables in the social sciences were measurable.[9] While he had used survey techniques, he for the most part relied on facts collected by others. But in all this it is impossible to say how much Titmuss was acting as a Fabian and how much his work was 'influenced' by Fabianism. In a sense Fabianism *was* the individuals who were members of the Fabian Society and they as much influenced it as the reverse.

Other developments in the 1950s

Outside the London School of Economics there were several other developments in empirical sociology in Britain in the early post-war years. Ruth Glass continued the regional town planning survey tradition pioneered by Geddes with her *The Social Background of a Plan. A Study of Middlesbrough* (1948). Ruth Glass was married to David Glass, but based in University College, London, so although strictly speaking she was outside the LSE, she had strong links with it. Her book was of note in the way it used a number of different sources – published statistics, unpublished administrative records, general field work and specific field inquiries. Among the latter were detailed surveys of the location of institutions, studies of institutional catchment areas and two questionnaire inquiries among particular groups in the Middlesbrough population. One was carried out by the Wartime Social Survey to obtain a picture of Middlesbrough's household structure. A systematic random sample of 1:23 households from the rating lists resulted in interviews with some 1,387 housewives and 1,209 other adults. Modified questionnaires for each were drawn up. Included in the schedule were questions on household size and composition, occupation and industry of the chief wage earners and their incomes, shopping habits and the use of post offices. A second questionnaire inquiry was carried out among the retailers themselves.

The study gave special weight to the use of a precise sociological concept of 'neighbourhood' which was defined, demarcated and graded in terms of multiple indices covering living conditions, industrial equipment (shops, schools and so on), neighbourhood integration and geographical demarcation. Living conditions were measured in terms of net population density, number of houses per acre, percentage of houses with rateable values of less than £11, percentage of owner-occupiers, percentage of chief wage earners with incomes of less than £5 per week, and the number of 'poverty' shops (junk shops, pawnbrokers, fried-fish shops and so on) per 1,000 people. Neighbourhood integration was measured by two indices: the number of outside institutions visited by people from a particular neighbourhood and the number of outside neighbourhoods to which they went for this purpose. Glass concluded that neighbourhood boundaries were determined by physical characteristics of the environment and the social characteristics of the people, although they were not boundaries of movement, and that social stratification had been accentuated by geographical separation.

In 1951 Rowntree (with Lavers) produced yet another social survey of York entitled *Poverty and the Welfare State: a third social survey of York dealing only with economic questions*. The authors stated that the purpose of the book was 'to throw light on the question of how far the various welfare measures which had come into force since 1936 have succeeded in reducing poverty'.[10] For the first time Rowntree was content with a sample survey (of 1:9 households), but the study otherwise followed very closely on the lines of the previous inquiries. The diets of 1936 were slightly modified, and there were changes in the estimates for clothing, fuel, light and sundries. The poverty line was set at £5 0s 1d for a family of husband, wife and three children. The book received considerable public attention; it was the first post-war survey wholly concerned with working-class poverty, while its findings suggested that the magnitude of the problem, which had been so startling in 1900 and even in 1935, had been reduced almost to vanishing point. In 1936 some 18 per cent of the total population of York (31 per cent of the working-class population) were in the poorest classes and in 'primary poverty', but by 1950 less than 2 per cent of the total population (2.8 per cent of the working-class population) were in this grim condition. In fact only 846 families in York were in 'primary poverty', while there was not a single family in York whose poverty was due to the unemployment of an able-bodied wage earner. Instead old age had become the main cause. Rowntree's book was very short and perhaps unduly optimistic. It did not linger on the deficiencies and inadequacies of the welfare state, but rested content on a summary of achievements. There were no recommendations for new policies; maybe this was not surprising for a man of 80 years of age.

In Scotland the four universities were engaged in producing a *Third Statistical Account*, following Sinclair's *Statistical Account of Scotland* of 1790 to 1799, and the *New Statistical Account of Scotland* of 1845. Each university assumed responsibility for a pilot study of a limited area, each carrying out the work in its own way. Glasgow University made a survey of Ayrshire. For the parish reports the survey officers roused the interest of the people of Ayrshire and hundreds of helpers collected data on many aspects of local life; even classes of schoolchildren were enlisted to help by doing simple local projects. A similar volume on Fife by St Andrew's University followed. In the cities the parish could no longer be viably used as the main unit of analysis and Aberdeen produced an account of its city based mainly on an interview survey. After the pilot work was completed, it was decided to continue the studies, each university being responsible for the counties in its region. The whole project was planned eventually to produce 29 volumes. Twenty have now been published. Some followed very closely the pattern set by Sinclair and most of the county reports included substantial parish accounts, while others were based on large-scale social surveys. The most recent was in 1979 on the counties of Perth and Kinross. This included 76 parish accounts, most of which were begun in the late 1950s and early 1960s. In spite of the delay in publication, no attempt was made to update the material.

Taken together, the three statistical accounts of Scotland cover a period of nearly 200 years and provide a unique record of social and economic changes in Scotland over that period. The implications of all these data either for future policy or for empirical sociology, however, have been very limited. The lack of purpose in all the research activity that the accounts involved is very striking and, in this respect at least, resembles the *West Ham* study carried out in 1907.

Another focus for empirical sociological research in the early post-war years was the Department of Social Sciences at Liverpool University. Team research in the Department dated back to 1947 when the additional funds made available from the Clapham Award were devoted to the creation of a number of research posts. The two main areas of the Department's concern were industrial organisation and community studies. The first two major industrial projects focused on the operation of joint consultation in manufacturing firms and on the Dock Labour Scheme in Liverpool. The results of these studies were published as *Industrial Leadership and Joint Consultation* by W.H. Scott in 1952 and *The Dockworker* (1954) by the Department as a whole. Later on Scott and Banks in their *Technical Change and Industrial Relations* (1956) examined the relationships between social structure and technical change over a lengthy period of the history of a large steel firm and included an intensive study of the most recent change. A substantial appendix contained a discussion of the framework of analysis that had been developing in industrial research and which was stated more precisely for use in the steel study.

Spin-offs from this study included publication of reports on the group interview technique[11] and on the impact of continuous shift-work on family life.[12] The Department took a leading part in the establishment in 1953 of the International Committee for Social Research in Industry which was to co-ordinate the execution of comparable researches in other countries. Liverpool's contribution was a more precise analysis, using material from the Department's study of the steel industry, of the attitudes to technical change of the steel-workers.[13]

In the field of community studies early attention was devoted to studying the social relationships of residents in a new housing estate; it then shifted to the social needs and conditions of the old urban areas from which such estates mainly draw their population. In an intensive study based on interviews with over 500 heads of households particular attention was paid to the socio-economic ranking of the local residents, to their participation in social and church activities, to the extent of residential mobility, and to their views about the locality, their opinion of their homes and their desire to move elsewhere. The results were published in 1960 as *Urban Redevelopment and Social Change* by Vereker and Mays. Attention then shifted to studying the institutional life of the district. One study by Mays looked into the operation of the local schools and emerged as *Education and the Urban Child* (1961), and another investigated how young people spent their leisure time. Mays also made special studies of delinquency in the area, and these were published as *Growing up in the City* (1954) and *On the Threshold of Delinquency* (1959). The first of these was concerned with establishing the hypothesis that delinquent behaviour was, in some of its aspects, a normal phase in the lives of urban boys living in the older, more deteriorated urban neighbourhoods and was more a function of their desire for social conformity than of a serious social or psychological disorder. The other study was an early example of action research and looked at the operation of special group work and casework techniques. It focused on a youth club that had been set up in 1953 and which was an experimental project 'concerned with discovering new ways of treating juveniles whose delinquency could for the most part be attributed to environmental and social causes . . . '[14]

One final strand of influence on empirical sociology in the 1950s was that of the anthropologists who came to hold many of the chairs of sociology as they were established in the 1960s. While many remained aloof from studying their home territory, others in the 1950s began a series of intensive studies of small communities scattered throughout Britain, using mainly anthropological methods and techniques. In one sense it could be seen as a re-awakening of social exploration — but without the imagery of unknown territories. A pioneer was Alwyn Rees,[15] who was a lecturer in geography and anthropology at Aberystwyth from 1946 to 1949 and then Director of Extra-Mural Studies. He carried out a study on a small, very rural, parish in mid-Wales and published the results in 1950 as *Life in a Welsh Countryside*. The community could hardly be described even as a 'village', but was a parish of three hamlets and scattered farmsteads occupying 15.5 square miles of rolling upland in Montgomeryshire with a population of about 500 in 1940.

Rees discovered that kinship played a dominant role in the local social structure; practically every household was bound to every other by kinship ties, or as he put it, perhaps a little more graphically, 'they are woven together like a pig's entrails'. He did not describe his techniques of investigation, except to comment in the Preface that his investigations extended over a period of eight years, the basic field work being carried out in the summers of 1939 and 1940 when questionnaires were completed for every household in the parish and other data were collected by means of interviews and observation. He had, furthermore, maintained contact with life in the community by frequent visits between 1940 and 1953 and periods of residence in 1944, 1945 and 1946.

One of Rees's students, W.M. Williams, carried out a comparable study in England in Gosforth, West Cumberland, which was published in 1956 as *The Sociology of an English Village: Gosforth*. This was based on field work carried out between 1950 and 1953. There was no particular issue or problem being investigated; Williams just attempted to describe the social structure by looking at the economy, the family, some aspects of the life cycle, social class, formal and informal organisations, religion, and relations with the outside world from an historical and social point of view. Again there was no comment on how the study was done. Williams had lived in Gosforth for a couple of years, but on the extent to which he participated in various activities there was no clarification. He apparently interviewed some people, but he did not say how many. The basic social and economic unit in Gosforth — a recognisable village with 723 inhabitants — was the family in which, once again, kinship was seen to play a very important role. However, unlike the Welsh parish, there was a very clear system of social stratification and Williams was able to distinguish several different social classes.

While Williams was in Gosforth, two anthropologists and a sociologist were looking at a mining town in the West Riding of Yorkshire that they called Ashton. The study was published in 1956 as *Coal is our Life: An analysis of a Yorkshire mining community* by Dennis, Henriques and Slaughter. Again the authors gave no account of how they proceeded nor any natural history of how the research developed. However, considerable use was made of secondary material, particularly the Census and other official statistics. The authors showed how the miner, engaged in dangerous work that needed close co-operation from his fellow workers, became steeped in trade union brotherhood. His leisure time was spent with his mates in long periods of weekend drinking, and he took little interest in his wife and family. However, while the men were thrown together by coal, it had exerted an opposite or centrifugal force on women; there was no work for them, other than housework. The idea of 'community' was thus no longer synonymous with some notion of idyllic, rural bliss. The authors thought of the miner and his family first as a member of the working-class, second as a member of the mining section of the working-class, and third as an Ashton miner whose life had a unique bias resulting from local factors.

In the summer of 1953 another anthropologist, Ronald Frankenberg, went to live in and make a socio-anthropological study of a parish in Denbighshire on the Welsh border. His published work was entitled *Village on the Border. A Social Study of Religion, Politics and Football in a North Wales Community* (1957). Frankenberg was based in the Department of Social Anthropology in Manchester and lived for a year in the village he called Pentrediweith (or 'village of no work'). While Williams had concentrated on the rural farming community around the village, Frankenberg focused on the village itself, showing how recreational activities built up, in the course of their existence, opposition to themselves. This resulted in increasing internal and external failure and the substitution of another activity as the focus of village life.

Following on his work in Gosforth, Williams investigated the village of 'Ashworthy', a pseudonym for an agricultural community in Devon. The village existed in a state of 'dynamic equilibrium': while the social structure as a whole appeared relatively unchanged and unchanging in the absence of external stimuli, within it constant and irregular changes were, in fact, taking place. Williams's central problem was to investigate how this equilibrium was maintained and how continuity was ensured. This, he emphasised, was accountable in terms of the relationship between man and the land, and he devoted the first half of the book to documenting the relationship of social and economic change to the context of family farming. The second part was devoted to the original aim of the research: the effects of demographic change on the structure of family and kinship within one small community.

An interesting development in terms of research technique was Williams's use of a pilot survey to choose the most suitable community out of four possibilities for his original purpose of studying the effects of rural depopulation on family and kinship. Using documentary sources — Parish Registers and Tithe Awards — he chose a community that had experienced a declining population for a relatively long period, was large enough to make a study worthwhile, and yet small enough to be intensively studied as a complete whole (having a population of between 500 and 700). Ashworthy was chosen because the others did not meet Williams's requirement or 'seemed on intuitive grounds, "unpromising"'. Williams went to great lengths to disguise the identity of Ashworthy:

> All the personal and place names used in this study are fictitious. All the dates, ages of individuals, sizes of farms and many other factual details have been systematically altered. Ashworthy is not a parish, although it is so described below, and the boundaries shown on the maps are not parish boundaries. All the maps and the statistical data refer to an area which is not an administrative unit.[16]

In spite of the author's claim that these changes 'had been made in a way which retains the validity of the material for analytic purposes', they did, nevertheless, appear to undermine the whole essence of a 'scientific' inquiry, particularly since, on Williams's admission, Ashworthy was not 'in any sense a *typical* rural community'.

Williams found that Ashworthy had a very poorly developed class

136

structure and as a result said very little about social class and social status. By contrast Littlejohn's *Westrigg: The Sociology of a Cheviot Parish* (1963) presented a detailed and dynamic account of social class in a rural community that was 'an upland parish in a mainly rural county in the south of Scotland'.[17] His techniques of research were first, 'listening in conversation with and among parishioners for words implying a conventional classification of persons and families falling within the various classes', second, 'noting friendships and cliques among parishioners and placing them within these classes', and finally, 'noting association and interaction among them on public occasions'. Littlejohn's study contained something comparatively rare in British studies — a strong historical bias — and he analysed the decline of the parish as a socio-economic unit, taking the turn of the century as his starting point, 'because many informants . . . could clearly recall social life as it was at that time'.[18]

All these studies were largely descriptive, and for the most part presented non-quantitative, often impressionistic, data. There were usually a few figures and perhaps some quotations, but most of the text was straight narrative, often with no conclusions or even main findings or even an introduction outlining the major objectives, purposes, or problems being investigated. Generalisations would be derived inductively, but on a low level of abstraction and specific to the community concerned. The result was that these studies were non-comparable and non-cumulative as far as empirical sociology was concerned. This may be one reason why the community study faded out in the 1960s. Another may be that younger generations of sociologists were simply less interested in this kind of work. However, in the mid-1970s community studies were to take on a new lease of life as anthropologists and sociologists investigated the social and economic impact of North Sea oil-related developments on rural communities in the Western Isles of Scotland.

Parallel with the traditional community study carried out by the anthropologists was an attempt by the Institute of Community Studies at the University of London to combine the strengths of both anthropological and sociological research methods and techniques. This was started in 1954 in a room in a settlement in Bethnal Green by Michael Young, Peter Willmott and Peter Townsend. Their original purpose was to study the relationship between the social services and working-class family life. The assumption was that policy makers and administrators were insufficiently aware of the needs or views of the working-class people who formed the bulk of users of social services. The hope was that social research would 'help to provide a more realistic basis for policy'.[19] It was decided to take the family as the unit of analysis and to focus initially on housing and in particular on the effects of building new estates outside the city, and on the provision made for old people. The latter inquiry was to be conducted by Townsend, the only one of the three founder members who had some 'relevant' training — in his case, anthropology. The aim was to combine the approaches of the anthropologist and the sociologist. 'We wanted', claimed Young and Wilmott, 'on the one hand, to study a smallish community in depth, drawing from people in informal talks the accounts which would make our "reports" as vivid as we could. We wanted, on the other hand, to collect some basic information from random samples of the population and to analyse it with proper statistical care'.[20] These two initial inquiries emerged as *Family and Kinship in East London* by Young and Willmott, and the other was Townsend's *The Family Life of Old People*, both published in 1957.

Many of the books since published by the Institute became standard texts for undergraduate courses in Departments of Sociology. In a review of the research in Bethnal Green Platt suggests that the 'old' tradition of research by the Institute used a mixture of fairly loose sampling and interviewing, was largely descriptive, sometimes impressionistic, and included some informal observation. She constructs a stereotype for a typical study as follows:

> The survey was, of course, done in Bethnal Green, and the book opens with a picturesque and graphic account of the area in general and of the more striking aspects of the lives of the people studied. The subject is a problem of social policy, and the survey is concerned with those at the receiving end of it, in particular as it affects and is affected by their family relationships. The research director himself, with the help of one or two colleagues, conducted 50—100 interviews, using a rather unstructured schedule with many open-ended questions. A team of hired interviewers, using a highly structured schedule with many closed and factual questions, interviewed a sample of 800—1,000 respondents in a more superficial way. Some data of a rather impressionistic nature were also collected by other means, such as informal observation and asking selected informants to keep diaries. The approach is mainly descriptive, with no formal hypothesis; the data are only very tentatively used to construct and test possible explanations of the observed facts, and there is little overt use of multivariate analysis or statistical tests. The main burden of the argument is carried by quotations from interviews, and the few tables are used chiefly as illustrations of the points made in this way. The conclusions are not merely summaries of the data, but contain policy recommendations. The strong orientation towards social policy is confirmed by the references given, only about

half of which are strictly social-scientific; the main traditions represented are those of social anthropology and of social arithmetic, with government reports bulking large.[21]

Platt comments that the extent to which Bethnal Green as a community or its inhabitants as individuals were representative of people in other areas was never treated in sufficient detail to suggest how far one could reasonably generalise from the studies carried out there. Furthermore, it was curious, she continues, that the Institute never actually did a full community study of the area looking at the community as a whole, nor did it make formal use of systematic participant observation. Instead these earlier studies used interviews to construct stereotypes of dubious validity, and as a substitute for inclusion in the sample questionnaires of questions on attitudes, meanings and the content of interaction. Platt concludes that the Institute's methodological intentions were good ones, namely, to combine the strengths of rigorous quantitative techniques with those of personal involvement and observation in depth. Unfortunately, the result was often to get the worst of both worlds, with data being used for purposes for which they were unsuitable. Large samples had been asked inappropriate questions, so that the answers were of little use, while small and unrepresentative samples had been used for making generalisations.

The experience of empirical sociology in Britain in the 1950s and early 1960s was, then, one of a continuation of social accounting, more or less explicitly tied to social policy and social reform, and community studies based primarily on participant observation. In both cases the role of theory was minimal, and implicit rather than explicit. As John Rex put it in 1974: 'On the level of method and data gathering and processing in the early 1950s, British sociology had not progressed very far . . . . There had been no Paul Lazarsfeld to call for the testing of sociological hypotheses by the techniques of the social survey'.[22] There were, however, signs that this was, in fact, beginning to happen. In articles in the *British Journal of Sociology* and the *Sociological Review* research *was* being applied to the testing of explicitly formulated generalisations. In the very first issue of the *British Journal of Sociology*, published in 1950, Kendall and Stuart tested the 'law of the cubic proportion' in election results, namely that the proportion of seats won by the victorious party varies as the cubic proportion of votes cast for that party over the country as a whole. In the same issue Benney and Geiss in a study of social class and political behaviour in Greenwich generated four hypotheses relating social class to party involvement and interest in politics from a random sample of 1,022 voters. The authors even used three- and four-way tables for some of which tests of significance were calculated, while Pearson's r was used to measure the degree of correlation between occupational grades (as measured by the Hall-Jones scale) and interviewer ratings. It was quite probably the earliest published research that used such techniques in a reasonably large survey. In the field of research monographs, Elisabeth Bott's *Family and Social Networks* (1957) was possibly the first to explicate the relationship between data and explicitly formulated hypotheses. Although the study was based on only 20 cases, it continued to be a popular book amongst students of sociology and was still being reprinted in 1971. Her main hypothesis, which was developed in the course of the study rather than stated in advance, was 'that the degree of segregation in the role relationship between husband and wife varies directly with the connectedness of the family social network'.[23]

Bott conducted a series of 13 interviews with each family in their own homes. Questions were developed as they went along. Later a series of clinical interviews was conducted on more intimate and personal matters. In addition there were some 'case conferences' and group discussions. For perhaps the first time a researcher discussed in detail not only the way in which the study was carried out, but also gave a natural history of the research itself. This had begun in 1950 and went through a number of stages, some of which were rather difficult, reflecting the different orientations of the research team and the difficulties that arose from the team's personal involvements with the families.

The 1950s also saw the beginnings of the institutionalisation of sociology on a new footing and its gradual acceptance as an academic discipline in the universities. Both the old Institute of Sociology and LePlay House found themselves in financial difficulties after the war. The *Sociological Review* had not appeared for some time due to shortages of paper, while Ginsberg withdrew his work from the *Review* because the LSE was just about to launch its own journal. In 1952 the journal was transferred to the University College of North Staffordshire (later to become Keele University) which began a *New Series* a year later. The Institute itself was finally dissolved in 1955.[24] Meanwhile the British Sociological Association had been established in 1951. The 13 founders — six of whom held chairs at the LSE at the time and included Glass and Ginsberg who acted as chairman — did not see the new body as a professional association. Rather, one of its major purposes was to encourage contact and co-operation between workers in 'all relevant fields of inquiry'.[25] There were others, however, who saw sociology as a clearly defined specialism and wanted careers in sociological research. At the first Annual General Meeting a resolution was passed asking the newly elected executive committee to appoint a sub-committee to study the recruitment, training and employment of sociologists. Although the sub-committee was established it never examined the facilities that already existed for training sociologists, nor did it make any recommendations for future policy. The fact was that the training of sociologists in Britain in the 1960s was woefully inadequate. There were fewer than 40 sociologists teaching in British universities and only 12 offered degrees in the subject. Such 'training' as there was took place at the LSE, and that emphasised the importance of historical and comparative reference to the systematic study of social institutions. There was no course in methods of sociological inquiry. Membership of the BSA itself, however, had grown considerably, and by 1960 stood at 600 and a Sociology and Social Anthropology Section of the British Association for the Advancement of Science had been formed in 1958.

Growing professionalism

In the 1960s and early 1970s the main theme of empirical sociology in Britain was one of attempts to increase the professionalism of sociological inquiry. This took three main forms: a focus on specialised substantive areas, a tendency to combine different research techniques in the pursuit of empirical investigations, and paying particular attention to the development and use of more sophisticated techniques of data collection and analysis. There were several major factors in this last trend. One was the rapid development of computer technology, which made the statistical analysis of the results of survey research a somewhat less tedious task and, furthermore, enabled sophisticated statistical techniques to be applied by those who were not statistical virtuosi. Second, there was official sponsorship through the Social Science Research Council, which had been set up in 1965, for the kind of quantitative inquiry that for many individual academics had hitherto been prohibitively expensive. Third, there was an increasing amount of survey research being conducted by government departments.[26] The Home Office Research Unit was established in 1958 and began to produce major reports on crime-related topics. At the same time a wide range of continuous multi-purpose governmental surveys developed. The Family Expenditure Survey, which had begun in the 1950s and was designed for a single purpose — to provide weights for the Retail Price Index — became multi-purpose in 1967. It was used by the Department of Health and Social Security to produce annual estimates of the numbers in poverty, by the Central Statistical Office to derive annual reports on the redistributive impact of income support measures on the distribution of income, and by the Department of the Environment to produce annual estimates of housing costs. The General

141

Household Survey was also set up in the 1960s designed explicitly for secondary analysis.[27] These surveys were conducted by the Government Social Survey, which had been founded in 1941 and which exerted a major influence in raising the standards of survey research and in persuading policy makers in government to pay attention to survey results.[28] It had been part of the Central Office of Information until 1967 when it became an independent department under the Treasury. However, in 1970 it was merged with the General Register Office for England and Wales into a single Office of Population Censuses and Surveys. The idea was that surveys and census concerned with individuals, families and households should be planned and conducted on an integrated basis. The Government Social Survey undertook and continues to undertake inquiries requested by government departments and other official bodies such as Royal Commissions.

Finally, the growth and spread of market research resulted in many refinements in research techniques, particularly those related to the interview survey. Developments in the measurement of attitudes and the use of quota sampling may be attributed to market researchers. Sociology students learning about research techniques frequently turned to Edwards's *Readings in Market Research* (1956) for instruction. Sophisticated techniques were not, however, sufficient on their own to produce sociological inquiry, and it is in this respect that the research conducted by the Government Social Survey and by market researchers was deficient. Their research was geared to purposes other than the development or testing of sociological theory.

Another form of professionalism in the 1960s was a tendency for different research techniques to be combined. One that combined survey research with participant observation along with the extensive use of documentary evidence was Birch's *Small-town Politics. A Study of Political Life in Glossop* (1959). Birch was interested not so much in social life as a whole, as in the specific problems of grass-roots politics in Glossop. There were two primary objectives: first to examine the problems of small-town government in a period that was generally recognised to be one of difficulty for all but the largest authorities; and second, to illustrate the nature of small-town party politics and to throw some light on the basis of party support. Information was collected in a number of ways: all documentary sources were explored including Census material, the files of the excellent local paper were read from 1918 onwards, influential persons — some 80 in all — were interviewed, while secretaries of voluntary associations and trade unions were sent questionnaires. Birch attended meetings of the Borough Council, political parties and some voluntary associations, while a random sample of about 600 townsfolk were interviewed in their own homes. The published work had chapters on the development of modern Glossop, on social structure and leadership, on political parties, local government, business and the trade unions, and on churches and voluntary associations. However, no specific hypotheses were suggested or tested and the conclusion was a summary of the main findings.

In 1960 Stacey published a study of *Tradition and Change* in Banbury, an inquiry that nicely straddled the line between community study and social survey. Frankenberg included Stacey's work in his book *Communities in Britain*[29] while accepting Stacey's own judgement that Banbury was not really a community. The work had begun as early as 1948, but some seven years were spent on field work and a further six on analysing and sifting the data. Stacey's purpose was to study the social structure and culture of Banbury with special reference to the introduction of large-scale industry. Apparently, when the study was first planned, 'attention was focused on the distinction between Banburians and immigrants. It seemed likely that there were important tensions between the two groups, even that the division might be the key to the social structure of the town'.[30] Since participant observation as a research technique was by itself inadequate for a town the size of Banbury, Stacey combined it with the use of published records and the survey technique. A research team of three made their homes in or near Banbury, and each took part in a different sphere of social life. A pilot questionnaire followed by a schedule inquiry into over 1,000 households covering some 3,387 individuals was used to determine population composition, family and household composition, and religious and political adherence. Additionally, leading members of all the formal organisations in Banbury were interviewed.

The main conclusion that emerged from the study was that Banbury's problem was not so much that of having to absorb a new influx of people, but that it had to face the challenge to the local tradition. This challenge was symbolised by the new ideas and ways of life that the workers of the newly established factories in this locality had brought with them. Banbury had ceased to be one community, while social change was loosening the ties of the in-turning traditional society and reducing the intensity of local relationships. Banbury was divided vertically between traditionalists and non-traditionalists and horizontally between the middle- and the working-classes.

In 1966 Stacey received a grant of £20,000 from the Nuffield Foundation to do a second study of Banbury. This was published as *Power, Persistence, and Change. A Second Study of Banbury* (1975). Stacey felt that this restudy was the first of its kind in Britain. One of its main aims was 'to assess the social systems present in Banbury particularly those associated with class and tradition and to assess the social changes which have taken place in these systems since 1950'. The research was by no means a replication in the manner of Rowntree or

Llewellyn-Smith; certainly there was an opportunity to test some of the predictions made in the first study and to discover the fate of the traditional society, but rather than reporting on all aspects of the structure, culture and processes that were analysed earlier, this work concentrated on those aspects where there was 'something particular to contribute to sociology as a whole or to a sub-discipline'.[31] Attention was paid to groups and quasi-groups, to the formation and collapse of groups, and to the joining, leaving and leading of groups by individuals.

If the substance was a little different, the research methods used were largely those of the earlier study. The field work was undertaken by a research officer and two assistants who lived in Banbury between 1966 and 1968. One of the methods of study was participant observation, each field worker participating in different aspects of the town. A 6 per cent random sample, this time of individuals, was drawn from the Electoral Register in 1967. Three sub-samples were later drawn from the main sample to provide data on the extended family, sex roles and social class images. Data were systematically collected about voluntary associations, their members and committee members, and their links with each other.

The book presented a complex picture of social class in Banbury with social categories that cross-cut in terms of positions in the system of production, in the consumption market and in the domestic housing market. Other cross-cutting categories related to familial statuses and to membership of age-sex groupings. Stacey concludes: 'Banbury . . . has no neat social class system but is dynamic, stratified, and cross-cut by ties within and without. It is an ordered society without a formal social order'. This research features in Bell and Newby's *Doing Sociological Research* (1977), which gives eight personal accounts that describe the actual practice of doing sociological research. Colin Bell, the research officer in the Banbury restudy, comments that *Power, Persistence, and Change* was finally published almost ten years after Stacey and himself began making preparations for restudying the town. Some of the delay was due to publishing problems, some to Bell's taking a lectureship at the University of Essex after two years of working on the restudy, but the rest was due to totally unforeseen difficulties arising from having four people working together, and their failure to face, let alone solve, the organisational and authority problems involved. There were three levels of hierarchy: Margaret Stacey, the director of the project living in Swansea; Colin Bell, a 'kind of foreman'; and two research assistants who, like Bell, both moved with their families to live in Banbury. The two research assistants were also registered for higher degrees in Swansea (under Stacey's supervision), giving them two masters and split loyalties. The project proved to be a particularly difficult one to handle and to bring to a conclusion, and there were rising levels of acrimony and recrimination between team members, only some of which are hinted at in Bell's 'Reflections on the Banbury Restudy' (Bell and Newby, 1977).

The sociology of eduction

The 1960s also saw the emergence of specialised substantive areas and in many of these empirical sociology made major strides. The sociology of education continued to focus on the relationships between social class, educational opportunity and social change. The empirical groundwork had already been laid by the various contributors to Glass's *Social Mobility in Britain* (1954), and later by Floud, Halsey and Martin in their *Social Class and Educational Opportunity* (1956). The dominance − even monopoly − by the London School of Economics of the sociology of education at this time resulted in a single structural-functional approach that lasted up to the mid-1960s. Lack of alternative models meant that there was very little discussion about its theoretical bases.[32] Douglas's national cohort studies continued to document the fact that at every stage in his schooling the working-class child was at a disadvantage through poorer home conditions and other environmental factors.

Empirical research in the 1960s turned to attempts to explain why this was so in terms of a range of social and socio-psychological factors. Some focused on the relationships between parents and children and stressed in particular the role played by parental attitudes. Wiseman, in a series of studies of over 13,000 14-year-olds in the Greater Manchester area, concluded that the important dimension was whether parents had a 'positive' attitude towards education, or whether they were indifferent or even 'actively hostile'.[33] The Plowden Report concluded that parental attitudes as expressed in a general interest in the school made a '28% contribution' to academic performance.[34] Bernstein launched the idea that it was the form of language used in the home that was the significant factor.[35] Unfortunately, in terms of empirical research, Bernstein found considerable difficulty in operationalising his concepts. Another group of researchers focused on the link between the home and the school. The Newsom Report[36] paid particular attention to imperfect home—school links, while Jackson and Marsden related parents' experiences with teachers and officials in Huddersfield and concluded that 'sheer ignorance and lack of mutual understanding, sympathy and tolerance can add up to disastrous failures of communication between schools and parents'.[37] Mays similarly examined the clash of norms between homes and schools in a lower working-class area of Liverpool.[38]

Other researchers studied peer group relationships to explain educational disadvantage. Hargreaves made a study of a streamed secondary modern school in the north of England where he found a process of 'subcultural differentiation' into the higher academically oriented 'A' and 'B' streams and the anti-academic or 'delinquescent' 'C' and 'D' streams. His book, *Social Relations in a Secondary School* published in 1967, has become almost folklore amongst sociologists of education. King, on the other hand, concentrated on the relationship between aspects of school organisation and pupil involvement in a questionnaire study of over 700 pupils covering 72 schools in England and Wales.[39]

There was, in short, a great deal of empirical work in this area, much of it oriented to very pragmatic concerns, but because it was geared to attempts to explain educational disadvantages, it built up in an inductive fashion a considerable body of theory. Towards the late 1960s the debate in the sociology of education moved towards the role of the new comprehensives in combatting inequalities. In her *Social Class and the Comprehensive School* Julienne Ford examined the reasoning behind the current pressure towards comprehensive reorganisation of secondary education. She suggested that such reform was based on an implicit theory about the effects of comprehensive education; a theory derived from the notion that early selection produced certain negative effects, and that the abolition of such discrimination would constitute a major step towards the creation of a 'fairer society'. Ford formulated five hypotheses — two referring to the 'academic', and three to the 'social' arguments — derived from this theory. These were first, that comprehensive schools would produce a greater development of talent than tripartite schools; second, that comprehensive schools would provide greater equality of opportunity for those with equal talent; third, that the occupational horizons of children in comprehensive schools would be widened relative to those of children in tripartite schools; fourth, that comprehensive schoolchildren would show less tendency to mix only with children of their own social type; and finally, that comprehensive schoolchildren would tend to have views of the class system as a flexible hierarchy, while tripartite schoolchildren would tend to see this as a rigid dichotomy. Ford then set out to test these hypotheses on a sample of London secondary schoolchildren. She selected three schools: a well established, relatively uncreamed comprehensive school of more or less average size, co-educational, streamed and with a 'house' system; a grammar school; and a secondary modern; all 'matched' as far as possible in relevant respects. Her 'sample', however, comprised the complete fourth years of these three schools — 320 boys and girls aged 14 to 15 (a procedure that made it very unclear what the sample was a sample *of*).

Questionnaires were administered in form groups and completed under supervision. By comparing the three schools against IQ scores and the various questions concerning, for example, occupational aspirations, Ford tested the hypotheses by computing (somewhat inappropriately) chi-square as a 'test' of significance. She also used sociometry to test the fourth hypothesis. However, no evidence was found to support any of the five hypotheses; Ford concluded that the theory itself must be faulty. Abolishing the eleven plus and educating all children in one building was not sufficient to produce a 'fairer society'. Most comprehensive schools were themselves streamed, so early selection was just as prevalent, if not more insidious, in the comprehensive school.

Looking back over her research in 1976, Ford, intimating the possibility of a new purpose for conducting social research, says:

> I am unable to avoid the conclusion that this is not the story of a vain or disinterested attempt to establish some 'facts'. There does not seem to be anything at all inductive about it. By her own admission the author was engaging in a rhetorical rather than an explorative game. She was disgusted and frightened by what she saw as the replacement of an overt form of educational inequality by a more subtle and tenacious kind of injustice. She believed that misguided or 'progressive' educationalists had started an unfortunate rumour. The idea was abroad that 'comprehensive' secondary education would somehow ameliorate the socially divisive effects of educational selection and assessment. She simply wanted to float a counter rumour that it might not.

Ford had simply used the 'scientific rhetoric' rather than a polemical one to 'aggravate, startle, or shock that counter-rumour into existence'. She admitted that 'no serious attempt' was made to test the first two of her hypotheses, and that her 'peremptory test of three hypotheses on a rather mysteriously selected sample of three London secondary schools did acquire the whiff to which conditioned nostrils react when admissible "evidence" is suspected. What was offered in the scientistic rhetorical arena as a rumour of "no reliable evidence", produced wider polemical circles'.[40]

Knowledge by itself, argues Ford, has no intrinsic value; the important issue is what such knowledge leads to. She comments on the various reactions to her book, finding, for example to her horror, Professor Cox, of Black Paper fame, using her research to support his own argument in favour of segregationist education. Yet, at the outset of her book, Ford had declared herself to be a socialist who was concerned that the comprehensive schools did not appear to be improving a very unequal and unjust situation. She comments: 'The theorist or researcher confronts his published statements as things apart from him, he no longer has autonomy over them, they exist in and of themselves and have a reality distinct from his solipsistic imaginings. He feels responsible for what he has said but impotent to intervene in the course of the dialogue'.[41]

Industrial sociology

Industrial sociology showed many of the same trends in the 1960s, but in its early years it was centred not on the London School of Economics, but at Liverpool. These studies have already been reviewed, but they were followed by a succession of monographs that attempted to analyse the class, status and market situation of different occupational groups. The seminal work here was by Lockwood who in 1958 published a study of white-collar workers. Using a variety of historical and contemporary sources, he looked at their class consciousness from three aspects: their economic position in relation to the labour market, the character of their work and the social relations arising out of it, and their social status. In particular he wanted to test whether the 'blackcoated worker' had a 'false' class consciousness. Lockwood located his study in an historical dimension by showing that the market, work and status situations of the clerks differed in the last century from those of the manual worker. Though not an owner of the means of production, the clerk was not really 'proletarian' either, and he enjoyed higher income, better job security and greater mobility than the manual worker. Lockwood concluded that the clerks were not an example of an occupational group having a false class consciousness since they did not identify with the 'labour movement'. Blackburn made a study of white-collar unionism, which he published as *Union Character and Social Class* in 1967. This used unstructured interviews with key informants and formal interviews with a sample of bank clerks. Considerable use was also made of documentary sources, again to put the situation in an historical context. Blackburn had a clearly formulated hypothesis: that unionisation was a function of 'unionateness' and of 'completeness', and he stressed that basically the reasons for trade unionism among white-collar workers were the same as for manual workers and arose out of a conflict of interests between workers and management.

The impact on British sociological thinking of the rediscovery of Weber and the debate with Marx and Marxism on the character of class relations was reflected in a number of studies of working-class embourgeoisement both in an industrial and in a political context. On the industrial front the classic study was that published in 1969 by Goldthorpe and his colleagues as *The Affluent Worker in the Class*

Structure. The project was initiated in 1962, although the book did not appear until five years after the data collection came to an end. The design of the study was to take a case study of a situation as favourable as possible to the confirmation of the hypothesis, that is to take a critical case. It was decided to study workers in a number of selected high-wage occupations who were employed at the Luton plants of three major manufacturing concerns. Attention was limited to married men regularly earning at least £17 per week, aged between 21 and 46, and resident in Luton. It was not a simple random sample, but a cluster sample of selected departments within each industry. In the end, 229 men were formally interviewed, both at work and at home.

The study concentrated on three major aspects of affluent workers' everyday lives — their work, their patterns of sociability and their aspirations and social perspectives. The authors concluded that

> in the case of the workers we have studied, there remain important areas of common social experience which are still fairly distinctly working-class; that specifically middle-class social norms are not widely followed nor middle-class life-styles consciously emulated; that assimilation into middle-class society is neither in process nor, in the main, a desired objective. In short, the results of our enquiry are not at all what might have been expected had the thesis of embourgeoisement been a generally valid one.[42]

Interest in the relationship between workers' attitudes and technical change continued at Liverpool. Banks published a study of industrial participation in 1963 and concluded that the more technical change results in smaller working teams and a general upgrading of skills, the greater was the extent of participation on the part of the work force that remained.[43] Most of the data were derived from a case study of a firm engaged in seed-crushing and animal foodstuffs. There were structured interviews (with some 340 process workers, 120 maintenance workers and all supervisors) which had been carried out in 1957 and 1958 and which focused on the manual workers' interest in promotion to the rank of supervisor and in serving as joint consultative representative or as a shop steward. There was also a great deal of observation by a team of researchers whose field work procedures were described in some detail in an appendix.

Using more specifically anthropological techniques, Tom Lupton engaged in open participant observation as an industrial worker in two workshops to show how different internal and external factors were related to the absence or presence of restrictive practices.[44] There were also studies of particular occupations like Tunstall's investigation of deep-sea fishermen,[45] Hollowell on long-distance lorry drivers[46] and Banton's studies of the police.[47]

Political sociology

Another major substantive area that blossomed as a sociological specialism in the 1960s was political sociology. In terms of empirical sociology, it was in studies of political behaviour that the significant developments took place. Opinion polls were, of course, non-sociological, but other studies have proceeded by establishing correlations between voting patterns and a variety of social and economic factors. Blondel's *Voters, Parties and Leaders* (1963) brought together many of the results. The relationship between voting and social class had already been established in the 1950s, but the focus of attention shifted to those members of the working class who voted Conservative. This appeared to be a classic case of Marx's false class consciousness working itself out in the political area. In 1962 Runciman, like Booth a shipping millionaire turned scholar, made a study of attitudes to social inequality and their relationship to positions of class, status and power. The results were published in 1966 as *Relative Deprivation and Social Justice* in which he reviewed the historical background of changing comparisons of class, attitudes to status and the inequalities of power between 1918 and 1962 (utilising some of the results of many of the studies reported in this book). An interview survey had been conducted in 1962 based on a stratified random sample of 2,000 names taken from two wards in each of 50 constituencies in England and Wales. A little over 1,400 were successfully interviewed using a questionnaire that had been previously tested on a quota sample of 100 respondents in four different areas. Respondents were asked to assign themselves to a class and then comment on what sorts of people they saw as 'working class' and 'middle class'. After a long analysis of the relationships between perceptions of class and the manual/non-manual occupational distinction, Runciman turns to the phenomenon of the working-class Conservatives who are shown to be largely manual workers who see themselves as 'middle class'. By the same token, non-manual workers who see themselves as 'working class' are much more likely to be Labour supporters. The analysis is long and complex, but the idea of statistical control is ever-present and he demonstrates how the results of social surveys can be used for purposes that go well beyond a descriptive reportage of the proportions that fall into specified social categories. Runciman concludes that the relationship between inequality and grievance only intermittently corresponds with either the extent and degree of actual inequality or with the magnitude and frequency of relative deprivation (or feeling of inequality). Further, such correspondence varies according to the dimensions of class, status and power.

A study that focused more specifically on the working-class Conservative was McKenzie and Silver's *Angels in Marble* published in 1968. This was a survey of working-class voters aimed at comparing working-class Labour and Conservative voters with respect to social characteristics like age, sex, income and occupation, and at comparing voters for the two major parties on topical questions and on a range of topical themes such as the distribution of power between groups and classes, the social origins of political leaders and the place of the working class in society. Another aim was to investigate the extent to which social 'deference' helps to account for the level of Conservative support in the working class.

The empirical material was gathered in four phases: an interview survey with a sample of 600 working-class people in large English cities who had voted at the previous election for one of the two major parties, re-interviews in depth with 50 of them, a sample survey of 36 municipal constituencies to analyse the opinions of various kinds of working-class Conservative during a period of decline in Conservative support, and intensive re-interviews with a very small number of these about their reaction to the Profumo affair.

The authors found that Labour and Conservative voters were very similar in terms of most social characteristics, although Conservative voters were somewhat better informed and convinced of the superior competence of the Party. There was a tendency among Conservative voters to defer to political leaders of elite social origins, but this was also apparent among Labour voters. The ideological basis for working-class Conservative voting was moving away from deference towards secularism, although women were more likely to be deferential than men.

* * *

Thus in the three key substantive areas of education, industry and politics there were many empirical enquiries carried out in Britain in the 1960s, many related deliberately and consciously to theoretical concerns, if not to explicitly. stated hypotheses. Some even set out to test the theories of others. Most, certainly in the early 1960s, emanated from the structural-functional school, which concentrated on socio-structural factors for the study of which the interview survey was a very useful tool and it was widely used, very often in combination with other techniques like participant observation and the use of official statistics and other documentary sources. Much the same was true of other sociological specialisms – in particular the study of religion,[48] race relations and minority groups,[49] crime and deviance, mass communications, and family and kinship. Worthy of special mention in the field of crime and deviance is the National Deviancy Conference, which was begun in 1968 and which has had considerable influence in moving concern away from law-based criminology towards a more radical form of deviancy theory.[50]

Empirical research and sociological theorising had finally come together in the 1960s; but it was an uneasy marriage that had not developed any codes of conduct about how the relationship was to develop. Following a survey of sociological research in Britain between 1950 and 1968, Krausz was able to conclude that the results were 'not unimpressive'.[51] He viewed the situation as a 'giant jig-saw puzzle with many pieces missing' with partial pictures of many areas, mostly un-related to the total scene of other social institutions in the social structure. Furthermore, the methodological immaturity of the subject placed limitations on overall results. There had, however, been a pro-liferation of research units such as the Centre for Urban Studies, the Tavistick Institute of Human Relations, the Population Investigation Committee, the Institute of Community Studies, and the Institute of Race Relations that had promoted at least a degree of continuity and cumulativeness in research. The Social Science Research Council Survey Archive or 'data bank' was set up in 1967 at the University of Essex. Its brief was to collect and preserve machine-readable data relating to social and economic affairs from academic, governmental and commercial sources, and to make those data available for secon-dary analysis. In the first decade of its existence the Archive activity sought data produced by opinion polls, commercial and market research companies such as NOP's National Political Surveys, although the great majority of its holdings consisted of *ad hoc* surveys, large and small, carried out by academics.[52] The Archive quickly became the largest of its kind outside North America, the largest in Europe, holding over 1,600 datasets by 1980 and adding to its collection at the rate of some 200 each year.[53]

Other trends in the 1960s

There were other perhaps less distinctive trends in the 1960s. One was for researchers, in the course of their careers, to show a tendency to revert to forms of social accounting as they became involved in the investigation of particular problems for official or organisational purposes. A striking illustration is the career of Pauline Morris who jointly with her husband published their study of Pentonville in 1963. This was based mainly on participant observation and the results were largely non-quantitative. The Morrises spent 15 months in Pentonville where they were allocated an office as a base from which to conduct their work. Their aim was to 'look at the prison of Pentonville as an ongoing social system, to attempt to identify its formal objectives and the means to their attainment, and sketch the broad outline of its social structure, and, by providing a descriptive analysis of its culture, to examine certain aspects of the dichotomy of its latent and manifest functions, that is to study the variations between the intended and unintended consequences of day-to-day behaviour within the institution'.[54] Both staff and prisoners were invited to visit them in the research office whenever the opportunity presented itself and they felt so inclined. The researchers were allowed to wander freely about the prison, observing and talking to prisoners and prison staff members. Many of the data were obtained from informal conversations; however, formal interviews were also carried out with about one-third of the staff. Each prisoner completed a 'census' form of his age, marital status, birthplace, age of leaving school and so on. Prison records were also analysed. The Morrises attended the morning conferences of the warden (or governor) with guards, as well as other prison meetings as and when they occurred. Some prisoners wrote essays, selections from which were reproduced as an appendix to the book. The main method of research, say the authors, consisted of 'being on the premises, visibly yet unobstrusively, and engaging in informal conversation whenever the opportunity presented itself'.[55] They kept a daily diary which, by the end of the study, ran to some 700,000 words.

The Morrises' main conclusion was that the negative effects of prison life on offenders were caused in the main by the adverse environment, including existing physical conditions, and the attitudes of prison staff and public, and that these environmental factors were conducive merely to controlling and containing the prisoner rather than attempting to improve him. Welfare provisions were made, but they were overshadowed by the pressing daily demands of feeding, clothing and housing a large body of men and keeping them out of mischief.

Pauline Morris went on to consider *Prisoners and their Families* (1965), a report written for Political and Economic Planning based on a representative sample of prisoners and their dependants. 'The survey', she says, 'has been both descriptive and analytic. We have attempted to portray objectively the conditions of life for a wide range of families of men in prison, first offenders, recidivists, and civil prisoners'.[56] The primary objective of the research was 'to elicit facts upon which penologists and administrators might base future policies'. Morris does, however, make specific recommendations in respect of financial position for prisoners' families, the improvement of social casework for prisons, and the improvement of facilities for contact between the prisoner and his family. Five hypotheses were set up in advance for testing and a typology of family situations into which each family could be placed was developed. Over 800 prisoners and their families were selected from 17 prisons, stratified by class of prison (central, regional or local), by type (open or closed), and by geographical region. They included 330 recidivists, 330 first offenders and 177 civil prisoners, all 'married' in the wider sense of the term. In addition a detailed study of 100 prisoners living in the London area was made. The prisoners were asked permission for their wives to be contacted (initially by letter) and 588 interviews were obtained in this way, but only after considerable difficulty in tracing them. The questionnaires used were closely structured and mainly precoded, being based on the results of a pilot study which had been carried out by means of completely unstructured, free-ranging interviews. The topics covered were family composition, finance, welfare, marital history, criminality, social contacts and future plans.

The processing and presentation of the material was very statistically-oriented; tests of significance, including chi-square, t-tests and analyses of variance, were conducted on all comparisons. There was even a statistical appendix written by Kalton. The results of the intensive interviews were presented as lengthy case studies under certain categories of situation. A similar research design, again highly quantitative, was seen in Pauline Morris's *Put Away. A sociological study of institutions for the mentally retarded* (1969). The study was carried out at the direct invitation of the National Society for Mentally Handicapped Children. Its objective was, once again, mainly descriptive, namely 'to examine the range and quality of institutional provision made in England and Wales for that group of handicapped individuals who are broadly known as "mentally deficient" '.[57] As before, there were detailed case studies to supplement the statistical material, but this time there were no hypotheses being specifically tested and there are no reports of significance tests having been carried out.

To some extent Ferdynand Zweig followed a similar path to that of the Morrises. His first book, *The Planning of Free Societies* (1942), had been reviewed enthusiastically by Seebohm Rowntree, who invited him to write a study for the Trust on spending habits and their influence on (secondary) poverty. Zweig was expected to use existing documentary sources; however, these had their limitations. He began to develop the habit of engaging all sorts of people in conversation, and from them he learned much of their background, lifestyles, hopes, fears and aspirations. Zweig saw himself as being engaged in the whole product and process of research, not just as one of a team where each individual knows only part of the process. His investigations, he says, 'never lose the character of a pilot survey, because they change all the time. I am master of my enquiry to the very end'.[58] The interview was for Zweig not a device for mechanically recording the responses to pre-set questions, but a conversation that was to be enjoyed by both participants and whose conduct was very definitely an art rather than a science.

In his earlier books Zweig was very informal, descriptive, making frequent use of quasi-statistics, and reluctant to come to any conclusions. The first of his books to possess a concluding chapter was *Women's Life and Labour*. There he says: 'I was asked to write a few conclusions out of my study. I am afraid a portrait or a sketch can never be conclusive, as life itself is not conclusive. However, a few general remarks can be substituted here for conclusions'. In his *The Worker in an Affluent Society* Zweig's methods were a little more formal; he used a more-or-less standardised interview schedule, although he personally conducted some 672 interviews, while his wife visited about 60 homes of those interviewed at work. Zweig offered some generalisations and conclusions at the end, suggesting a principle of 'emotional homeostasis', and epitomising the affluent worker in terms of his general conservatism and his ambivalence. He saw new trends that appeared to be characteristic of the welfare state — a rise in security-mindedness and a general process of 'feminisation'.

Zweig's latest book, *The Student in an Age of Anxiety*, was much more conventional in its approach. He selected a random sample of students from Oxford and Manchester, quoting figures derived from an interview schedule which was reproduced at the end of the book. As a conclusion he built a model of the typical student and reviewed the general trends of thought and preferences revealed by the students' opinions. He pointed to the new conservatism, the wave of internationalism, the pro-Russian trend, Britain as a moral force and so on. Zweig even made 'tentative suggestions' for future policy including the development of the mental health services, advice on the subject of careers, a greater emphasis on physical exercise and team games, and the constructive use of vacations.

All too often, during the careers of empirical sociologists, the lure of institutionally or officially backed empirical inquiry resulted in work that was decreasingly sociological and more in the tradition of the social accounting of statistical aggregates. The inclination to draw conclusions about sociological theory declined in proportion as the temptation to make recommendations for future policy increased.

Action research

One last trend in the 1960s that might be mentioned was for some researchers to depart more explicitly from the canons of 'objective' and 'scientific' inquiry by deliberately making changes in the social environment, the effects of which are then studied. Such 'action research' had in fact been used in some fields of social science for a long time. Researchers and consultants in work organisations have made regular use of it and have produced a considerable body of literature on the subject.[59] The application of action research to social problems began with Mays's *On the Threshold of Delinquency* referred to earlier. Later examples, both published in 1964, are Spencer's *Stress and Release in an Urban Estate* and Jephcott's *A Troubled Area. Notes on Notting Hill*. The former looked at the effect of the introduction of an adventure playground and other facilities on various forms of urban stress as reflected in delinquency, truancy, child abuse and adult crime in certain selected areas of Bristol. Jephcott's study arose out of the Notting Hill riots of 1958. Beginning in 1962, she spent four months in a preparatory stage consulting some 60 people in official positions. This helped to delineate the main problems of the borough and put the researcher into contact with her future respondents. Jephcott's resources were too limited to allow the drawing of a random sample, but she nevertheless made an attempt to adopt some kind of selection procedure into which subjectivity was unlikely to enter. She decided to narrow her area to the district lying within a radius of about seven minutes' walk from Ladbroke Grove tube station. She says: 'A circle was drawn with a radius of 1,000 feet from the local tube station on a 1:2500 map of Kensington; this circle contained a certain number of streets, from each of which house numbers x, x + 1, and x - 1 were selected'.[60] As a result she covered some 39 streets with a population of between 11,000 and 12,000. She obtained personal introductions through officials to the people of about 90 households living in the area, the great majority of whom lived in multi-occupied houses. A couple of months later Jephcott began a second project involving action research: she attempted to induce local residents to co-operate in short-term and small-scale action regarding such problems as the provision of outdoor play facilities for small children, household rubbish disposal and old people.

A perhaps better known instance of action research had its origins in the immediate aftermath of the publication of the Plowden Report in 1967. The Plowden Committee had drawn attention to the schools in run-down areas that were facing a 'vicious circle' of 'cumulative deprivation'.[61] Positive discrimination in favour of these 'educational priority areas' was advocated to make schools in the most deprived areas 'as good as the best in the country'. The Plowden Committee had also made a plea for 'research to discover which of the developments in the educational priority areas have the most constructive effects so as to assist in planning a longer term programme'. Halsey, who at the time was part-time adviser to the Secretary of State (Anthony Crosland) at the Department of Education and Science, was impressed by the principle of positive discrimination and the call for action research, and began a project which was sponsored partly by the Department itself and partly by the Social Science Research Council. Its terms of reference were to carry out and to evaluate an action programme with four objectives: first to raise the educational performance of the children, second to improve the morale of teachers, third to increase the involvement of parents in their children's education, and finally to increase the 'sense of responsibility' for their communities of the people living in them. Four districts were chosen in London, Birmingham, Liverpool and the West Riding, and parallel Scottish arrangements were made at Dundee. A balance had to be struck between two aims: on the one hand there was the unitary principle of an action research team based in Oxford having as its main aim the production of a working policy for Educational Priority Area practice which would, at least in principle, be national in its scope; and on the other the principle of local diagnosis and local autonomy, which would take account of the variations in needs and possibilities arising from the peculiar characteristics of each of the four districts.

During the project's first year a series of descriptive surveys were carried out covering teachers, parents and pupils in the project schools. Their purpose was both to provide the project directors with relevant information to help them plan their strategies, and also to enable the project areas to be compared systematically one with another, thereby indicating why a policy that was successful in one might be inappropriate in another. All teachers in the project schools were sent a postal questionnaire asking about career histories, their attitudes towards various aspects of teaching and the degree of their job satisfaction. A study was made of a random sample of 800 mothers of children in the project schools who were interviewed at home while a survey of the ability and attainments of all the children in the project schools administered standardised tests of verbal ability and reading.

Key features of the projects were developments in pre-schooling (in particular a programme aimed at language improvement), the introduction of community schools (including the provision of community education centres, home—school liaison teachers and an educational visitor service), and developments in the curriculum. The results of the research programme were published in 1972 in five volumes entitled *Educational Priority*. Halsey concluded that the Educational Priority Area was, socially and administratively, a viable unit through which to apply the principle of positive discrimination, that pre-schooling was the outstandingly economical and effective device in the general approach to raising standards, that the idea of the community school, as outlined by Plowden, had been shown to have powerful implications for community regeneration, that there were practical ways of improving the partnership between families and schools and of improving the quality of teaching, and that action research was an effective method of policy formulation and practical innovation. Halsey recognised, however, that the Educational Priority Area could be no more than part, though an important one, of a comprehensive social movement towards community development and redevelopment in a modern industrial society.[62]

The Newsons

While empirical research and sociological theorising had, in various ways, come together, the traditions of social accounting and social exploration certainly did not die out in the 1960s. The notion of descriptive fact gathering by means of the social survey was still very prevalent and may be seen in the work of John and Elisabeth Newson, who in 1963 published their *Infant Care in an Urban Community*. This research figures both in Banks's *Studies in British Society* (1969), studies chosen because they were 'rich in their sociological content or implications' and 'exemplify major areas of importance in contemporary English life',[63] and also in Shipman's *The Organisation and Impact of Social Research* (1976), which included six of 'the most quoted books in behavioural science related to education'.[64] The Newsons studied the child-rearing practices of 700 mothers in Nottingham based on a sample drawn at random from records kept by the City of Nottingham Health Department. The data were derived almost entirely from intensive interviews, the majority of which, as in the Douglas studies, were conducted by health visitors. However, Elisabeth Newson herself conducted nearly 200 interviews in order to be able to compare the results with those of the health visitors. In a sequel, published as *Four Years Old in an Urban Community* (1968), the Newsons followed up 275 families and added 425 new cases whose mothers were seen for the first time as the children reached four years old. This time, however, a grant from the Nuffield Foundation enabled the Newsons to pay for a team of professional interviewers, each with a tape-recorder.

In a commentary that looks back on their work from the perspective of 1976 the Newsons explain that their interest in the research began with the arrival of their own baby, who 'we soon discovered was also the focus and excuse . . . for a cultural bombardment designed by society to initiate us into our new status as young parents'.[65] There was no shortage of (conflicting) advice particularly from 'baby-books' on how they should look after their infant, but little knowledge on what parents actually did and thought about child-rearing. The Newsons admitted that no hypotheses were being tested; nevertheless the study had 'a certain value as a descriptive sociological investigation'. In a comment strikingly reminiscent of Sir Frederick Eden's *The State of the Poor* (1797), the Newsons say, '. . . we make no attempt, in this particular field, to investigate change or to become involved with policy-making, because we do not see this as consonant with the observer's role as we chose to play it . . . we provide the ammunition for others rather than supplying the motive force for firing it'.[66] Eden's 'hewers of stone' and 'drawers of water' were still very much alive even in the 1970s.

From the standpoint of research methods the Newsons saw their most radical innovation as their 'attempt to fashion the interview itself into a more reliable tool of investigation'.[67] The use of tape-recorders was developed, probably for the first time, into a purposefully integrated research tool, rather than being used as a simple *aide-memoire* to avoid writing down responses first hand. The interviewers had a pencil and schedule, which was used not only to ensure that the questions were asked in the same way, but also to note essential information to cut down processing time later, and to note at which points on the tape there were 'quotable' quotes. This situation allowed the interviewer 'to give all her mind to the relationship and to probe effectively and flexibly'.[68] All the interviews were transcribed and the results sorted and cross-referenced. Apparently, some ten large volumes were filled with this material. The questions were all very carefully phrased; some were deliberately loaded to offset the tendency to give expected answers. Thus mothers were asked (counter to all the worldly advice in the texts on questionnaire design): 'I expect he still wets the bed sometimes, doesn't he?' This was loaded in the direction of the answer 'yes', but, say the Newsons, no mother will say that her child wets the bed if he does not. Schedule and pencil also facilitated the control of eye contact by enabling the researcher to look down and write the odd word or two if eye contact was raising the level of anxiety.[69]

Poverty studies

Following the tradition of Rowntree's inquiries in York, Townsend in the early 1960s conceived the idea of carrying out a national survey of poverty in Britain (having already made a re-analysis of the 1953 and 1960 Family Expenditure Survey data to assess the numbers of people below the poverty line, the results of which were published in 1965 as *The Poor and the Poorest* in collaboration with Abel-Smith). In 1964 he successfully applied to the Joseph Rowntree Memorial Fund for £32,000 and after extensive pilot work between 1965 and 1968 the

main survey was carried out in 1968 and 1969. This involved interviews with over 4,000 individuals in over 2,000 households in 51
constituencies throughout Britain, collecting data on over 6,000 people
including children. The questionnaire ran to 39 pages with sections on
housing and living amenities, employment, occupational facilities and
fringe benefits, cash income, assets and savings, health and disability,
the use of social services, and style of living. The sample was a multi-
stage stratified random sample of households of a very complex kind,
and no effort was spared to make it nationally representative. Some
four-fifths of the interviews were carried out by a small group of about
25 interviewers who were instructed to interview the housewife and
all wage earners (and other income recipients) in the household. This
averaged out at two people per household, but it took up to three calls
to complete a household with an average interview time of two hours.
Some 76 per cent of the households selected gave complete information
and a further 6 per cent did so 'substantially'. In addition, some information was obtained about the great majority of the 385 households
refusing an interview. While the main survey was being carried out,
four local surveys were conducted in Salford, Glasgow, Belfast and
Neath, producing data on 1,208 households and 3,950 individuals. In
total there were data, mostly of a very elaborate kind, for 3,260 households and 10,048 individuals.

The results of this inquiry, however, were not published until 1979.
Entitled *Poverty in the U.K. A survey of household resources and
standards of living*, it was a massive volume of 1,216 pages. The field
work had used up much of the budget and in spite of further sub-
vention from the Rowntree Trust, 'the protracted final stages of
analysis and writing had to be conducted on a shoestring'.[70] Townsend
argued that the results were still relevant in 1979 because the structure
of society 'does not change significantly in a short span of years'. While
there had been vast technological and cultural changes, the division of
society into classes, patterns of community, family and neighbourhood
social groupings − all aspects of social structure − remained largely
unaltered. In particular, one of the major findings of the study was that
the structure of inequality had changed very little. One trend, however,
had been the growth of the professional, managerial and executive
classes accompanied by a growth in the dependent population of
retired, unemployed and disabled. More people had been 'pushed to
the bottom', while the proportion with low incomes had 'definitely
grown since 1969'. Such a trend, claimed Townsend, represented 'an
advanced stage in the history of the conflict between classes'.[71]

Poverty, according to Townsend, referred to individuals, families
and groups in the population who lacked 'the resources to obtain the
types of diet, participate in the activities and have the living conditions

160

and amenities which are customary, or at least widely encouraged or approved in the societies to which they belong. Their resources are so seriously below those commanded by the average individual or family that they are, in effect, excluded from ordinary living patterns, customs, and activities'.[72] All conceptions of poverty based on some form of absolute standard were 'inappropriate or misleading' and 'deserve to be abandoned'. Even Rowntree's 'physical efficiency' standard did not take into account a whole range of factors, in particular dietary customs. The wider concept of 'resources', argued Townsend, should replace that of income, while 'style of life' should replace 'consumption' (or, more narrowly still, 'nutritional intakes').

In the study Townsend looked at subjective and social definitions of poverty by asking respondents if there was 'real poverty these days' and what they would describe as 'poverty'. Most saw it as something that afflicted particular minority groups like 'old age pensioners' or 'people out of work', or they saw it in terms of subsistence — not having enough to eat, unable to afford clothes, pay the rent and so on. Three 'objective' measures of poverty were taken: the state's standard, the relative deprivation standard, and what Townsend coined as the 'deprivation' standard. The first was very complex because account had to be taken of *all* the rules that applied to the giving of various benefits and the stopping of them. Townsend took an amount 40 per cent above Supplementary Benefit Commission levels as an adjustment to the basic rates allowing for various forms of discretionary payments that were often added, and the income and assets of households normally disregarded in determining eligibility. He found 37 per cent in poverty according to this standard. The relative income standard was defined in terms 'first, of a number of types of household, and secondly, of levels of 50 per cent (very low) and 80 per cent (low) of the mean income for each type'.[73] Some 10.6 per cent were in poverty according to the 'very low' standard and 40 per cent according to the 'low'.

The deprivation standard was Townsend's claim to conceptual innovation. He hypothesised that there was a point at which, for different types of family, 'a significantly large number of families reduce more than proportionately their participation in the community's style of living'.[74] He built up a list of 60 indicators of style of living[75] covering diet, clothing, fuel and light, home amenities, housing environment, work benefits, recreation, education, health, and social relationships. From these a 'summary index' of 12 indicators was selected on the basis that they applied to the whole population. A score of deprivation was then simply added up, the higher the score the higher the deprivation. The mean individual score for the entire sample was 3.5, while 'a score of five and six or more is regarded as highly suggestive of deprivation. Twenty percent of households scored an average of six or more'.[76] Townsend then showed that this index of deprivation was highly correlated with annual net disposable income and, furthermore, tended to increase sharply at certain levels for particular household compositions. These levels then indicated approximately the incomes below which deprivation occurred, and a 'deprivation standard' was accordingly constructed. Townsend found 25 per cent of households and 23 per cent of individuals in the sample were living on incomes below this standard, representing about 4.8 million households and 12.5 million persons throughout the UK. The proportion of people who experienced poverty some time during the year was even higher. The incidence of poverty was highest in one-person households, in Northern Ireland, the north-west of England and the south-west of Scotland, amongst children, women, the separated and widowed, and amongst the elderly.

Using a number of different measures of social class Townsend found that on all measures class uniformly correlated with poverty, and he concluded 'that the nature and degree of differentiation of occupational class is a predominant determinant of poverty – especially . . . when we take into account the class origins and occupational experiences of both husband and wife'.[77] In terms of feelings of poverty 8 per cent of chief wage earners and heads of households said they felt poor all the time; 41 per cent of those aged 35 and over said they were not as well off as they had been 10 years previously. There was a strong correlation between objective and subjective deprivation so that attitudes closely reflected resources. Accordingly, the 'myth of the contented poor is not borne out by the data'.[78]

Deprivation at work, in housing, in the environment and in poor areas is extensively detailed as is deprivation amongst categories in the population most prone to poverty – social minorities, the unemployed and the underemployed, the low paid, the older workers, the disabled and the long-term sick, handicapped children, one-parent families, and old people. As a scheme for alleviating poverty, the supplementary benefits scheme existed 'as much to control behaviour in conformity with what is regarded as desirable socially as to meet need'.[79] Further-more, some 4.4 per cent of the people in the sample (representing about 2.4 million people) seemed on the basis of a careful check to be eligible for, but were not receiving, benefit. There were also more than 40 other schemes that were unco-ordinated, while there were marked variations in the point on the income scale at which families of different composition qualified.

The chief conclusion of Townsend's book is that 'poverty is more extensive than is generally or officially believed and has to be under-stood not only as an inevitable feature of severe social inequality but also as a particular consequence of actions by the rich to preserve and enhance their wealth and so deny it to others'.[80] The part played by the rich is, to Townsend, the key to explaining poverty. Even the popular conception of poverty in terms of subsistence is a misconception 'fostered by motives of condescension and self-interest as well as duty by the rich'.[81] Poverty is rooted in class relations, in the institutional structure of society, and in the policies of access and exclusion that are operated. After 925 pages Townsend outlines in one page the policies that would represent an 'effective assault on poverty'. These include the abolition of excessive wealth and income by statutory maxima, the abolition of unemployment by means of statutory obligations on the government and local authorities to provide employment, a more comprehensive incomes policy, a more co-ordinated social security benefits scheme with higher levels of benefit, further innovations in public ownership, industrial democracy, restraints on professional and managerial autonomy, higher levels of universal education, and abolition of the distinction between owner-occupiers and tenants. By explaining poverty in terms of class relations, and in his focus on the contrast between the rich and the poor, the exploiters and the exploited, Townsend is implicitly Marxist, but he stops short of advocating the overthrow of the capitalist system and opts for radical socialism instead. For a study that purports to be firmly in the tradition of Booth and Rowntree, Townsend not only makes scant reference to either, but makes no comparisons of his findings with theirs. The book reflects both the strengths and weaknesses of the social accounting tradition in British empirical sociology: its meticulous attention to gathering mountains of correct 'facts' painstakingly collected and copiously presented, and recommendations for policy that reflect more the researcher's ideological position than the results of the survey. Conceptually and sociologically the study is less innovative than Booth's, and in terms of the statistical analysis of the causes of poverty is less precise than that of Rowntree.

Using participant observation

Apart from those studies based on the formal survey as the main technique of analysis, there were in the 1960s many that used participant observation. Some of them not only combined this technique with others, but also showed a self-conscious concern for theoretical considerations. An early example was Bryan Wilson's *Sects and Society* (1961). He looked at the history, doctrine, social teaching and social composition of three minority religious groups in Britain, and attempted to show how each aspect of the life of these bodies interacted with the others. He says: 'Each is examined in terms of its

163

teaching and practices; its organisation; its self-interpretation and relation to the wider society, and the changes experienced in these regards; its grounds and techniques of recruitment; its social class, age, sex, and educational structure'.[82] Wilson worked on his own by participant observation, asking members for information about the organisation and its doctrines, and undertaking interviews to obtain life histories. He read journals, biographies of the leaders, tracts, sermons and other documents to obtain a deep appreciation of what membership entailed. He found that winning the confidence of the sectarian was a lengthy and delicate process. Much of the resulting research monograph was descriptive with frequent use of quasi-statistics, but there was a concluding chapter that contained his sociological analysis. Wilson constructed an ideal-type established sect in Christianity, and compared his three sects with that model, taking into account both static and dynamic elements such as the processes of institutionalisation, denominalisation and schism. He then turned to a consideration of the type of functions that the sect performed for its adherents, and suggested a relationship between socio-economic conditions and religious expression. The poor, the socially neglected and the culturally deprived were those who, in the main, and especially in the early days, were drawn into the Elim and Christadelphian movements, both of which offered compensations for lack in this world by a promise of a bright future for the faithful. By contrast, for the Christian Scientist, the hope was this-worldly and immediate; his optimism in the prevailing social order accurately reflected the social standing of the bulk of the adherents to the sect, most of whom were from the middle and the striving lower middle classes. It was the expression of the well-to-do and comfortable, or those who would be so.[83]

Another important example is Rex and Moore's *Race, Community, and Conflict* (1967) which Krausz gives as an example of a piece of research which 'started off with a clarification of existing concepts and theories, had a theoretical conception, and led through fieldwork to empirical study and new theoretical conclusions'.[84] The authors rejected earlier theoretical orientations on race relations and focused instead on conflict, seeing 'a class struggle over the use of houses' a struggle that was 'the central process of the city as a social unit'.[85] They saw the conflicts and the realistic adjustments leading to truce situations as taking place within a special kind of social system. This was the 'zone of transition' in the industrial city, where tension management usually achieved some kind of reconciliation between the various opposing interests. This 'balance of power' situation was not to be confused with the host—immigrant framework of accommodation or assimilation advanced by earlier researchers. Rather, 'the particular aspects of race relations with which we have been concerned are explicable only in terms of the sociology of the city'. The zone of transition was not so much an exclusively immigrant 'ghetto' as a special area of the city with peculiar problems of its own which included that of the coloured immigrant in his urban setting. Rex and Moore used three field work techniques: participant observation of the routine life and special 'events' of Sparkbrook, informal interviewing of apparently important or interesting members of various groups who often provided other contacts and introductions, and an interview survey of 386 English and immigrant residents that was conducted mainly by students and members of the Society of Friends. The authors had experienced considerable difficulties in finding interviewees; initially they had drawn a sample of over 1,500 persons, yet they claimed to be 'confident that our findings are not significantly different from those that would have resulted from a larger or more complete sample'.[86]

In-depth interviews

The work by Sheila Patterson exemplified another trend in the 1960s towards the long, informal, in-depth interview that was neither survey research in the conventional sense nor was really participant observation, and it produced mainly qualitative data. In her book, *Dark Strangers* (1963), she argued that in interviewing relatively unsophisticated people the production of paper and pencil by the interviewer would have an inhibiting effect on the interviewee. Between 1955 and 1958 she spent four or five days and often evenings each week in the area, interviewing, observing or participating in various local or immigrant activities. She did not live in the area 'for family and personal reasons'. She found a representative sample impossible to obtain 'by reason of the recent arrival of most members, of the changing demographic structure of the groups and of its high mobility'.[87] Instead she sought the point of contact in the various major areas of association — jobs, housing and social activities. Eventually some 250 white and 150 coloured people were interviewed.

Patterson looked at the situation of the West Indian immigrant in South London as an immigrant–host relationship, regarding colour as 'only one of a number of major factors involved in the various processes of absorption'. She suggested certain indices of accommodation in the areas of association; for example, in the economic sphere, she had hoped to find the immigrant workers becoming more settled in their jobs, conforming generally to the customs of British workers like joining unions, whilst in social relationships she would expect local people to be used to the presence of coloured people. Her study could then gauge, although not very accurately, the degree of immigrant accommodation in the various areas of association.[88] She concluded that, 'on the whole, then, it seems that the accommodation of West Indians in the economic life of South London was, despite some checks, proceeding slowly but not unsatisfactorily in view of all the factors involved'.[89] Her studies showed a 'fair degree of immigrant accommodation in work, somewhat less in housing, and the modest beginnings of migrant acclimatisation and local acquiescence in casual and formal social contacts − this, then, was the general position in Brixton in mid 1959'.

Attacks on empiricism and survey research

By the end of the 1960s empirical sociology in Britain looked distinctly promising. Yet storm clouds − blown in from the USA and from the Continent − were gathering in an ominous fashion. In France sociology had been slow to institutionalise after its brilliant beginnings in the 1890s, but by the middle 1950s, following the installation of the Fifth Republic, a striking development took place. Marxists like Alain Touraine were very influential and their influence was felt on the British scene. Some British sociologists like John Rex saw Marxism as a challenge to sociology itself. Its effect on empirical sociology, however, is less clear since Marxists were not necessarily anti-empirical. The great master himself had, after all, made great use of official statistics and reports to describe working-class conditions in England. Some Marxists, however, have argued that such data are the creations of political bureaucratic structures that support the interests of a capitalist society.[90] At the end of the 1960s and in the early 1970s Louis Althusser's critique of empiricism was also very influential in Britain and his ideas have been taken up by people like Barry Hindess at Liverpool University. Hindess has argued[91] that the basis of knowledge is not to be found in human 'experience' or in empirical knowledge of any kind, but in concepts and rationalist forms of proof and demonstration.

The general cynicism of intellectual life in post-war Germany had the effect in sociology of a rejection of macro-sociological ideas and a retreat into the narrowly defined questions of empirical research. However, the early 1970s saw the resurgence of the critical Marxist sociology of the Frankfurt School, centred about Jurgen Habermas, whose *Knowledge and Human Interests* (1972) became influential in Britain. Undoubtedly the major influence on British sociology at this time, however, was from the USA. The arrival of symbolic interactionism, phenomenology and ethnomethodology threw doubt on the kinds of 'facts' that empirical sociology was currently producing. These

166

'interpretative' perspectives tended to give primacy to actors' meanings, understandings, interpretations and explanations of social phenomena for the analysis of which the traditional techniques of the formal survey were not only inadequate, but assumed that there was some kind of empirical 'truth' to be discovered. The idea that data were artificial constructions of the sociologist received further support from Thomas Kuhn's influential *The Structure of Scientific Revolutions*, which was published in 1962. Kuhn suggested that the rules of sociological method were merely the conventional practice of scientists and were specific to whatever paradigms were currently in fashion. Cicourel's book *Method and Measurement in Sociology*, published in 1964, was a systematic and influential critique of much that passed for empirical sociology. Feyerabend and Phillips[92] in the early 1970s were for abandoning methods altogether since methodological rules inhibited the growth of knowledge, and they argued for a methodological anarchy in which 'anything goes' in the production of new ideas. Further credence to this idea was given by the growing recognition that much sociological research was effectively carried out in a very *ad hoc* way as evidenced in Hammond's *Sociologists at Work* (1964).

In Britain survey research came in for attack. Bechhofer (1967) complained that there were too many surveys in Britain and that too much attention was, in any case, being given to mere head counting. In 1968 Carter, from a questionnaire inquiry conducted amongst British Sociological Association members and university lecturers in sociology in 1966, found that many sociologists echoed these feelings. Peel and Skipworth looked at 163 reports of surveys which appeared in the major American and British journals of sociology between 1967 and 1970 and found wide differences in sample sizes amongst surveys designed to explore broadly comparable phenomena; they found considerable variation in the extent to which sample findings were extrapolated to wider populations, and a 'surprisingly cavalier attitude to the reporting of significance testing'.[93] Peel and Skipworth complained that in many reports there was no attempt to fulfil the most elementary sampling criteria, while researchers were prepared to accept very low response rates. What was surprising about the findings and the comments on them, however, was that the strictures of the authors applied equally to American and British researchers. Even in terms of sample sizes there was very little difference between the two countries.

The position had apparently not changed a decade later. Harrop, from an analysis of research reports in the *British Journal of Sociology* and *Sociology* between 1968 and 1978, found that the technical quality of the surveys was generally poor. The most frequent problem was failure to sample from a theoretically significant population – only 28 per cent of survey reports were based on national studies of the population in question and none had been drawn from the entire adult population in Britain — the standard universe for many market research studies. In fact, argues Harrop, sample surveys organised by academics are generally less satisfactory than those conducted by market research agencies. They will have less money, less technical skill, less experience of conducting and commissioning surveys, 'while their future careers are not likely to depend on the production of reliable results'.[94] In terms of technical quality Harrop may well be correct; but it is just as empirical sociology that market research is defective. Perhaps the solution would be for sociologists to employ market researchers to conduct their surveys for them, but some experiences of doing that have not been at all happy.

Mark Abrams has recently bemoaned the fact that policy makers take very little notice of survey research, in spite of its rapid development in the 1960s. The explanation, he suggests, lies in the inadequate and amateurish training in survey methods and in a contempt for numeracy on the part of social scientists. Much survey research is, in any case, mindless empiricism.[95] Marsh, in a paper to the 1980 British Sociological Association Conference, has argued that, despite the establishment of the Social Science Research Council in 1965, and despite the enormous growth in the volume and sophistication of survey research, the improvement that this should have made possible in empirical studies of a sociological nature has not occurred. 'If anything', she continues, 'the number of theoretically relevant surveys has declined, and the interest of sociologists in surveys has suffered an eclipse'.

That survey research and other forms of empirical inquiry have largely disappeared from the scene seems to be the current 'story' of what is happening to sociology in Britain today. Such views were fuelled by the experience of attempts to set up survey centres within the universities. William Belson ran his Survey Research Centre from the LSE, but it was never integrated into the teaching and research life of the University. In 1970 the Social Science Research Council Survey Unit had been set up with Mark Abrams as Director. The idea was that it should become a repository for survey skills which would then be made available to others through advice, involvement and teaching. However, when Abrams retired in 1976 the Unit was closed. Whatever the reasons for such an action — and there has been much speculation on the subject — it represented to many empirically minded sociologists an attack on survey research methods. The 1980 British Sociological Association Conference was devoted to the theme 'Development and Diversity: British Sociology 1950–1980'. One of the general topics that was suggested was 'positivism and after', implying that there had been a positivist phase, and that it was now dead.[96] Significantly, most of the papers devoted to this theme accepted that this was so, and then attempted to explain why or how this state of affairs came about. However, one paper questioned this interpretation of events. Platt argued that both in terms of textbook definitions of 'positivism' and in terms of who writers on positivism included as 'positivist', there was considerable variation. It was a term used by many to describe those works from which authors wished to dissociate themselves. However, taking a pragmatic definition of positivism as the presentation of quantitative data, and claims to be testing hypotheses, Platt found that in the three main British journals of sociology there was no reduction in the proportion of quantitative articles. These constituted between a third and a half of all articles in each decade. Furthermore, there was a steady increase in the proportions claiming to be testing hypotheses from 13 per cent in the 1950s to 25 per cent in the 1970s. The proportion of articles that were both quantitative and tested hypotheses rose steadily from 9 per cent in the 1950s to 19 per cent in the 1970s. Platt concludes that the evidence is quite inconsistent with a picture in which there was a solid dominance of positivism which was eroded in the 1960s and had been undermined by the 1970s. From a look at textbooks on research methods and syllabuses at universities Platt found that in the teaching of research methods there certainly had been a move away from positivism with a greater consideration given to alternatives to 'orthodox' methods. Curiously, Platt found that the term 'positivism' became more conspicuous in the 1970s both in teaching and in philosophically oriented books.

Marsh has argued that surveys are not, in any case, inherently positivistic.[97] The 'logical status' of a survey is that they are one of two possible ways of testing causal hypotheses (the other being experimentation), and this involves notions like 'necessity' and 'mechanism' that go beyond experience and observation to which positivists assert that all knowledge is limited. The analysis of data is positivistic only if causal significance is seen to be a purely technical problem of measuring intercorrelations. The schedule questionnaire without extensive piloting, and the notion of 'response error' and its relation to an 'individual true value', are positivistic, but a greater sensitivity to the wording of questions and to the contextual situations in which responses arise would help to avoid such positivistic pitfalls.

Whatever may have happened to positivism in the 1970s (and much of that argument will depend on what is meant by that term), the key question remains: how much empirical sociology was there in Britain in the 1970s, and was it a declining proportion of the sociological enterprise as a whole? A precise answer to this question is probably impossible since, once again, it will depend on definitions — of 'the sociological enterprise', of 'empirical sociology' — and how the 'importance' or 'significance' or 'size' of any empirical inquiry is measured. Monographs that report the results of an inquiry conducted by the authors themselves after 1970 are not difficult to find. Some have been in the social accounting tradition of descriptive, fact-finding inquiry, some have been based on participant observation, or on a mixture of the two. Many have been based on relatively small samples, while some have been more grandiose in their scale. Some have made significant theoretical contributions to the discipline and others have attempted to test theories previously advocated.

Social mobility research

Perhaps the most comprehensive large-scale study based primarily on survey research to be carried out in the 1970s was by a team of researchers at Oxford who, following the tradition established by Glass in the 1950s, were investigating trends in intergenerational mobility in England and Wales. The group, who had set themselves up in 1969 as the Oxford Social Mobility Group, were also concerned to make comparisons of the processes of occupational achievement in British and American society. The initial idea was to repeat the Glass inquiry of 1949 and to replicate Blau and Duncan's *The American Occupational Structure*, which had been published in 1969. Two early publications of the group by Hope (1972) and Ridge (1973) made it clear that there were problems in measuring social class and social mobility in the way Glass had done, while the idea of replication was only one of many interests when the group undertook a national mobility inquiry in 1972 as a collective enterprise.

The inquiry took the form of a stratified two-stage sample survey among men aged between 20 and 64 and resident in England and Wales at the time. In the first stage a sample of 16,563 was drawn using information on population density of groups of wards and parishes from a list compiled by the Office of Population Censuses and Surveys, and in the second stage Electoral Registers were used. After removing those who did not fit the requirements of the specified population, a target sample of 12,598 remained of whom 10,309 were successfully interviewed, a response rate of 82 per cent. After a series of pre-pilot studies carried out in the Oxford area, a commercial agency was contracted to carry out small pilot studies, a final 'full' pilot, and the main survey itself. Questions were designed to collect detailed information on the occupations held by respondents at various stages in their working lives, on their education and on all forms of occupationally relevant training, on their qualifications, and to a more limited extent on the occupations, education, training and qualifications of various of their relatives. There were also questions on areas of residence, current income, friendship patterns, political affiliations and so on.

Great care was taken over the briefing and supervision of the interviewers at both the pilot and main interview stages. At the start of the main inquiry interviewers were instructed to complete three interviews, to return their schedules to their supervisors, and to wait until these had been edited before undertaking further interviews. These were used as a basis for further briefing on the completeness and clarity of the information they had recorded. Out of 339 interviewers who had worked on the survey 45 were not retained or withdrew after the three interviews. The major limitation of the sample was its exclusion of women, which the researchers justified on two grounds: that to include them would have required a much larger sample (which they could not afford) or would have been at the expense of the number of men (which would not have enabled them to carry out certain analyses on the basis of five-year birth cohorts with reliable results); second, the degree of relevance of information on the occupational mobility of women for an analysis of class mobility and class formation was doubtful. Scotland had been excluded on the grounds that this really required a separate study which was, in any case, in process of being carried out.[98]

A large number of publications has emerged from the group,[99] but the main results have recently been published in two separate books, one by Goldthorpe (1980) which concentrates on occupational mobility, and the other by Halsey and his colleagues (1980) who concern themselves with the educational dimension. Both studies base their class scheme on a scale developed earlier by the group itself which was published in Goldthorpe and Hope (1974), and which comprises seven overall categories that combine occupational function with employment status. The two top classes, which include higher- and lower-grade professionals, administrators and officials, managers and proprietors along with supervisors of non-manual employees and higher-grade technicians, they call the 'service' class. Classes III to V, the 'intermediate' class, include routine non-manual workers, small proprietors and self-employed artisans, and lower-grade technicians and foremen, while the 'working class' includes all grades of manual workers.

Goldthorpe suggests that his inquiry represents a return to a relatively old tradition of social mobility research: the study of mobility in relation to class structure and its implications for class formation and class conflict. This departed from 'the usual practice of post-war mobility research' which was influenced mainly by Glass's earlier study and which was concerned with mobility only in terms of social status or prestige and which showed little concern with the issue of the implications of mobility within a growing capitalist economy of working-class homogeneity and cohesion.[100] In an introductory chapter Goldthorpe reviews briefly the variety of interests out of which, over the last century or so, the study of social mobility has sprung, and then turns to an examination of three theses that relate mobility to the form of the class structure and to the character of its class relations. The 'closure' thesis argues that there is least mobility near the peak of the hierarchy because privilege brings along with it the ability to perpetuate privilege. Proponents of the 'buffer zone' thesis claim that there are restrictions on the extent of mobility across the division between manual and non-manual occupations and that this is of major importance in preventing mobility of a long-range kind. Lastly, the 'counterbalance' thesis proposes that different forms of mobility tend to offset one another; in particular, increased mobility through educational opportunity has been largely offset by a decline in mobility through training 'on the job'.

Goldthorpe found from his data that all three theses tended to under-estimate the degree of upward mobility that existed. Their proponents have tended to make inferences about absolute mobility — the actual extent of movement into and out of the various social classes — from measures of relative mobility which compare rates of mobility either one class with another or against some criterion of 'perfect' mobility. Changes in the occupational structure, in particular the expansion of the 'service' classes, have created more upward mobility, so that men of all class origins in the younger class cohorts in the sample have tended to have better chances than men of similar origins in the older cohorts of gaining access to higher-level positions. Relative mobility rates, however, have remained remarkably stable, so that the lower classes are now no better off relative to the higher ones in terms of the chances of upward mobility; in fact, there is evidence of a widening of differences in class chances. Goldthorpe suggests that a model of 'constant social fluidity' would fit the data rather well.

Goldthorpe and his colleagues undertook a follow-up inquiry in 1974 which was aimed at looking in some detail at the experiences of those who had undergone long-range mobility. A sub-sample of 896 was selected of whom 652 were reinterviewed. Each of these was invited in addition to submit a written life history in their own words, but only 247 did so. An analysis of these life histories suggested that there was widespread awareness of having been socially mobile — even amongst those categorised as being stable in class position.

Goldthorpe concludes that British society 'is still very far removed from the goal of openness' despite continuous and sustained economic growth, despite large-scale educational reforms, and despite the transformation of the occupational structure in a direction that created more 'room at the top'.[101] The main function of economic growth can 'best be regarded as being not that of facilitating egalitarian reform but rather that of obscuring its failure'.[102] Only class conflict will result in significant modifications of class inequalities. In terms of class formation, both the service classes and the working classes have become more homogeneous and self-recruiting whereas in the range of the intermediate class positions the extent and nature of mobility is such that the existence of classes as collectives that retain their identity through time is problematical.

Despite deriving their analyses from the same survey, Halsey et al. claim that their study of educational mobility is in a very different tradition: that of political arithmetic, with its concerns for educational selection, the idea of 'wastage' of talent and of 'pools of ability'. Such concerns may be traced back to the Glass study of 1949, to Hogben's *Political Arithmetic* of 1938, and even to the political arithmeticians of the seventeenth century like Petty and Graunt. The authors include Booth, the Webbs and Mayhew amongst their forebears, but this would be to widen the definition of 'political arithmetic' to include the whole social accounting tradition and even the idea of social exploration − a tradition which the researchers certainly do not follow.

It was clear that the idea of replication was more important to the Halsey team than it had been to Goldthorpe. They admit that the content of the interviews 'was dominated by the decision of the research team to replicate as far as practicable the questions asked by David Glass . . . . At the same time the team also attempted a similar replication on the American study by Blau and Duncan carried out in 1962'.[103] Having said that, there are no further references to Glass in the remainder of the book and no attempt is made to compare their findings with his. Furthermore, while the authors borrow some techniques from Blau and Duncan, in particular their path analysis, there is only a very brief comparison of the British data with the American findings.[104]

The Halsey team based their analyses on a sub-set of the original inquiry, namely 8,529 after excluding men aged 60 and over and those not resident in England or Wales at age 14. This makes any comparison between the Halsey and Goldthorpe findings problematic, and neither, in fact, attempts any such comparisons. In particular, the age cohorts on which the analyses are based do not correspond to Goldthorpe's. The youngest men in the sample were aged 20 in 1972 and may have left school in 1967 or 1968, so the study, apart from a brief look at post-secondary education, really only covers the period up to the late 1960s, well before the introduction of comprehensive schools had had any impact. The book, then, is more an historical analysis of the English tripartite system of grammar, technical and secondary modern schools of the pre-war and early post-war years rather than a contemporary analysis of educational opportunities. The eight-year gap between survey and publication of the results had done little to enhance the book's relevance to contemporary issues.

The authors use cohort analysis to reconstruct the experience of those who entered the educational structure in Britain at various dates from early in the century to the 1960s, following respondents' educational careers from primary to secondary school and for the 'fortunate minority' to further education and university. The data are treated as a series of 'flows' through 'educational pathways', but the use of sophisticated statistical techniques of path analysis and multiple regression serves only to rediscover the already well-rehearsed arguments in the debate over equality of educational opportunity as between social classes, namely that while there has been a considerable expansion of opportunities, the service classes have profited most from them. The result is that, on a number of different measures, the gap between the working classes and the rest has remained much the same, or has even widened a little. The authors found evidence of considerable upward mobility and concluded that the state (tripartite) system gave 'superior' education to vast numbers from 'uneducated' homes. This leads them to question Bordieu's theory of cultural capital whereby only the higher social classes have the cultural wherewithal to succeed in the system. As the authors put it: 'It is the dissemination rather than the reproduction of cultural capital that is more apparent here'.[105] In passing, the researchers also use their data to refute the speculations of Hoggart, Jackson and Marsden, and Bantock in Britain, Boudon in France, and Jencks in America.

Halsey et al. argue that the most glaring aspect of inequality of opportunity is the continued existence of private education. Even though fewer than 5 per cent of the age group go to private schools, they have an importance 'far beyond their numerical strength' and 'exact their uncalculated but enormous toll of reduced political pressure from middle class parents, on stimulus from expert teachers and response from motivated pupils. The private market starves the comprehensives of the resources they need to attain high standards'.[106] Accordingly, the integration of the private sector into the national system 'is essential if the ideals of either meritocracy or equality are to be realised'. Finally, in looking at the question of the link between quality and expansion of the educational system, the authors advance the hypothesis that expansion leads to greater equality only in the later stages of educational growth when opportunities for the higher class have reached saturation point and will increase little relative to those with ability from points lower on the scale.

The Oxford Social Mobility Group, then, has produced extensive analyses of occupational and educational mobility in England and Wales up to the early 1970s. However, the separation of these two aspects into two books that are in many respects independent studies with non-comparable results is unfortunate. In particular, the important question of the relation between schooling and the nature of adult mobility is pursued by neither. Furthermore, the results of both studies turn crucially on the nature of the class scheme adopted, and neither pursued the idea of testing what would happen if a different classification had been used.

Interest in theory

Other less grandiose survey research was also conducted in the 1970s but, like the Halsey and Goldthorpe studies, was more geared to the testing of theoretical formulations than was evident in the social accounting tradition. Thus Blackburn and Mans (1979), after an examination of neo-classical, dual labour market and radical theories of the labour market, sought to test them in the Peterborough area. They took a sample of almost 1,000 unqualified male manual workers in semi-skilled and unskilled jobs in nine firms in Peterborough, and studied the beliefs, attitudes and general orientations of the workers. Smith (1977) made a study of racial disadvantage in England and Wales derived from several interrelated surveys and case studies carried out between 1973 and 1975. From a survey of 3,300 Asians and West Indians, together with a comparison survey of 1,239 white men, he looked at inter-locking networks of disadvantage. These he explained in terms of the interaction between migrants and the principal institutions in the fields of housing and employment. On the latter there was a national survey of 300 firms, there were detailed case studies of 14 firms, and interviews with 27 of the country's largest employers at head office level and with eight of the major trade unions. The field work on housing comprised detailed case studies of council housing allocation in ten local authority areas.

An empirical researcher with a keen interest in sociological theory is George Brown. His work began in the early 1960s, but it culminated in a book written in collaboration with Tirril Harris called *The Social Origins of Depression*, published in 1978. In this book the authors develop a causal model of depression that has three major components: the provoking agents (e.g. losing a job) which influence when the depression occurs, the vulnerability factors (e.g. being in a state of unemployment) which influence whether the provoking agents will have an effect, and the symptom formation factors which influence the form and severity of the depression. They examine the model empirically using two groups of women: 114 psychiatric in- and out-patients living in Camberwell in south-east London, and two separate random samples totalling 458 women living in the same community. They look at the class differences in the incidence of depression and find an inverse relation only among women with children, and account for this in terms of provoking agents and vulnerability factors. The way the book focuses on conceptually abstract social factors involved in the production of mental states is strongly reminiscent of Durkheim's study of *Suicide* published in 1897 — to which the authors make frequent reference. The analysis is long and careful and restricted to graphs, histograms, cross-tabulation, three-variable analyses, with chi-square as the test of significance and gamma as the main measure of association. As a piece of classical sociology in the fullest sense of that term, Brown and Tirril's study has few equals.

There were many empirical studies in the 1970s that were based widely on participant observation as the main technique of investigation; but these, too, were more concerned with theoretical issues than had been many of the community studies of the 1950s and 1960s. Burton, in his *The Politics of Legitimacy: Struggles in a Belfast Community* (1978), reports how he spent eight months as a participant observer in 'Arro', a tight-knit Catholic working-class area in west Belfast. He outlines the three main components of the Catholic world view — communalism, sectarianism and republicanism — and shows that support for the activity of the IRA has its roots in the wider social consciousness of the Catholic community.

Jason Ditton's study of fiddling and pilfering amongst bakery personnel (1977), Paul Willis's study of a small group of working-class, non-academic, disaffected white males in a small-town secondary school showing how working-class kids ended up with working-class jobs (1977), and James Patrick's *A Glasgow Gang Observed* (1973), may be seen as following the tradition of participant observation that had begun in the USA with William Whyte's *Street Corner Society* (1955). These and many others exemplified a trend in the 1970s towards more interpretative methods of sociological research in which the techniques of interviews, observation, participation, and the use of documentary sources were all brought to bear on uncovering actors' meanings. Many of the data are qualitative, and the ultimate criterion of validity is no longer with the scientist, but with the subjects of investigation both in terms of the reasons they give or have given for their actions, and in terms of the language and thought categories that they use to interpret the world around them. Formal causal analysis is avoided so that the dignity and integrity of those being studied is retained by not encapsulating them in the thought process of others. Thus Gerald Grace in *Teachers, Ideology and Control* (1978) studied the social construction of the 'good teacher' and the 'good school' as defined by headmasters and their deputies in inner city comprehensive schools catering mainly for working-class pupils. The data were derived from interviews and formal discussions not only with the heads and their deputies, but also with those so defined as 'good teachers'. Their perceptions of the nature of their pupils and their backgrounds, their own educational and pedagogic aims and practices, their attitudes towards curriculum change, and their experiences of autonomy and constraint were all studied.

Newby et al. (1978) considered ideologies about land ownership and property based on intensive interviews with about 200 mostly very rich East Anglian farmers, while Coxon and Jones (1979) looked into the subjective aspects of various processes of description, classification and evaluation of occupations. This represented an attempt to develop, through an examination of individual subjects' ways of dealing with occupational concepts and terminology, models of collective belief systems about occupations. Nancy Foner (1979) in a non-random sample of 45 male and 45 female Jamaicans who in 1973 had been living in London for at least three years, focused on status changes and the meanings ascribed to them by the Jamaicans. Cook et al. (1977) in *The Fragmentary Class Structure* reported the results of a survey carried out in Liverpool in 1972 with 474 economically active males in a variety of manual and non-manual occupations to determine the bases and consequences of images or perceptions of class and class structure. They managed to show how class images were becoming more complex and more fragmented.

Sociology in Scotland

In Scotland academic sociology began rather later than it did in England and publications by sociologists in Scotland and about Scotland did not begin to emerge until after about 1974.[107] The tradition has been rather more strongly empirical than it was south of the border and was often located in departments other than sociology in the universities. The major growth points have been in political sociology and in particular in studies of the rise of Scottish nationalism, analyses of the socio-economic structure, investigations into the social impact of North Sea oil-related developments, the sociology of education, medical sociology, and sociological investigations in the area of social work, social administration, and the Scottish children's panel system. A major feature of these developments is the extent to which they have been dominated by the work of various research institutes like the Medical Research Council Medical Sociology Unit at Aberdeen; the Centre for Educational Sociology at Edinburgh, which began a unique enterprise in collaborative research based on the Scottish Education Data Archive and which was based on extensive surveys of school leavers between 1967 and 1978; the North Sea Oil Panel, which was set up to co-ordinate research into the impact of oil-related developments; the Strathclyde Area Survey, which carries out economic and social research by survey methods and on contract for outside bodies; and the Scottish Council for Research in Education. There have been some large-scale social surveys of the largely descriptive fact-finding type. Thus Jackson and Hanby (1978) focused on participant attitudes towards job creation and work experience programmes in Scotland. They took a stratified random sample of nearly 1,000 who were interviewed while they were on the project. Hendry (1979) made a study of the relationship between school, sport and leisure which involved the conduct of about 3,000 interviews with teenagers throughout central Scotland.

Using lengthy in-depth interviews, Dobash and Dobash (1980) investigated marital violence against over 100 women who sought aid from the Scottish Women's Aid Federation between 1974 and 1977. They present a detailed account of the forms of violence men directed against their wives and cohabitees, and from a reading of all police records of Edinburgh and one district of Glasgow in 1974 looked at the responses of various social, legal and medical agencies to the womens' requests for help. A major development in Scotland has, however, been the rebirth of community studies which have looked largely at the social impact of North Sea development in the Western Isles. These have tended to be carried out by anthropologists, but ones with a keen eye on utilising what can be gained from sociological perspectives, methods and techniques. These studies are reviewed extensively by Condry (1980), who shows that much of the work is not just ethnographic, but has pursued the implications of the social changes that are taking place for theories of development, and for people's perceptions of change and its relationship to the problem of social identity.

Secondary analysis

One other development of note in the 1970s was in secondary analysis. An early study by Abel-Smith and Townsend had re-analysed raw data on households and individuals from the 1953 and 1960 Family Expenditure Surveys provided by the then Ministry of Labour in order to assess the numbers of people below or close to the poverty line. Using a 25 per cent sub-sample of the 1953 data set (which had originally been a sample of 13,000 households throughout the UK who had provided records of their expenditure during a three-week period) and the full data set for the later enquiry, the authors found from the earlier survey that 10 per cent of the households and 7.8 per cent of persons, representing about four million people in the UK, were below 140 per cent of basic national assistance levels. These figures increased markedly for the 1960 data, partly due to differences between the two samples, but also partly due to an increase in the proportion of the aged, in the numbers of large families, and of the long-term sick.

A more comprehensive study of trends in poverty was carried out by the National Institute of Economic and Social Research for the period 1953–1973,[108] while the greater wealth of information in the General Household Survey on the personal and household characteristics of respondents resulted in another more detailed study of the characteristics of the poor and the correlates and causes of poverty in the mid-1970s by a research team at the London School of Economics that had been commissioned by the Royal Commission on the Distribution of Income and Wealth. This study effectively brought together theoretical approaches to the explanation of poverty with policy-related concerns; it studied poverty within particular social groups (such as the elderly and one-parent families), and assessed the relationship between poverty, unemployment and ill-health.[109] Le Grand also made a secondary analysis of General Household Survey data to study the distributional effects of non-monetary income, in particular from the National Health Service and education. He found that the higher socio-economic groups benefited most from these services because of their greater use of them.[110] There has also been a number of secondary analyses on *ad hoc* surveys which initially were largely descriptive, but the data were subsequently used to test further hypotheses.[111]

The 1970s – conclusion

If there were cries of anti-positivism and expressions of disdain for empirical research and for survey research in particular in the 1970s, there were also many whose actions, at any rate in terms of the way they pursued the sociological enterprise, were unaffected by the hubbub. There has been a lot of empirical sociology in the last decade, some of it of very good quality, much of it perhaps a little mediocre. There was no distinctive 'style' of research as there had been to some extent a decade before. The formal, fact-finding, large-scale, quantitative social survey, and the quasi-anthropological mode of participant observation had given way to researches conducted in whatever ways sociologists saw fit to pursue answers to their problems, to satisfy their curiosities, or' to achieve their goals. To a degree, methodological anarchy was already a reality. But was there a discrepancy between the way sociologists conceived the sociological enterprise in abstract terms and what they actually did in practice? There is little evidence on this point, but perhaps some inkling may be derived from a series of interviews conducted by the author with a sample of 24 sociologists in university departments of sociology in Scotland in 1973. These showed that there was little agreement on what 'the scientific method' involved, on how they perceived or defined an 'empirical' article in a journal, and on the role that statistics, sampling and tests of significance should play in empirical inquiry. While there was considerable awareness of 'indiscriminate' use of significance tests, many said they would nevertheless still use them in circumstances that most textbooks on research methods would claim to be wrong or inappropriate, for example on non-random samples and total populations. Many did not relate statistical usage to the measurement characteristics of the data concerned, and views on whether hypotheses should be spelled out at some stage in the process of inquiry showed considerable variation. What counted as a 'sociological explanation' seemed to be a matter of personal and individual preference; the textbook assumption that 'sociological explanation' meant causal analysis was not one that many sociologists could accept in view of the epistemological assumptions involved. Nearly all had used survey research at some point in their careers, but many were clearly more dubious about its role in some kinds of situations.

What was striking about the answers expressed in the interviews was the sheer diversity of opinion. There was little consensus on anything and for just about every view expressed, somebody else averred exactly the opposite. There was even little polarisation into 'schools' of thought; rather there was a scattering of opinion individually expressed. Questions on research method and technique were approached in a highly pragmatic fashion and sociologists would for example ask of themselves, regardless of textbook strictures on their use: 'Will tests of significance nevertheless tell me something I would not otherwise know?' or even 'Will they nevertheless help to get the article published?' Enquiries about how they came to learn most of what they knew about research methods revealed that in their student days they had not attended any formal course on research methods but had learned 'on the job' as they went along. Doing sociological research did not mean following textbook accounts of 'how-to-do-research'. Many had a copy of Galtung's *Theory and Methods of Social Research* (1967) on the shelf but had not glanced at it since their student days. Clearly, they had not been socialised early in their careers into a normative methodology, and apparently did not feel the need to consult books on the subject before embarking on empirical investigations.

Sociology in the 1970s was more complicated and more contested than in previous decades. Doubts about its practical relevance were legion, as were misgivings about its status as a science. The structure of norms and values for the conduct of empirical inquiry that had been to some extent built up on the 1960s had crumbled again in the 1970s. The theoretical synthesis of structural-functionalism fell apart with the revival of Marxism, the renewed interest in symbolic interactionism, and the importation of structuralism, phenomenology and ethnomethodology. Empirical sociology seemed to be going everywhere and nowhere. In the words of one commentator on the sociological scene in Britain, sociology was

> . . . vast and amorphous, disjointed and self-contradictory; anything can be said about it. There is no intellectual foible it does not contain, no *gaucherie* of which some sociologist is incapable, no political ideology which some version of it cannot defend. Sociologists range from educated and cultivated men to leaden-footed philistines, they write about everything from the nature and destiny of man to fallen women. They thus provide any comer with particular excuses for venting general grudges. Sociology is the great intellectual grab-bag of our time: everybody from the Provost of King's to the Professor of Logic at the London School of Economics, can reach into it, certain to find precisely what he wants.

What is most striking about this commentary, however, is that it was made by Norman Birnbaum in 1960, talking about sociology in Britain and America in the 1950s![112] The 'story' of what was happening to sociology in the 1970s could be constructed in any way according to one's perspective. While the empirical researchers were screaming their cries of anti-positivism, theorists were at the same time bemoaning the paucity of sociological theory in Britain because of what was seen as the pervasiveness of empiricism. Thus Morgan in 1975 was commenting that British sociology 'continues to be influenced by a tradition of common-sense empiricism tempered to the concerns of middle range domestic problems and enlightened social policy'.[113] At the same time academic sociology in Britain is 'marked by a conspicuous absence of a coherent body of theory concerned with the structure and culture of society whose complex inequalities have been documented repeatedly since the pioneering investigations of Booth and Rowntree'.

The most recent history is the most difficult to write; the 'true' perspective of long-term trends remains very much beneath the surface. Certainly the post-war period leaves some puzzles unresolved. The new and the older 'civic' universities were in the 1960s more receptive to sociology than were the ancient universities of Oxford, Cambridge and St Andrews. Yet while St Andrews has continued to drag its feet about teaching sociology at all, the Oxford Mobility Group has produced two of the major research projects in recent years. This makes the question of sociological leadership very complex. There are no clear leaders. Added to this is the role of the polytechnics whose concern for the applied, socially and vocationally 'relevant' side of academic learning has had some influence on the way in which the subject has been taught. The trend since the setting up of the Council for National Academic Awards has been towards a reduction in the supply of degree courses leading to named awards in sociology, but an increase in those resulting in social science, social studies or applied social science awards. There has also been a considerable increase in service teaching for a wide range of courses. However, the polytechnics in the 1970s became the focus for the younger and more radical of the recently graduated sociologists. This often put them at odds with the prevailing ideology and in the end was counter-productive in terms of emphasising the practical role of a strongly empirical sociology.

Notes

1   See Westergaard's obituary, 1979.
2   The classification that emerged turned out to be very similar to that already used by the Government Social Survey and not very different from the one designed by the Population Investigation Committee working in close association with the Statistical Committee of the Royal Commission on Population. All these scales may be seen as modifications or extensions of the Registrar General's five-fold classification. The standard classification has seven categories as follows:

   1 Professional and high administrative
   2 Managerial and executive
   3 Inspectorial, supervisory, and other non-manual, higher grade
   4 Inspectorial, supervisory, and other non-manual, lower grade
   5 Skilled manual and routine grades of non-manual
   6 Semi-skilled manual
   7 Unskilled manual

A full list of the actual occupations under each category is given by Oppenheim, 1966, pp 275-84.
3   Glass, 1954, p.80.
4   Douglas and Rowntree, 1948, p.5.
5   Ibid., p.207. The study used a social class classification based on the husband's occupation. Initially there were 10 categories, but these were for the most part reduced to five — professional and salaried, black-coated wage-earners, manual workers, agricultural workers, and others. This was not a very satisfactory scheme since some 60 per cent fell into the manual workers category.

6   Douglas, 1976, p.20.
7   Cole, 1961, p.326.
8   Hobsbawm, 1964, p.252.
9   Reisman, 1977, p.27.
10   Rowntree and Lavers, 1951, p.1.
11   J.A. Banks, 1957.
12   O. Banks, 1956.
13   O. Banks, 1960.
14   Mays, 1959, p.9.
15   A still earlier study was that of Little (1947), who set out 'to examine the social interactions and reactions resulting from the presence of coloured people in Britain, choosing as a specific example a coloured community in the dockland of Cardiff' (Preface).
    Little was an Assistant Lecturer in Anthropology at the London School of Economics, and at least one of his purposes was 'to draw attention of anthropologists in Britain in concrete terms to the possibilities of applying their discipline more positively to the study of urban society' (Preface).
16   Williams, 1963, p.xiv.
17   Littlejohn, 1963, p.1.
18   Ibid., p.39.
19   Young and Willmott, 1961, p.203.
20   Ibid., p.204.
21   Platt, 1971, p.76.
22   Rex, 1974, p.2.
23   Bott, 1957, p.60.
24   See Farquharson, 1955, for an account of the dissolution of the Institute.
25   See Banks, 1967, for an account of the Association's first fifteen years.
26   See Bulmer, 1978, for a full review.
27   Hakim, 1980.
28   Moser and Kalton, 1971, p.13.
29   Frankenberg, 1966, p.154.
30   Stacey, 1960, p.165.
31   Stacey et al., 1975, p.6.
32   Reid, 1978, p.22.
33   Wiseman, 1964, p.170.
34   Plowden Report, 1967, Table I, p.33.
35   Bernstein's ideas on language are to be found in a number of places. Two of the clearest statements are Bernstein 1961 and 1965. His most recent statements are in Bernstein, 1971.
36   Newsom Report, 1963.
37   Marsden, 1967, p.48.

38   Mays, 1961.
39   King, 1973.
40   Ford, 1976, p.55.
41   Ibid., p.59.
42   Goldthorpe et al., 1969, p.157.
43   Banks, 1960, p.134.
44   Lupton, 1963.
45   Tunstall, 1962.
46   Hollowell, 1968.
47   Banton, 1964.
48   See J.A. Banks, 1967.
49   See Richmond, 1966.
50   For an account of British criminology and the National Deviancy Conference, see Cohen, 1975.
51   Krausz, 1969, p.184.
52   Hakim, 1980, p.1.
53   Ibid., p.2.
54   T. and P. Morris, 1963, p.4.
55   Ibid., p.8.
56   P. Morris, 1965, p.9.
57   P. Morris, 1969, p.3.
58   Zweig, 1965, p.4.
59   Much of this is reviewed by Rapoport, 1970.
60   Jephcott, 1964, p.36.
61   Plowden, 1967, p.50.
62   Halsey, 1972.
63   Banks, 1969, p.4.
64   Shipman, 1976, p.ix.
65   J. and E. Newson, 1976, p.23.
66   Ibid., p.26.
67   Ibid., p.30.
68   Ibid., p.37.
69   The Newsons' early studies in fact became the core of what is now the Child Development Research Unit at Nottingham University. While most of the research was concerned with 'ordinary' children and 'ordinary' families, the Newsons did move into the field of handicap when the Spastics Society asked them to make a comparative study of the upbringing of cerebral palsied children. There have also been studies of Punjabi children, children without fathers, the visually and the hearing impaired. At the same time, the Newsons continued their studies of ordinary children. The results of their findings concerning the children at seven were published in 1976 as *Seven Years Old in the Home Environment*.
70   Townsend, 1979, Preface.

71 Ibid., p.29.
72 Ibid., p.31.
73 Ibid., p.248.
74 Ibid., p.249.
75 He does not say how, except that the indicators were selected 'on the basis of pilot interviews'.
76 Townsend, 1979, p.252.
77 Ibid., p.412.
78 Ibid., p.431.
79 Ibid., p.849.
80 Ibid., p.893.
81 Ibid., p.914.
82 Wilson, 1961, p.6.
83 Ibid., p.317.
84 Krausz, 1967, p.207.
85 Rex and Moore, 1967, p.273.
86 Ibid., p.291.
87 Patterson, 1963, p.20.
88 Ibid., p.17.
89 Ibid., p.390.
90 See Irvine et al., 1979.
91 See Hindess, 1973.
92 See Feyerabend, 1975 and Phillips, 1973.
93 Peel and Skipworth, 1970.
94 Harrop, 1980.
95 Abrams, 1979.
96 Cohen, 1980, argues that, at least for certain traditional species, positivism really is dead (and feels that it is a good thing too).
97 Marsh, 1979.
98 The Scottish Mobility Study was in fact carried out by a group at the University of Aberdeen, but few publications have as yet emerged. Some interim results were given by Payne et al., 1976.
99 These include Hope, 1972, Ridge, 1974, Goldthorpe and Hope, 1974, Goldthorpe and Llewellyn, 1977a, 1977b, Halsey, 1975, 1977, 1978, Thorburn, 1977, and Raffe, 1979.
100 Goldthorpe, 1980, p.22.
101 Ibid., p.251.
102 Ibid., p.252.
103 Halsey et al., 1980, p.16.
104 Ibid., pp 167-71.
105 Ibid., p.199.
106 Ibid., p.213.
107 See Kent, 1980, for a brief account and bibliography of empirical research on Scotland.

108 Fiegehan et al., 1977.

109 Layard et al., 1978. Quoted from Hakim, 1980, p.10.

110 Le Grand, 1978. Quoted from Hakim, 1980.

111 For example Lancaster's analysis of a national survey of the unemployed commissioned by the Department of Employment to test theories on the job search behaviour of the unemployed, and to assess the impact of unemployment benefits on the duration of unemployment. See Lancaster, 1979 and Daniel, 1974.

112 Birnbaum, 1960, p.460.

113 Morgan, 1975, p.119.

6 Conclusion

Empirical sociology in Britain has had a long history. Its foundations were laid in the 1830s by the social accountants, not from any concern to develop or to test sociological theory, but as a by-product of attempts to determine the causes of the sufferings (and the short-comings) of the urban working classes. Indeed, Comte had not even coined the word 'sociology' until after the statistical societies had carried out most of their house-to-house inquiries, while Spencer's writings on sociology did not appear until the 1870s. From 1844 on-wards the social explorers developed the role of the scientific investigator beyond that conceived by the social statisticians. From a collector and analyst of numerical information the empirical sociologist became an interpreter of systematically observed social life. In the 1890s Charles Booth joined these two roles together to produce a formidable piece of sociological investigation, while the Webbs in the same period developed the study of social institutions in a way that was grounded in historical analysis.

The path of development that empirical sociology took was marked by three main factors: a detachment from the concerns of the social theorists, periods of sporadic activity alternating with periods of dis-continuity, and the failure of many innovative ideas and techniques to diffuse over time and amongst contemporaries. To say that the empirical sociologists were 'detached' from the concerns of the social theorists is by no means to argue that they were uninfluenced by them. There is little doubt that the works of Comte had considerable influence on Booth. Booth's two cousins, Harry and Albert Crompton, were leading members of Comte's 'Church of Humanity', and through them, wrote Beatrice Webb in the first of her two autobiographies, he 'came under the influence of Auguste Comte. Perpetually discussing the philosophy of positivism and the theories arising out of it with such leading positivists as Dr Bridges, Professor Beesley, the Harringtons and the Lushingtons, Charles Booth was fairly captivated, and his formal adhesion to the ranks of Positivism was held to be only a matter of time'.[1] The prediction proved to be unfounded, but Booth's general scientific approach to the study of poverty, his basis of observed or recorded fact, and the law-like generalisations that he developed, made his *Life and Labour of the People of London* closer to a practical application of Comte's ideas than is commonly supposed. Unfortunately, nowhere in his 17 volumes of published findings did Booth actually refer to Comte; if he had more specifically related his findings to Comptist ideas he might have received more readily the recognition for his pioneering sociology so long denied him.

In a similar way Beatrice Webb had undoubtedly been influenced by her early relationship with Herbert Spencer. According to Simey (1961) Beatrice had read Spencer's *First Principles of Sociology* with 'a kind of fervid enthusiasm' — but then rejected his ideas. She complained in *My Apprenticeship* that Spencer irritated her 'by trying to palm off illustrations as data', and treating his deductions as 'laws' rather than suggestive hypotheses.[2] Nevertheless, what the Webbs later described as their 'speciality' — presenting 'an analytical history of institutional forms' — was certainly something that Beatrice had learned from Spencer.[3]

The detachment of empirical sociology from sociological theorising was more one of differing objectives than a lack of influence. Theorists like Comte and Spencer wanted to create a discipline that would study society in a scientific manner. The aims were to discover the laws that governed the structural relationships between social phenomena and the patterns of social evolution. Such a science would facilitate prediction and control in the same way that natural scientists were increasingly able to do with physical phenomena. The empirical sociologists, by contrast, had one overriding aim: the improvement of the social conditions under which the vast majority of the working classes lived. This is not to argue that the theorists were uninterested in social reform; it is just that the empirical sociologists had reform as their immediate objective, and saw the task of documenting exactly how people lived and discovering the immediate causes of poverty, drunkenness, disease and prostitution as the most effective way of bringing about efficient reform. The theorists on the other hand probably felt that effective reform was possible only after the discipline of sociology had made some progress. To the political economists of the period, the difference between empirical inquiry and theoretical analysis was mainly a convenient division of labour — perhaps a little too convenient since as far as sociology was concerned this division of labour began to break down only in the 1960s, and even then only as far as the research practice of sociology was concerned. For the teaching and training of future sociologists separate courses in sociological theory and research methods are still the norm today.

Sporadic activity

The second main feature that characterised the path of empirical sociology in Britain was its sporadic and discontinuous nature. Three main periods of relatively intense activity may be distinguished: 1834–1851, 1890–1907 and the 1960s. In the first the statistical movement took shape not only in the form of statistical societies, but also in statistical activity in government departments. The work of the two social explorers Engels and Mayhew also fits into the latter part of this period. The second period was dominated by the researches of Booth and Rowntree, but it also saw the founding of the Sociological Society and the intense exchange of ideas that followed. It also saw the founding of the first department and the first chair in sociology at the London School of Economics. The third period — the 1960s — saw the development of empirical research into many specialised substantive areas, attempts to develop the professional nature of sociological inquiry, and efforts to relate empirical activities to the work of the social theorists. The periods in between were not, however, ones in which empirical sociology lay dormant. Between 1851 and 1890 Mayhew continued, somewhat spasmodically, his inquiries into the London 'street folk' and into the criminal prisons of London, the criminologists carried on until 1857, while other social explorers, in a rather more journalistic fashion, still made their voyages of discovery into the unknown culture of the urban poor. The period from 1907 to 1960 was, in many respects, quite active, although little actual progress was made. Before 1914 empirical inquiries were split between divergent schools of thought and practice, and in the inter-war period there were several replications of earlier studies and a number of quite large-scale social surveys. There was also the attempt at Mass Observation by Madge and Harrison. In the 1950s there were a number of key pioneering studies, but not in such quantities as were seen in the following decade, while the 1970s have been characterised more by self doubts than by cumulative progress.

The only literature specifically on the development of empirical sociology in Britain suggests that discontinuity is a result of lack of institutionalisation. Both Cole (1972) and Elesh (1972) argue that intellectual continuity is difficult to maintain in a non-institutionalised setting, that is, one that lacks channels of communication such as journals and learned societies, and has no formal place in the institutions of higher education where formal training in the subject is available and where research itself becomes the primary technical function of specialised roles. Only when these appear is there a cumulative development of ideas and techniques with researchers referring to and building upon the work of their predecessors. Only then is there an internal generation of theoretical and practical problems and a substantial measure of agreement on goals, tools and theories. The main problems with this explanation are first that each factor aids the others so that indicators of institutionalisation become confused with its causes and effects, second that it begs the question about why institutionalisation did not occur in the first place and third that it does not explain the periods of activity in which some of the features of institutionalisation temporarily appeared.

The typical paths of development for the sciences in general have been the subject of attention for philosophers and sociologists of science for a long period. The most influential model to emerge has been that proposed by Thomas Kuhn (1962) in which periods of 'normal science' alternate with periods of 'crisis' in which a scientific revolution occurs. Normal science, says Kuhn, 'means research firmly based on one or more scientific achievements that some particular scientific community acknowledges for a time as supplying the foundation for its further practice'.[4] It is characterised by the existence of a 'paradigm', which amounts to a set of scientific achievements that have two main characteristics: they are sufficiently unprecedented to attract an enduring group of adherents away from competing modes of scientific activity, and they are sufficiently open-ended to leave all sorts of problems for the redefined group of practitioners to resolve. Paradigms act for a time as a common point of reference for all investigations in the area, shaping the discipline's sense of where its problems lie, what its appropriate tools and methods are and the kinds of solutions it might accept as warranted.

Kuhn notes that 'a sort of' scientific research is possible without a paradigm. There is a 'pre-paradigm' stage which is characterised by competing schools of thought. Since there is no basis for assessing the relevance of facts, 'early fact-gathering is a far more nearly random activity than the one subsequent scientific development makes familiar' and is 'usually restricted to the wealth of data that lie ready to hand'.[5] The result is a morass of facts. The initial consolidation of a discipline about a single paradigm is typically accompanied by its recognition within the larger scientific community, by the acquisition of its own journals, by the foundation of specialists' societies and by its elaboration into specialised sub-disciplines, while brief articles rather than books become the major vehicle for research communication. The individual scientist need no longer begin each empirical or theoretical venture anew, creating his own first principles, his own language, methods and standards; rather, the common base is made clear in textbooks and by the way the subject is taught.

Whether the periods in the history of empirical sociology in Britain in which a distinctive style of research became popular for a while represented 'normal science' in Kuhn's sense is doubtful. In the period of the statistical movement, for example, it would not be possible to point to any paradigmatic studies that became the focal point or 'exemplar' for future work. Previous studies were seldom, if ever, referred to, and although the accepted method of inquiry between 1834 and 1848 was the house-to-house survey, there were very few commentaries or even isolated comments on how these were actually carried out. Frequently the researcher did begin anew and such evidence as was available suggested that the interpretation of what a house-to-house inquiry meant varied considerably from project to project. Certainly there were no textbooks on methods of sociological inquiry at the time, and only in the case of the Manchester and London Statistical Societies did a specialised journal emerge which was intended to keep members informed of developments in the field. The activities of participants in the statistical societies did not really fit Kuhn's description of normal science as basically a puzzle-solving activity. The main characteristic of a puzzle is that a solution assuredly exists (as with a jig-saw puzzle or a crossword puzzle). The test is of a person's skill in finding it — but within the set of accepted rules that define both the nature of the acceptable solution and the steps by which it is to be obtained.[6]

It can be plausibly argued that no piece of empirical sociology in Britain ever attained paradigmatic status in this sense. The prime candidate was probably Booth's study of the life and labour of the people of London, but why it never became an exemplar for the future conduct of inquiry is a question that Kuhn's theory does little to answer. Empirical sociology, even in the periods of relatively intense activity, seemed closer to Kuhn's 'pre-paradigmatic' stage. In a later edition of his book (1970) he wrote in a postscript in which he attempted to respond to his critics by clarifying the notion of a 'paradigm'. A paradigm was whatever members of a scientific community shared. Since, by the same token, a scientific community consisted of men who shared a paradigm, it could not *be* in a pre-paradigm stage. What changed with the transition to maturity of a science was not the acquisition of a paradigm, but the development of puzzle-solving research. On this basis Kuhn would presumably argue that empirical sociology was simply 'immature'; but that would mean that his model could not be applied to events that had already taken place.

The dynamic for change, according to Kuhn, is the appearance of anomaly. Novelties of fact (or 'discoveries') somehow violate the paradigm-induced expectations that govern normal science.[7] In fact it is only against such expectations that anomaly manifests itself. The process by which scientists become aware of anomaly is crucial, since counter-instances are really only the 'puzzles' with which the paradigm began. Anomalies are often only puzzles that, over time, have become intractable. Some anomalies are incorporated into the existing paradigm by making adjustments to the paradigm itself — often against some resistance. Eventually, a sense of crisis develops and new theories emerge, but the existing paradigm is not rejected until an alternative appears. A scientific revolution occurs when the older paradigm is replaced in whole or in part by an incompatible new one. The new paradigm expresses an entirely new world-view, but the way these changes are typically reported in textbooks disguises revolutions as mere additions to scientific knowledge. In consequence, revolutions tend to be nearly invisible.

Kuhn's idea of a 'scientific revolution' is, like the notion of normal science, difficult to apply to British empirical sociology. Rather than competing or alternative paradigms there were often gaps between one style of empirical inquiry and the next. There was usually no confrontation, argument or debate over the 'correct' procedures; rather new styles emerged and operated as if the previous ones never existed. Earlier work was generally not referred to and different ways of doing research were seldom compared. A Mayhew or a Booth just proceeded with whatever methods seemed appropriate for their own particular problems. Only at the turn of the nineteenth century were there simultaneously existing schools of thought — the town planners, the eugenicists, the social reformers, the social explorers and the social accountants — yet these schools for the most part developed independently of one another. Not one of them represented a kind of 'normal science' that some new paradigm could overturn in a scientific revolution.

Significantly, Friedrichs (1970) did attempt to apply Kuhn's model to American sociology. Parsons's *The Social System* (1951) was, he argued, an exemplar which initiated a period of normal science. However, after examining various subsequent revolutionary currents in American sociology, Friedrichs was forced to conclude that Kuhn's theory 'would be insufficient to the task of analysing revolutions in the social and behavioural sciences'.[8]

A model which attempts to combine Kuhn's stencil with the idea that science grows as a process of diffusion of innovation is put forward by Crane (1972). She emphasises that social interaction and integration play an important role in the growth and diffusion of scientific knowledge by facilitating the diffusion of ideas that in turn make possible cumulative growth in a research area. The typical pattern of growth of scientific knowledge is a logistic or S-shaped curve, and Crane suggests that the various stages in the growth of a research area are accompanied by a series of changes in the characteristics of both scientific knowledge and in the scientific community that is studying the area. In the first stage when interesting discoveries provide models for future work — a paradigm in Kuhn's sense — new scientists are attracted to the area but there is little or no social organisation. In the second stage, in the period Kuhn would call 'normal science', groups of collaborators and communication networks (or 'invisible colleges' as Crane calls them) appear. This is a highly productive period producing an exponential growth in publications and in new members to the area. In the third and fourth stages the implications of the seminal ideas are exhausted and become increasingly difficult to test due to the appearance of anomalies that cannot be explained by the original model. Membership of the 'invisible college' declines accompanied by increasing speculation and controversy amongst those who remain.

The period of exponential growth can be interpreted as a 'contagion' process in which the more scientists are interacting with one another the more of them will adopt an idea. This will be reflected in the growth of numbers of publications, and in the numbers of new authors publishing for the first time in the research area. However, in the history of British empirical sociology it is doubtful, even during the period of the statistical movement or at the time of cumulative growth in English criminology between 1839 and 1857, whether there was anything that resembled an 'exponential' growth. In both cases only a handful of individuals were actively engaged in conducting empirical investigations, and although there were some developments that were built upon by others, for example the practice of using age-specific rates of crime, these individuals hardly constituted an 'invisible college' in the sense proposed by Crane.

Instead of looking for the dynamic forces within science itself, it may be tentatively suggested that the degree of activity in empirical sociology is at least to some degree a reflection of social, economic, political and literary activity elsewhere in society. The 1830s were years of intense political unrest. The activities of the social accountants may be seen as but one manifestation among many of the tumultuous events of the time. By contrast, the 1850s and 1860s were decades of great material progress during the Victorian boom when the sense of crisis and upheaval had somewhat abated. Again, the industrial turmoil of the 1880s was reflected in renewed vigour amongst empirical sociologists. The reformist Liberal government years leading up to the First World War were times of social optimism and strands of empirical sociology went their own way. The inter-war years were ones of relative depression and unemployment. Scope for new ideas and new institutions were rather limited and empirical sociology shared in the general malaise. The period of intense activity in the 1960s was probably a reflection of the general economic optimism of the time. Expansion seemed a possibility on all fronts, not least in the universities where departments of sociology were established and grew with remarkable rapidity.

Diffusion of innovations

If adequate explanation for the sporadic and discontinuous nature of empirical sociology in Britain presents some difficulties — and the above is intended only to sketch some directions in which the answer may rest — then the failure of innovative ideas and practices to diffuse over time and amongst contemporaries offers some intriguing possibilities about the nature and role of innovation in sociology as a whole. Chapter 1 showed how the amount and quality of empirical research carried out in the years between 1834 and the middle of the 1850s was rather impressive — yet the development was rather uneven. Some researchers for example were clearly aware that it was the rate of crime and the proportion educated that had to be compared if the relationship between such variables was to be explored, while others were content to make comparisons on the basis of simple frequencies. Some were concerned with the statistical reliability of the conclusions they drew from their analyses; others just presented uninterpreted tables of figures as the 'facts' on which others could (so they thought) base social reforms. The criminologists engaged in quite sophisticated secondary analyses of official data, while Plint was aware of the limitations of crime statistics: that they measured only detected crime, not actual crime, that certain crimes rarely came to the attention of the police, that changes in statistics frequently reflected changes in judicial procedures, in the law, and in police policy and detection rates. Yet others just took figures derived from court proceedings and made comparisons on an ecological basis. Plint was aware of what would nowadays be called 'spurious' interpretations between variables, while others were content to show some connection simply between levels of crime and levels of education in particular areas in order to confirm their prejudgement that lack of education was the 'cause' of crime. Sampling, replication, three-variable and causal analysis, the testing of specifically formulated hypotheses, the use of family budgets, house-to-house inquiries, interview schedules — all these were tried in the 1830s and 1840s. Yet there was little agreement on what constituted the 'best' methods and techniques of inquiry, there was no accumulating body of 'principles' of research and there were no norms and values for the conduct of empirical inquiry. Much of what the social accountants did was simply lost to posterity.

This is all the more curious when it is remembered that Charles Booth some 50 years later became a member of the Statistical Society of London in whose journal the results of much of the work of the social accountants had been published. Booth was even the Society's President for two years between 1892 and 1894. Yet there is no hint in any of the 17 volumes of Booth's *Life and Labour of the People of London* that he had ever read any of these reports. If he had, he certainly made little use of them to develop his own techniques of inquiry. Just as curious was that although Booth made increasing use of experiential and qualitative evidence in his later studies of religious influences, he made no reference to the pioneering studies of Engels and Mayhew — yet both had been concerned to explain the industrial causes of low wages.

Booth's work itself contained many innovations — both conceptual and methodological — yet many of these were ignored by his followers like Rowntree and Bowley. The innovations in correlational statistics made by Galton, Pearson and Yule in the 1890s failed completely to diffuse to Booth, Rowntree and Bowley who, as Professor of Statistics at the London School of Economics, one might have expected to be at least aware of these developments. Yule even criticised some of Booth's interpretations of his own findings; but neither Booth nor Rowntree nor Bowley responded. The techniques of statistical correlation were never applied to the analysis of survey data until over half a century later. Lastly, one might mention the Webbs's study of industrial democracy which represented a radical departure from the ahistorical fact-finding or exploratory empirical sociology of their predecessors. The historically analytic study of the dynamic aspects of social institutions was certainly a major innovation, yet such studies were not seen again in Britain until the 1960s.

Innovations made by the pioneers of empirical sociology in Britain, then, often failed to diffuse either to their contemporaries or to their successors. The only study in this area is by Selvin (1976), who attempts to explain why the techniques of correlation developed by Yule diffused neither to Booth nor to Durkheim, whose study of suicide appeared in 1897 just as Yule was publishing his major articles on statistical correlation. Selvin concludes that there were channels of communication between Yule and Booth by way of the Royal Statistical Society (and somewhat more indirectly by way of Beatrice Webb) and that Booth would probably have been able to understand Yule's paper (or could easily have had it explained to him). However, Selvin doubts whether Booth would have found Yule's work important and useful. As to why this should be so, Selvin suggests only that Booth was a man of 'limited intellectual powers'. Whether or not this is true, it is inadequate as an explanation. In the case of Yule it was likely that his work was too closely associated with that of the eugenicists, Galton and Pearson, to be palatable to Booth. But why it was that Yule's techniques did not diffuse to Rowntree or to Bowley is, however, not so easily explained.

The problem which is glossed over both by the proponents of models of scientific growth and by diffusionists relates to the initial recognition, definition or perception of an idea or a practice *as* new. Crane, for example, defines an innovation in the research area she identifies as 'rural sociology' as 'the first use of a dependent or independent variable in a publication in the form of a new hypothesis or revision of a previous hypothesis'.[9] In another research area in a branch of mathematics the frequency of citation is used as a measure of innovativeness. What counts as an 'innovation' is thus defined externally to the individual researcher. The first use of a particular variable may not be seen as an innovation by perhaps even a minority of members of an invisible college. In fact Crane herself found that 21 per cent of the innovations in the rural sociology area were used by only one individual – the innovator himself – while 48 per cent were used by five or fewer members of the area. Some 40 per cent of the publications in the mathematics area were never cited at all.

If Selvin had concentrated on the stages of adoption of an innovation that have been developed by Rogers (1962), and Rogers and Shoemaker (1971), he might well have concluded that Booth probably never even reached the first stage of 'awareness' of Yule's correlation coefficients. Rogers defines an innovation as 'an idea *perceived* as new by the individuals' (my italics), but he does not pursue the notion that there may be a stage prior to awareness in which a potential adopter *comes* to perceive or define an area as new or as an innovation in the first place. Rogers limits himself to saying that at the awareness stage 'an individual is exposed to the innovation, but is not yet motivated to seek further information'.[10] In a later edition of the book Rogers and Shoemaker admit that perception is selective; even if individuals are exposed to messages about an innovation (as Booth almost certainly was to Yule's work on correlation), 'there will be little effect of such exposure unless the individual perceives the innovation as relevant to his needs and as consistent with his existing attitudes and beliefs'.[11]

However, the authors do not consider the circumstances under which ideas or practices come to be defined as innovatory. Most researchers looking at the diffusion of innovation have implicitly seen the awareness stage as a random, non-purposive occurrence; individuals become aware of an innovation quite by accident.

By 1971 Rogers and Shoemaker had distilled the results of more than 1,500 diffusion publications to provide a list of generalisations that gave a summary of what was known about the diffusion of innovations. From a number of such generalisations it is clear that early knowledge and later adoption of innovation is facilitated by a high degree of social participation and integration into the scientific community as well as by greater exposure to the channels of communication. It seems highly plausible that the perception of an idea or practice as new or innovatory by any one individual will, too, depend on the degree of his integration into a scientific community of scholars.

Novelty (like anomaly in Kuhn's theory) may be perceived only against a background of normal practice from which it is seen to be a 'departure'. Normal practice, however, will exist only when there is a relatively structured set of norms and values for the conduct of inquiry. In their absence everything is new, but nothing is recognised as 'an innovation'. Innovation will, in short, remain imperceptible until such times as 'current practice' defines an historical idea or procedure as an early example. Such structures of norms and values for the conduct of empirical inquiry crystallise and dissolve over time, so the salience or visibility of ideas or practices as 'new departures' grows and fades. This may help to explain why the criminologists between 1839 and 1857 could recognise and use age-specific crime rates as a useful 'innovation', while the visitation of every other house in a defined geographical area by an agent of the Manchester Statistical Society in 1834 was not perceived either by the organisers of the research or by other members of the Society as a departure from the current practice of complete enumerations.

Similarly it may be argued that while Booth almost certainly did know about Yule's article of 1895 that questioned Booth's interpretation of his own tables, it is possible that he just did not see the potential in using correlation coefficients to measure the degree of relationship between poverty and other variables. Like Rogers and Shoemaker's farmer who could 'drive past 100 miles of hybrid corn and never "see" the innovation',[12] so Booth and Rowntree and even Bowley after him did not see the applicability of the work of Galton, Pearson and Yule to the analysis of quantitative social data. Unfortunately, evidence about whether researchers actually knew about earlier investigations of similar areas or those using similar techniques of inquiry is scarce. It did not appear to be a feature of the style of reporting the results of empirical research to footnote earlier studies. However, in many instances it was a question of not relating an empirical investigation to anything that had gone before. This did not mean that Booth, for example, did not know about or know of the surveys of poverty conducted by members of the Statistical Society of London, about Mayhew's investigations of the London poor, about Engels's inquiries in Manchester or about Yule's criticisms of the way he had read his own tables. Although there was nothing in Booth's 17 volumes to suggest that he had deliberately consulted any of these works, it is plausible that he knew of them, but just did not 'see' the relevance of calculating Pearsons's r or Yule's Q for the kinds of problems he was investigating. He probably never studied Mayhew's work and if he had come across the 1861 edition of *London Labour and the London Poor* he may well not have seen in it the basis for coping with the problem of how to find out how many people there were living in poverty. It is possible, of course, that Booth was well aware of Yule's work, but deliberately ignored it because of its association with eugenics, and because the conclusions about the effects of giving out-relief that Yule had come to were not the kinds of conclusions that were welcome to him. It is certainly unlikely that Booth would have had the wherewithal to criticise Yule's use of his own statistics; the phenomenon of the 'spurious relationship' had not been discovered at the time, and the ideas of 'correlation surfaces' and 'scatter plots' were not ones that were likely to appeal to Booth, even if he were able to understand them. In short, the calculation of correlational statistics quite probably just did not strike Booth as 'an innovation' as far as interpreting the results of empirical surveys was concerned.

Whatever reasons Booth may have had for deliberately ignoring Yule, it seems unlikely that Bowley would have chosen consciously and deliberately to ignore the work of Pearson and Galton as well as that of Yule. Bowley wrote *An Elementary Manual of Statistics* (1909), which subsequently went into six editions and in which he was concerned mainly to show how to use and handle official statistics. He saw statistical methods (as opposed to statistics, which were 'numerical statements of facts in any department of inquiry, placed in relation to each other') as 'devices for abbreviating and classifying the statements and making clear their relations',[13] and he covered the use of ratios, percentages, averages, the use of diagrams, tabulation and sampling. However, he made no mention of or reference to Galton, Pearson or Yule. It can reasonably be inferred only that Bowley just never 'saw' the relevance of developments in correlation for the kinds of problems with which he was dealing. Curiously, Yule also wrote *An Introduction to the Theory of Statistics* (1911). Most of the book was, of course, concerned with correlation, and even though he covered the topic of sampling in several chapters he made no reference to Bowley. He had clearly come across Bowley's work later on, for in the 1937 edition of the book a number of Bowley's writings appear as a separate set of references at the end. It could well be that Bowley identified himself with the tradition of Booth and Rowntree, and Yule with the eugenicists, whose work would almost certainly have been an anathema to him. It probably made him very sceptical of the statistical techniques used by the eugenicists. On the other hand, Yule had no apparent reason to be particularly wary of Bowley's sampling techniques and he was certainly interested in social problems. Yule may well have been disappointed at the lack of reaction to his work from Booth, Rowntree and Bowley, but it must also be remembered that the survey itself was not a particularly well-standardised technique. There were no text-books at the time on how to conduct surveys, and there was no place where students or anybody interested in conducting surveys could learn from the experience of others. In short there was no structure of norms and values for the conduct of such inquiries so that Bowley's 'innovation' of taking samples instead of making complete enumerations was possibly just not perceived as a radical departure from anything that could be conceived as 'current practice'. There was no sociological community at the time in which new ways of doing things could be discussed or even passed on from individual to individual.

The imperceptibility of innovation

The hypothesised link between the perception of ideas and practices as innovations and the structure of norms and values for the conduct of empirical inquiry allows for the possibility that innovations may remain unperceived for long periods of time and may accumulate without recognition by any one individual, but ultimately will amount to significant developments in the field; developments which, although apparently obvious today, at an earlier stage were unrecognised. This is an idea suggested by Baldamus (1976) in the context of methods of sociological theorising. He argues that there are often unintended by-products of collective activity which arise from unconscious, haphazard, fumbling individual activities. A newly emerging phenomenon may be overlooked or remain unrecognised simply because it is unexpected or unanticipated. As an example he gives the sociologist's preoccupation with terminological precision. By consistently and consciously trying to invent new concepts and new connections between concepts in terms of their descriptive content, unintentionally a new form of speaking has arisen. This is the use of dualistic word-connections that are expressed either as paradoxical or pleonastic phrases like 'unconscious methods' or 'subjective meanings'.

It is useful, however, to make a distinction between 'innovation' and 'discovery' at this stage. Discoveries refer to the results of inquiry — to something that has been revealed by observation and measurement in the real world. Innovations on the other hand are products of the mind; they may be new ideas or new practices used in the conduct of inquiry. Thus Booth may be said to have 'discovered' that 30.7 per cent of the people in London lived 'in poverty' in the 1890s, but that his use of school board visitors to obtain information on every inhabitant in London with children was an 'innovation'. Baldamus himself suggests that discoveries as well as innovations may remain imperceptible. He suggests for example that the extensive and complex knowledge that sociologists nowadays have of the process of 'primary socialisation' is a major discovery, and came about as a series of unintended and unanticipated events, confused, erratic and beset with countless errors. Nothing about primary socialisation was known, presumed or conjectured at the time of the 'founding fathers' of sociology. Such discoveries are the consequence of a collective enterprise and are accumulated by a community of scholars so unobtrusively and slowly that they remain imperceptible even over long periods. However, the very notion of an 'unperceived discovery' is a contradiction in terms — one of Baldamus's own paradoxical word-connections perhaps. To discover something is to reveal it and to make it perceptible. Only innovation can remain unperceived.

Books such as those by Bell and Newby (1977), Bell and Encel (1978) and Platt (1976) suggest clearly enough that even in contemporary Britain there is little agreement amongst sociologists about norms and values for the conduct of inquiry. If this is so, are there not 'innovations' that are currently taking place, but which as yet have not been perceived as such by sociologists? It could be suggested, for example, that the growing use of computers and the availability of computer packages like SPSS have produced a crop of innovations that remain largely unperceived. The sheer ease with which vast quantities of data can be handled and very sophisticated statistics produced by researchers who may not themselves be particularly numerate has resulted in techniques of analysis that amount to a very rampant form of data dredging. Although this is a term already used by some textbooks, it is generally given as a kind of warning about what to avoid (and, by implication, *is* avoided by experienced researchers); yet the extent to which data dredging exists as a 'standard' technique may not be perceived by the contemporary sociologist as a radical departure from the kind of analyses carried out in the 1960s.

Data dredging arises in two main forms. One consists in the sheer quantity of items of information that may be transcribed on to a computer card. A study of 300 respondents covering over 1,000 variables is by no means unusual, yet that amounts to a data matrix of some three million cells each of which may arise from one or two (or more) column variables, so that each variable may have 100 values or more. Just obtaining a print-out of frequency distributions for each variable results in a document that may take weeks just to look through, but all produced by including a very simple control card in the SPSS job-deck. If the researcher is just 'looking for something interesting' in his mountains of data, this amounts to a form of fact gathering that is just as mindless as some of the inquiries carried out in the heyday of the statistical movement. The only difference is that instead of data relating to four million inhabitants of London each mapped on to, say 300 variables, the researcher now takes 300 respondents and maps each on to a matrix of three million items. The number of variables handled has increased in proportion as the number of cases has decreased. Intensive analysis has tended to replace extensive analysis.

The other form of data dredging consists in the use of sophisticated statistical techniques to uncover patterns of relationships between variables. The use of 'dummy' variables to create interval data from nominal categories in order to use factor analysis or multiple regression analysis, and the facility of factor and regression sub-programs on SPSS has enabled researchers to produce factors of no theoretical relevance, or to make nonsensical statistical 'explanations' of dependent variables. This makes the overall analysis as inductive as it ever was in the days of Booth, even though the contemporary researcher may pretend to the contrary by seeking a theory that 'fits' his data, and then presenting the results of his research as if the whole operation had been a deductive exercise.

It was suggested in the introduction that a science ignorant of its founders and of its history does not know how far it has travelled nor in what direction. This situation is likely to perpetuate the imperceptibility of innovation since innovations can be recognised only in the perspective of long-term trends, trends which themselves are likely to remain unperceived if the history of empirical social research continues to be ignored. Data dredging, it has been suggested, amounts to such an unperceived long-term trend. Furthermore, as a technique for the analysis of surveys, it tends to minimise the role of theory and of theorising. When Baldamus (1972) analysed the contributions in Hammond's *Sociologists at Work* (1964), he discovered that side by side with the official methodology that one found in the textbooks on systematic theory, formal logic, statistical methods, survey design or interview procedure, there existed a reservoir of unofficial, non-formalised techniques of inquiry that arose from the 'know-how' of social scientists acquired through constant practice. In each of the contributions there was an expression of a preoccupation with informal theorising in which both the theory and the evidence were constantly restructured, redefined, reinterpreted, and reformulated in a process of trial and error that the contributors recurringly referred to as 'constantly moving back and forth from theory to data'. This process, which Baldamus called 'double-fitting', made nonsense of hypothesis construction in the accepted sense and flatly contradicted the whole idea of scientific testing since hypotheses were fabricated to fit the facts.[14]

What is most striking from a glance at the recent British equivalent of Hammond's book by Bell and Newby (1977) is the absence in such accounts of any concern with theorising at all, and a concentration instead on the practical social contingencies involved in getting the research project to completion. Instead of the unceasing search for an 'integrating principle', a 'new theoretical amalgam', a 'basic conceptual framework', a 'crucial insight', a 'major idea' or a 'relevant typology' that Baldamus found for the American contributors in 1964, there is Atkinson concerned with the way in which publication can affect the course of the research, Bell with the difficulties of establishing a working relationship between members of a hierarchical research team, Cohen and Taylor on analysing 'talk', Pahl on the role of the sociologist as a hired expert, and Wallis on the morality of researching groups of people who do not wish to be studied. These practical social contingencies are presented as the 'real stuff' of research; gone apparently are the agonies of finding a theoretical framework for the data, of searching for an appropriate technique of inquiry to be used for collecting them, of deciding how many variables and how many cases to analyse, and what statistical techniques to use. A number of contributors to the Bell and Newby book comment that textbooks on research methods do not 'tell it how it is', and that their own procedures departed in significant ways from such formal accounts. Most admit to having made 'blunders' or 'mistakes' at some point yet, apparently, not crucial ones. Most of the accounts give narratives of sequences of events that punctuated the conduct of the inquiry, yet few describe what they were actually doing in terms of research techniques, practices and skills from an analytic viewpoint, nor how they attempted to match theory with evidence. Moore does mention that he and Rex 'rejected a functionalist approach to the study of Sparkbrooke' and instead began 'from an action point of reference',[15] but he does not discuss how they came to develop their theory of the balance of power between conflicting interests. Only Newby admits to engaging in 'double-fitting' — he changed his theory in a period of extended post field work reflection and the data he presented 'were selected accordingly'.[16]

Bell (1974) argues that even the 'warts and all' portraits of research projects are reconstructions written by an active participant and are therefore accounts that are problematic in their own right. They enable the researcher still to conceal the actual practice of empirical inquiry. Bell hints that such concealment is deliberate — that 'we don't want to be caught with our scientific trousers down'. After all, 'double-fitting' really amounts to 'cooking the facts' as far as the textbooks on research methods are concerned.

Data dredging, inductive reasoning from vast matrices of data and a concern for the practical social contingencies of carrying out research, then, possibly constitute the 'new' unperceived innovations in techniques of empirical inquiry used by sociologists in the 1970s. Yet, from an historical perspective, it is possible to see that these are changes more of form than of substance. Instead of facts as collections of data speaking for themselves, as in the days of the social accountants, data are now manipulated statistically before being made to speak, and to sound scientific in the rhetoric of tests of significance, factor analysis, multiple regression, analysis of variance, multi-dimensional scaling, cluster analysis, discriminant analysis and log-linear models. Inductive reasoning itself is nothing new in empirical inquiry, but the products of such processes are added to 'sociological theory' rather than to policy recommendations. Empirical investigators from Mayhew onwards have always been concerned with the practical social contingencies of bringing their inquiries to a successful conclusion, but instead of constituting merely a hindrance to speedy inquiry, these contingencies are now becoming part of an explicated 'lore' of science to be used for didactic purposes.

Bell came to the conclusion that unless sociology obtained a more secure epistemological base grounded in a well-researched descriptive methodology, it will have no future. Yet it may well be that the unarticulated research practices are not so much deliberately concealed, as Bell would have it, as unrecognised and unperceived even by the researcher himself. Research practices become cumulative only as a result of the unconscious and unintended by-products of collective activity. Newly emerging practices may be overlooked in the short term simply because they are unrecognised. 'Progress' materialises only as a disorderly and imperceptible sequence of false starts, errors, discoveries and innovations that become recognisable only over a period of time.

It has been suggested earlier that the sporadic and discontinuous nature of empirical sociology in Britain has had more to do with the social, political, economic and ideological environment than with any internal dynamic within the discipline itself. At the same time the likelihood of ideas or practices coming to be perceived as 'innovations' does to a large extent depend on the internal structure of norms and values for the conduct of inquiry within specific sub-areas of sociology. These two elements may now be combined into a new model of scientific growth which suggests that activity within an area may be sparked off by activity in society at large, but its perpetuation and ultimate institutionalisation requires that it break out of a vicious circle whereby inadequate institutionalisation in the form of structures of norms and values for the conduct of inquiry results in a lack of perception and hence cumulation about what counts as a 'development' in the area, while at the same time the very lack of such developments will hamper institutionalisation. Only in periods of relatively intense activity is this circle likely to be broken and the discipline seen to progress. At other times progress is indeed taking place, but it remains unperceived.

Notes

1   B. Webb, 1926, p.182.
2   Ibid., p.270.
3   See Spencer's comments on institutional analysis in his *The Study of Sociology* (1873). They are reprinted in Simey, 1968, p.203, n.8a.
4   Kuhn, 1962, p.10.
5   Ibid., p.15.
6   Ibid., p.38.
7   Ibid., pp 52-3.
8   Friedrichs, 1970, p.290.
9   Crane, 1972, p.18.
10   Rogers, 1962, p.82.
11   Rogers and Shoemaker, 1971, p.105.
12   Loc.cit.
13   Bowley, 1909, p.1.
14   Baldamus, 1972, p.291.
15   Moore, 1977, p.90.
16   Newby, 1977, p.126.

Bibliography

N.B.   All publishers are in London unless otherwise indicated.

Abel-Smith, B. and P. Townsend (1965), *The Poor and the Poorest*, G. Bell and Sons.

Abrams, M. (1961), *Social Surveys and Social Action*, Heinemann.

Abrams, M. (1979), 'Social Surveys, Social Theory and Social Policy', *Quantitative Sociology Newsletter*, 21, pp 15-23.

Abrams, P. (1968), *The Origins of British Sociology: 1834-1914*, Chicago, The University Press.

Allen, R.G.D. (1968), 'A.L. Bowley' in D.L. Sills (ed.), *International Encyclopedia of the Social Sciences*, Macmillan.

Aron, R. (1967), *Main Currents in Sociological Thought*, Harmondsworth, Penguin, 1970. Two vols.

Ashton, T.S. (1934), *Economic and Social Investigations in Manchester, 1833-1933*, P.S. King and Son. Republished by Harvester Press, 1977.

Bakke, E.W. (1933), *The Unemployed Man. A Social Survey*, Nisbet.

Baldamus, W. (1972), 'The Role of Discoveries in Social Science' in T. Shanin, *The Rules of the Game*, Tavistock.

Baldamus, W. (1976), *The Structure of Sociological Inference*, Martin Robertson.

Banks, J.A. (1957), 'The Group Discussion as an Interview Technique', *Soc. Rev.*, vol.5, no.1, pp 75-84.

Banks, J.A. (1969), *Studies in British Society*, Routledge.

Banks, O. (1956), 'Continuous Shift-Work; Attitudes of Wives', *Occupational Psychology*, vol.30, no.2, pp 69-54.

Banks, O. (1960), *The Attitudes of Steel Workers to Technical Change*, Liverpool University Press.

Banton, M. (1953), 'The Economic and Social Position of Negroes in Britain', *Soc. Rev.*, vol.1.

Banton, M. (1964), *The Policeman in the Community*, Tavistock.

Barnes, H.E. (1927), 'The Fate of Sociology in England', *Proceedings of the American Sociological Society*.

Bechhofer, F. (1967), 'Too Many Surveys', *New Society*, no.245.

Bell, C. (1974), 'Replication and Reality, or the Future of Sociology', *Futures*.

Bell, C. and S. Encel (eds) (1978), *Inside the Whale: Ten Personal Accounts of Social Research*, Pergamon.

Bell, C. and H. Newby (1972), *Community Studies*, Allen and Unwin.

Bell, C. and H. Newby (1977), *Doing Sociological Research*, Allen and Unwin.

Benney, M. and P. Geiss (1950), 'Social Class and Politics in Greenwich', *Brit. Jour. Soc.*, vol.1.

Berlin, Sir I. (1948), *Karl Marx: His Life and Environment*, Oxford University Press.

Bernstein, B. (1961), 'Social Class and Linguistic Development: A Theory of Social Learning' in A.H. Halsey, J. Floud and C.A. Anderson, *Education, Economy and Society*, New York, Free Press.

Bernstein, B. (1971), *Class, Codes, and Control*, Routledge.

Bernstein, B. (1974), 'Sociology and the Sociology of Education. A Brief Account' in Rex, 1974.

Birch, A.H. (1959), *Small-Town Politics. A Study of Political Life in Glossop*, Oxford University Press.

Birch, A.H. and P. Campbell (1950), 'Voting Behaviour in a Lancashire Constituency', *Brit. Jour. Soc.*, vol.1.

Birnbaum, N. (1960), 'Friends and Enemies', *The Twentieth Century*, vol.167, part 999.

Blackburn, R.M. (1967), *Union Character and Social Class. A Study of White-Collar Unionism*, Batsford.

Blackburn, R.M. and M. Mans (1979), *The Working Class in the Labour Market*, Macmillan.

Blau, P.M. and O.D. Duncan (1967), *The American Occupational Structure*, New York, Wiley.

Blondel, J. (1963), *Voters, Parties, and Leaders*, Harmondsworth, Penguin.

206

Boardman, P. (1944), *Patrick Geddes — Maker of the Future*, University of North Carolina Press. Rewritten as *The Worlds of Patrick Geddes. Biologist, Town Planner, Re-educator, Peace Warrior*, published by Routledge, 1978.

Booth, C. (1887), 'The Inhabitants of Tower Hamlets (School Board Division), their Condition and Occupations', *Jour. Roy. Stat. Soc.*, vol.50.

Booth, C. (1889), *Life and Labour of the People*, Williams and Norgate.

Booth, C. (1891), *Labour and Life of the People*, Williams and Norgate.

Booth, C. (1892-7), *Life and Labour of the People of London*, Macmillan, 9 vols.

Booth, C. (1894), *The Aged Poor in England and Wales*, Macmillan.

Booth, C. (1902-3), *Life and Labour of the People of London*, Macmillan, 17 vols.

Booth, C. (1913), *Industrial Unrest and Trade Union Policy*, Macmillan.

Booth, W. (1890), *In Darkest England and the Way Out*, Salvation Army.

Bott, E. (1957), *Family and Social Network. Roles, Norms, and External Relationships in Ordinary Urban Families*, Tavistock.

Bottomore, T.B. and R. Nisbet (1979), *A History of Sociological Analysis*, Heinemann.

Bottomore, T.B. and M. Rubel (1963), *Karl Marx: Selected Writings*, Harmondsworth, Penguin.

Bournville Village Trust (1941), *When We Build Again*, Allen and Unwin.

Bowley, A.L. (1910), *An Elementary Manual of Statistics*, Macdonald and Evans.

Bowley, A.L. (1912-13), 'Working Class Households in Reading', *Jour. Roy. Stat. Soc.*, vol.76.

Bowley, A.L. (1915), *The Nature and the Purpose of the Measurement of Social Phenomena*, P.S. King.

Bowley, A.L. and A.R. Burnett-Hurst (1915), *Livelihood and Poverty. A Study in the Economic Conditions of Working-Class Households in Nottingham, Warrington, Stanley and Reading*, Bell and Sons.

Bowley, A.L. and M.H. Hogg (1925), *Has Poverty Diminished?*, P.S. King.

Branford, V. (1914), *Interpretations and Forecasts*, Duckworth.

Branford V. and A. Farquharson (1924), *An Introduction to Regional Surveys*, Le Play House.

Briggs, A. (1961), *Social Thought and Social Action. A Study of the Work of Seebohm Rowntree, 1871-1954*, Longmans.

Briggs, A. (1965), *Victorian People. A Reassessment of Persons and Themes 1851-67*, Harmondsworth, Penguin.

Brothers, Joan (1964), *Church and School. A Study of the Impact of Education on Religion*, Liverpool University Press.

Brown, G. and T. Harris (1978), *The Social Origins of Depression. A Study of Psychiatric Disorder in Women*, Tavistock.

Bulmer, M. (1978), 'Social Science Research and Policy Making in Britain' in Bulmer (ed.), *Social Policy Research*, Macmillan.

Burton, T. (1978), *The Politics of Legitimacy: Struggles in a Belfast Community*, Routledge.

Butterfield, H. (1963), *The Wing Interpretation of History*, G. Bell and Sons.

Carneiro, R. (1968), 'Herbert Spencer' in *International Encyclopedia of the Social Sciences*, New York, Free Press.

Carter, M.P. (1968), 'Report on a Survey of Sociological Research in Britain', *Soc. Rev.*, vol.16, pp 5-40.

Cartwright, A. (1964), *Human Relations and Hospital Care*, Routledge.

Chadwick, E. (1842), *The Sanitary Condition of the Labouring Classes of Great Britain*, Edinburgh University Press.

Cicourel, A.V. (1964), *Method and Measurement in Sociology*, Free Press.

Clark, Sir G.N. (1972), 'Social Science in the Age of Newton' in Oberschall, 1972.

Clark, T. (1972), *Prophets and Patrons: The French University and the Emergence of the Social Sciences*, Cambridge University Press.

Clay, Rev. J. (1839), 'Criminal Statistics of Preston', *Jour. Stat. Soc. Lon.*, vol.2.

Cobbett, W. (1830), *Rural Rides*, Everyman Library.

Cohen, P. (1980), 'Is Positivism Dead?', *Soc. Rev.*, vol.28, pp 141-76.

Cohen, S. (1975), 'From Psychopaths to Outsiders: British Criminology and the National Deviancy Conference' in H. Bianchi, M. Simondi and I. Taylor (eds), *Deviance in Europe, Papers from the European Group for the Study of Deviance and Social Control*, New York, Wiley.

Cole, M. (1945), *Beatrice Webb*, Longmans.

Cole, M. (1961), *The Story of Fabian Socialism*, Heinemann.

Cole, S. (1972), 'Continuity and Institutionalisation in Science: A Case Study of Failure' in Oberschall, 1972.

Condry, E. (1980), *Scottish Ethnography*, SSRC Report.

Cook, F.G., S.C. Clark and E. Semeonoff (1979), *The Fragmentary Class Structure*, Heinemann.

Coxon, A.P. and C.L. Jones (1979), *Class and Hierarchy. The Social Meaning of Occupations*, Macmillan.

Crane, D. (1972), *Invisible Colleges: Diffusion of Knowledge in Scientific Communities*, University of Chicago Press.

Cullen, M.J. (1975), *The Statistical Movement in Early Victorian Britain. The Foundations of Empirical Social Research*, New York, Harvester Press.

Daniel, W.W. (1974), *A National Survey of the Unemployed*, Political and Economic Planning.

Darwin, C. (1859), *The Origin of Species: By Means of Natural Selection of the Preservation of Favoured Races in the Struggle for Life*, Collier Books, 1962.

Davies, M. (1909), *Life in an English Village. An Economic and Historical Survey of the Parish of Corsley in Wiltshire*, T. Fisher Unwin.

Defoe, D. (1724-6), *Tour Thro' the Whole Island of Great Britain*, Davies, 1927.

Dennis, N., F. Henriques and C. Slaughter (1956), *Coal is Our Life: An Analysis of a Yorkshire Mining Community*, Tavistock.

Ditton, J. (1977), *Part-Time Crime. An Ethnography of Fiddling and Pilfering*, Macmillan.

Dobash, R.E. and R.P. Dobash (1980), *Violence Against Wives. A Case Against the Patriarchy*, Open Books.

Douglas, J.W.B. (1964), *The Home and the School*, Macgibbon and Kee.

Douglas, J.W.B. (1976), 'The Use and Abuse of National Cohorts' in M. Shipman (ed.), *The Organisation and Impact of Social Research*, Routledge.

Douglas, J.W.B. and J.M. Bloomfield (1958), *Children Under Five*, Allen and Unwin.

Douglas, J.W.B. and G. Rowntree (1948), *Maternity in Great Britain*, Oxford University Press.

Durant, R. (1939), *Watling: A Survey of Social Life in a New Housing Estate*, P.S. King.

Dyos, H.J. (1967), 'The Slums of Victorian London', *Victorian Studies*, vol.XI.

Easthope, G. (1974), *A History of Research Methods*, Longmans.

Eden, Sir F.M. (1797), *The State of the Poor*, Frank Cass and Co.

Edwards, F. (ed.) (1956), *Readings in Market Research: a Selection of Papers by British Authors*, The British Market Research Bureau.

Elesh, D. (1972), 'The Manchester Statistical Society: A Case Study of Discontinuity in the History of Empirical Social Research' in Oberschall, 1972.

Engels, F. (1845), *The Condition of the Working Class in England in 1844*, first published in England in 1892.

Farquharson, D. (1955), 'Dissolution of the Institute of Sociology', *Soc. Rev.*, vol.3.

Feyerabend, P. (1975), *Against Method*, New Left Books.

Fiegehan, G.C., P.S. Lansley and A.D. Smith (1977), *Poverty and Progress in Britain 1953-73*, National Institute of Economic and Social Research Occasional Paper, Cambridge University Press.

Fletcher, J. (1843), 'Progress of Crime in the U.K.', *Jour. Stat. Soc. Lon.*, vol.6, pp 218-40.

Fletcher, J. (1848), 'Moral and Educational Statistics of England and Wales', *Jour. Stat. Soc. Lon.*, vol.11, pp 344-66.

Fletcher, R. (1971), *The Making of Sociology: A Study of Sociological Theory*, Nelson.

Foner, N. (1979), *Jamaica Farewell. Jamaican Migrants in London*, Routledge.

Ford, J. (1969), *Social Class and the Comprehensive School*, Routledge.

Ford, J. (1976), 'Facts, Evidence and Rumour: A Rational Reconstruction of "Social Class and the Comprehensive School"' in M. Shipman (ed.), *The Organisation and Impact of Social Research*, Routledge.

Frankenberg, R. (1957), *Village on the Border: A Social Study of Religion, Politics, and Football in a North Wales Community*, Cohen and West.

Frankenberg, R. (1966), *Communities in Britain*, Harmondsworth, Penguin.

Fried, A. and R.M. Elman (eds) (1969), *Charles Booth's London*, Harmondsworth, Penguin.

Friedrichs, R.W. (1970), *A Sociology of Sociology*, Free Press.

Galbraith, V.H. (1961), *The Making of Domesday*, Oxford University Press.

Galton, Sir F. (1883), *Inquiries into Human Faculty*, Dent.

Galtung, J. (1967), *Theory and Methods of Social Research*, New York, Columbia University Press.

Geddes, P. (1903), *City Development. A Study of Parks, Gardens, and Culture Institutes*, Edinburgh, Geddes Press.

Glaser, B.G. and A.L. Strauss (1968), *The Discovery of Grounded Theory. Strategies for Qualitative Research*, Weidenfeld and Nicolson.

Glass, D.V. (1952), 'The Population Controversy in Eighteenth Century England. Part I: The Background', *Population Studies*, vol.6, pp 69-91.

Glass, D.V. (1954), *Social Mobility in Britain*, Routledge.

Glass, D.V. (1965), 'Two Papers on Gregory King' in D.V. Glass and D.E.C. Eversley (eds), *Population in History. Essays in Historical Demography*, Chicago, Aldine.

Glass, D.V. and J.L. Gray, (1938), 'Opportunity and the Older Universities. A Study of the Oxford and Cambridge Scholarship System' in Hogben, 1935.

Glass, R. (1948), *The Social Background of a Plan: A Study of Middlesbrough*, Routledge.

Glazer, N. (1964), 'The Rise of Social Research in Europe' in D. Lerner (ed.), *The Human Meaning of the Social Sciences*, Meridian.

Goldthorpe, J.H. (1980), *Social Mobility and Class Structure in Modern Britain*, Oxford University Press.

Goldthorpe, J.H. and K. Hope (1974), *The Social Grading of Occupations: A New Approach and Scale*, Oxford, Clarendon Press.

Goldthorpe, J.H. and C. Llewellyn (1977a), 'Class Mobility in Modern Britain. Three theses examined', *Sociology*, vol.11, no.2.

Goldthorpe, J.H. and C. Llewellyn (1977b), 'Class Mobility: Intergenerational and Worklife Patterns', *Brit. Jour. Soc.*, vol.28, no.3.

Goldthorpe, J.H., D. Lockwood, F. Bechhofer and J. Platt (1969), *The Affluent Worker in the Class Structure*, Cambridge University Press.

Grace, G. (1978), *Teachers, Ideology, and Control. A Study in Urban Education*, Routledge.

Graunt, J. (1662), *Natural and Political Observations Mentioned in the Following Index and made upon Bills of Mortality. With Reference to the Government, Religion, Trade, Growth, Ayre, Disease and the several Changes of the said City*, reprinted by Arno Press, New York, 1973.

Greenwood, J. (1866), *A Night in a Workhouse*, reprinted in Keating, 1976, pp 33-54.

Guy, W.G. (1839), 'On the Value of the Numerical Method as Applied to Science, especially to Psychology and Medicine', *Jour. Stat. Soc. Lon.*, vol.2, p.25.

Guy, W.G. (1843), 'An Attempt to Determine the Influence of the Seasons and Weather on Sickness and Mortality', *Jour. Stat. Soc. Lon.*, vol.6, p.133.

Guy, W.G. (1850), 'On the Relative Value of Averages derived from different Numbers of Observations', *Jour. Stat. Soc. Lon.*, vol.13, p.30.

Habermas, J. (1972), *Knowledge and Human Interests*, Heinemann.

Hakim, C. (1980), 'Secondary Analysis and the Relationship between Official and Academic Social Research', Paper given to the British Sociological Association Conference, Lancaster, 1980.

Hall, J. and D.S. Jones (1950), 'The Social Grading of Occupations', *Brit. Jour. Soc.*, vol.I.

Halliday, R.J. (1968), 'The Sociological Movement, the Sociological Society, and the Genesis of Academic Sociology in Britain', *Soc. Rev.*, vol.16, pp 377-98.

Halsey, A.H. (1972), *Educational Priority*, HMSO, 5 vols.

Halsey, A.H. (1975), 'Education and Social Mobility in Britain since World War II' in *Education, Inequality and Life Chances*, vol.I, Paris, OECD.

Halsey, A.H. (1977), 'Towards Meritocracy? The Case of Britain' in J. Karabel and A.H. Halsey (eds), *Power and Ideology in Education*, Oxford University Press.

Halsey, A.H., A.F. Heath and J.M. Ridge (1980), *Origins and Destinations: Family, Class and Education in Modern Britain*, Oxford University Press.

Hamilton, S. (1933), *Sidney and Beatrice Webb. A Study in Contemporary Biography*, Boston, Houghton-Mifflin.

Hammond, P.E. (1964), *Sociologists at Work: Essays on the Craft of Social Research*, New York, Basic Books.

Hanham, F.G. (1930), *Report of an Inquiry into Casual Labour in the Merseyside Area*, Liverpool, Henry Young.

Hargreaves, D. (1967), *Social Relations in a Secondary School*, Routledge.

Harper, E.B. (1943), 'Sociology in England', *Social Forces*, vol.11, pp 335-42.

Harrison, B. (1967), 'London's Lower Depths', *New Society*, 2 November.

Harrison, T. (1970), Preface to new edition of *The Pub and the People: A Worktown Study*, Mass Observation, 1943.

Harrop, M. (1980), 'Social Research and Market Research: A Critique', *Sociology*, vol.14, pp 277-81.

Hawthorn, G. (1976), *Enlightenment and Despair. A History of Sociology*, Cambridge University Press.

Henderson, W.O. and W.H. Chaloner (1958), Editorial introduction to F. Engels, *The Condition of the Working Class in England*, Oxford, Basil Blackwell.

Hendry, L. (1979), *School Sport, and Leisure. Three Dimensions of Adolescence*, Lepurs.

Hennock, E.P. (1976), 'Poverty and Social Theory in England: the Experience of the Eighteen Eighties', *Social History*, vol.1.

Heywood, J. (1838), 'Report of an Enquiry, conducted from house-to-house, into the State of 176 Families in Miles Platting within the Borough of Manchester in 1837', *Jour. Stat. Soc. Lon.*, vol.1, p.34.

Hilton, J. (1924), 'Enquiry by Sample: An Experiment and its Results', *Jour. Roy. Stat. Soc.*, vol.LXXXVII, part IV.

Hilton, J. (1925), 'Some Further Enquiries by Sample', *Jour. Roy. Stat. Soc.*, vol.XCI, part IV.

Hilts, V. (1978), 'Aliis Exterendum or, the Origins of the Statistical Society of London', *Isis*, vol.69, pp 21-43.

Himmelweit, H.T. and A. Summerfield (1951), 'Student Selection. An Experimental Investigation', *Brit. Jour. Soc.*, vol.2.

Hindess, B. (1973), *The Use of Official Statistics in Sociology. A Critique of Positivism and Ethnomethodology*, Macmillan.

Hirschi, T. and H.C. Selvin (1967), *Delinquency Research: An Appraisal of Analytic Methods*, New York, Free Press.

Hobsbawm, E.J. (1964), 'The Fabians Reconsidered' in *Labouring Men. Studies in the History of Labour*, Weidenfeld and Nicolson.

Hogben, L. (1938), *Political Arithmetic. A Symposium of Population Studies*, Allen and Unwin.

Hollowell, P. (1968), *The Lorry Driver*, Routledge.

Hope, K. (ed.) (1972), *The Analysis of Social Mobility: Methods and Approaches*, Oxford, Clarendon Press.

Hopkins, E. (1979), *A Social History of the English Working Classes, 1815-1945*, Edward Arnold.

Howarth, E.G. and M. Wilson (1907), *West Ham: A Study in Social and Industrial Problems*, Dent.

Humpheries, A. (1971), Introduction to *Voices of the Poor: Selections from the Morning Chronicle* by Henry Mayhew, Frank Cass.

Humpheries, A. (1980), *Travels into the Poor Man's Country. The Work of Henry Mayhew*, Firle, Sussex, Caliban Books.

Irvine, J., I. Miles and J. Evans (1979), *Demystifying Statistics*, Pluto Press.

Jackson, B. and D. Marsden (1962), *Education and the Working Class*, Routledge.

Jackson, M.P. and V. Hanby (1979), 'Work Creation Programmes: Participant Responses', *Industrial Relations Journal*, vol.10, no.2, pp 23-30.

Jennings, H. (1934), *Brynmawr: A Study of a Distressed Area*, Allenson and Co.

Jephcott, P. (1964), *A Troubled Area: Notes on Notting Hill*, Faber and Faber.

Jones, D.C. (ed.) (1934), *The Social Survey of Merseyside*, University of Liverpool Press.

Jones, D.C. (1948), *Social Surveys*, Hutchison.

Katz, E., M.L. Levin and H. Hamilton (1963), 'Traditions of Research on the Diffusion of Innovation', *Am. Soc. Rev.*, vol.XXVIII.

Kay-Shuttleworth, J.P. (1832), *The Moral and Physical Condition of the Working Classes, Employed in the Cotton Manufacture in Manchester*, James Ridgeway, reprinted by Irish University Press, 1971.

Keating, P. (1971), *The Working Classes in Victorian Fiction*, Routledge.

Keating, P. (1976), *Into Unknown England: Selections from the Social Explorers*, Fontana.

Kendall, M.G. and A. Stuart (1950), 'The Law of the Cubic Proportion in Election Results', *Brit. Jour. Soc.*, vol.7.

Kent, R. (1980), 'A Survey of Empirical Research on Scotland', paper presented to the British Sociological Association Conference, Lancaster, to be published as 'Sociological Research on Scotland: A survey of Empirical Inquiries 1950 to 1980', *Transactions of the 1980 Conference*, BSA.

King, R. (1973), *School Organisation and Pupil Involvement*, Routledge.

Krausz, E. (1969), *Sociology in Britain: A Survey of Research*, B.T. Batsford.

Kuhn, T.S. (1962), *The Structure of Scientific Revolutions*, University of Chicago Press.

Lacey, C. (1970), *Hightown Grammar: The School as a Social System*, Manchester University Press.

Lancaster, T. (1979), 'Econometric Methods for the Duration of Unemployment', *Econometrica*, vol.47, no.4.

Layard, R., D. Piachaud and M. Stewart (1978), *The Causes of Poverty, Background Paper No.5*, Royal Commission on the Distribution of Income and Wealth, HMSO.

Lazarsfeld, P.F. (1972), 'The Sociological Study of the History of Social Research' in Oberschall, 1972.

Lazarsfeld, P.F. and A.R. Oberschall (1965), 'Max Weber and Empirical Social Research', *A.S.R.*, vol.30, pp 185-99.

Lecuyer, B. and A.R. Oberschall (1968), 'Sociology: Early History of Social Research' in D.L. Sills (ed.), *International Encyclopedia of the Social Sciences*, Macmillan.

Le Grand, J. (1978), 'The Distribution of Public Expenditure in the Case of Health Care', *Econometrica*, vol.45, pp 125-42.

Little, K.L. (1947), *Negroes in Britain. A Study of Racial Relationships in English Society*, Kegan Paul.

Littlejohn, J. (1964), *Westrigg: The Sociology of a Cheviot Parish*, Routledge.

London, J. (1903), *The People of the Abyss*, New York, Macmillan.

Lupton, T. (1963), *On the Shop Floor: Two Studies of Workshop Organisation and Output*, Pergamon.

McCulloch, J. (1825), *Principles of Political Economy: With a Sketch of the Rise and Progress of Science*, reprinted by Alex Murray, 1872.

Mackenzie, D. (1976), 'Eugenics in Britain', *Soc. Sci. Studs.*, vol.6, pp 499-532.

McKenzie, R.T. and A. Silver (1968), *Angels in Marble: Working Class Conservatives in Urban England*, Heinemann.

McKibbin, R.I. (1978), 'Social Class and Social Observation in Edwardian England', *Trans. Roy. Hist. Soc.*, vol.28, pp 175-99.

Madge, C. and T. Harrison (eds) (1938), *First Year's Work, 1937-38*, Mass Observation, Lindsay Drummond.

Madge, J. (1963), *The Origins of Scientific Sociology*, Tavistock.

Malthus, T. (1798), *First Essay on Population*, Macmillan, 1926.

Marris, P. (1958), *Widows and Their Families*, Routledge.

Marsden, D. (1967), 'Education and the Working Class' in M. Craft, J. Raynor and L. Cohen, *Linking Home and School*, Longmans.

Marsh, C. (1979), 'Problems with Surveys: Method and Epistemology', *Sociology*, vol.13, no.2, pp 293-305.

Marsh, C. (1980), 'Underdevelopment and Compartmentalisation: Survey Research in British Sociology', paper read to the British Sociological Association Conference, Lancaster.

Marshall, T.H. (1938), *Class Conflict and Social Stratification*, Le Play House Press.

Marshall, T.H. (1975), Introduction to *Methods of Social Study* by Sidney and Beatrice Webb, Cambridge University Press.

Mass Observation (1937), *May 12th*, Faber and Faber.

Mass Observation (1938), *Britain*, Harmondsworth, Penguin.

Mass Observation (1940), *War Begins at Home*, Faber and Faber.

Mass Observation (1943), *The Pub and the People*, Gollancz.

Mass Observation (1948), *Puzzled People. A Study in Popular Attitudes to Religion, Ethics, Progress and Politics in a London Borough*, Gollancz.

Mass Observation (1954), *The Voters' Choice: A Special Report*, Gollancz.

Mass Observation (1961), *Britain Revisited*, Harmondsworth, Penguin.

Mayer, G. (1936), *Friedrich Engels. A Biography*, Chapman Hall.

Mayhew, H. (1861), *London Labour and the London Poor*, first published in four volumes by Griffin, Bohn and Co., reprinted by Dover Publications Inc., New York, 1968.

Mayhew, H. (1862), *The Criminal Prisons of London and Scenes of Prison Life*, Griffin, Bohn and Co., reprinted by Frank Cass and Co., 1968.

Mayhew, H. (1880), *The Morning Chronicle Survey of Labour and the Poor: The Metropolitan Districts*, Sussex, Caliban Books, 6 vols.

Mays, J.B. (1954), *Growing Up in the City*, Liverpool University Press.

Mays, J.B. (1959), *On the Threshold of Delinquency*, Liverpool University Press.

Mays, J.B. (1961), *Education and the Urban Child*, Liverpool University Press.

Mess, H.A. (1928), *Industrial Tyneside: A Social Survey*, Benn.

Michels, R. (1915), *Political Parties: A Sociological Study of the Oligarchical Tendencies of Modern Democracy*, Jarrold.

Mitchison, R. (1962), *Agricultural Sir John, the Life of Sir John Sinclair of Ulster, 1754-1835*, Geoffrey Bless.

Morgan, D. (1975), 'British Social Theory', *Sociology*, vol.9, no.1, pp 119-24.

Morris, P. (1965), *Prisoners and their Families*, Allen and Unwin.

Morris, P. (1969), *Put Away: A Sociological Study of Institutions for the Mentally Retarded*, Routledge.

Morris, T. and P. Morris (1963), *Pentonville: A Sociological Study of an English Prison*, Routledge.

Moser, C.A. and G. Kalton (1971), *Survey Methods in Social Investigation*, Heinemann.

Mumford, E. and O. Banks (1967), *The Computer and the Clerk*, Routledge.

Newby, H., C. Bell, D. Rose and P. Saunders (1978), *Property, Paternalism and Power: Class and Control in Rural England*, Hutchison.

Newsom, F. (1963), *Half Our Future. A Report of the Central Advisory Council for Education*, HMSO.

Newson, J. and E. Newson (1963), *Infant Care in an Urban Community*, Allen and Unwin.

Newson, J. and E. Newson (1968), *Four Years Old in an Urban Community*, Allen and Unwin.

Newson, J. and E. Newson (1976a) 'Parental Roles and Social Contexts' in M. Shipman (ed.), *The Organisation and Impact of Social Research*, Routledge.

Newson, J. and E. Newson (1976b), *Seven Years Old in the Home Environment*, Allen and Unwin.

Oberschall, A. (1965), *Empirical Research in Germany 1848-1915*, The Hague, Mouton.

Oberschall, A. (1972), *The Establishment of Empirical Sociology: Studies in Continuity, Discontinuity, and Institutionalisation*, New York, Harper and Row.

Oppenheim, A.N. (1968), *Questionnaire Design and Attitude Measurement*, Heinemann.

Patrick, J. (1973), *A Glasgow Gang Observed*, Eyre Methuen.

Patterson, S. (1963), *Dark Strangers: A Sociological Study of the Absorption of a Recent West Indian Migrant Group in Brixton, South London*, Tavistock.

Payne, G., G. Ford and C. Robertson (1976), 'Changes in Occupational Mobility in Scotland. Some Preliminary Findings of the 1975 Scottish Mobility Study', *Scottish Jour. Soc.*, vol.1, no.1, pp 57-79.

Peel, J. and G. Skipworth (1970), 'Sample Size: An Innovatory Procedure in Survey Analysis', *Sociology*, vol.4, pp 385-93.

Petty, W. (1690), *Political Arithmetick*, first written in 1671, first published surreptitiously in 1683 as *England's Guide to Industry*. The first authorised edition was published posthumously in 1690 by Petty's son.

Pfautz, H. (1967), *Charles Booth on the City: Physical Pattern and Social Structure*, Chicago University Press.

Phillips, D. (1973), *Abandoning Methods*, San Francisco, Jossey-Bass.

Platt, J. (1971), *Social Research in Bethnal Green*, Macmillan.

Platt, J. (1974), *Realities of Social Research. An Empirical Study of British Sociologists*, Sussex University Press.

Platt, J. (1980), 'The Social Construction of "Positivism" and its Significance in British Sociology' in P. Abrams, R. Deem, J. Finch and P. Rock (eds), *British Sociology 1950 to 1980*, Allen and Unwin (forthcoming).

Plint, T. (1851), *Crime in England: Its Relation, Character, and Extent, as Developed from 1801 to 1848*, Charles Gilpin.

Plowden, Lady B. (1967), *Children and their Primary Schools. A Report of the Central Advisory Council for Education (England)*, vol.1, Report, HMSO.

Popper, K. (1963), *Conjectures and Refutations*, Routledge.

Raffe, D. (1979), 'The "Alternative Route" Reconsidered: Part Time Further Education and Social Mobility in England and Wales', *Sociology*, vol.13, no.1.

Rapoport, R.N. (1970), 'Three Dilemmas in Action Research', *Human Relations*, vol.23, no.6.

Rawson, R.W. (1839), 'An Inquiry into the Statistics of Crime in England and Wales', *Jour. Stat. Soc. Lon.*, vol.2, pp 316-44.

Rees, A.D. (1950), *Life in a Welsh Countryside*, University of Wales Press.

Reid, I. (1978), *Sociological Perspectives on School and Education*, Open Books.

Reisman, D. (1977), *Richard Titmuss. Welfare and Society*, Heinemann.

Rex, J. (1961), *Key Problems in Sociological Theory*, Routledge.

Rex, J. (1974), *Approaches to Sociology. An Introduction to Major Trends in British Sociology*, Routledge.

Rex, J. and R. Moore (1967), *Race, Community and Conflict. A Study of Sparkbrooke*, Oxford University Press.

Richmond, A.H. (1966), 'Britain' in *Research on Racial Relations*, UNESCO.

Ridge, J.M. (1973), *Mobility in Britain Reconsidered*, Oxford, Clarendon Press.

Rogers, E.M. (1962), *Diffusion of Innovations*, New York, Free Press.

Rogers, E.M. and F.F. Shoemaker (1971), *Communication of Innovations*, New York, Free Press.

Rosenberg, J.D. (1968), Introduction to the 1968 reprint of the 1861 edition of *London Labour and the London Poor* by Henry Mayhew, New York, Dover Publications.

Rowntree, B.S. (1901), *Poverty. A Study of Town Life*, Macmillan.

Rowntree, B.S. (1941), *Poverty and Progress. A Second Survey of York*, Longmans.

Rowntree, B.S. and B. Lasker (1911), *Unemployment. A Social Study*, Macmillan.

217

Rowntree, B.S. and G.R. Lavers (1951), *Poverty and the Welfare State: A Third Social Survey of York Dealing only with Economic Questions*, Longmans.

Runciman, W.G. (1966), *Relative Deprivation and Social Justice. A Study of Attitudes to Social Inequality in Twentieth Century England*, Routledge.

Schad, S. (1972), *Empirical Sociological Research in Weimar Germany*, The Hague, Mouton.

Scott, W.H. (1952), *Industrial Leadership and Joint Consultation*, Liverpool University Press.

Scott, W.H. and J.A. Banks (1956), *Technical Change and Industrial Relations*, Liverpool University Press.

Selvin, H.C. (1976), 'Durkheim, Booth, and Yule: the Non-diffusion of an Intellectual Innovation', *Archives of European Sociology*, vol.XVII, pp 39-51.

Semmel, B. (1958), 'Karl Pearson: Socialist and Darwinist', *Brit. Jour. Soc.*, vol.IX, pp 111-25.

Shipman, M.D. (1972), *The Limitations of Social Research*, Longmans.

Simey, T.S. (1961), 'The Contribution of Sidney and Beatrice Webb to Sociology', *Brit. Jour. Soc.*, vol.XII, pp 106-230.

Simey, T.S. and M.B. Simey (1960), *Charles Booth, Social Scientist*, Oxford University Press.

Sims, G. (1883), *How the Poor Live*, Chatto and Windus.

Sinclair, C. (1853), *Memoir to the Rt Hon. Sir John Sinclair with an Account of his Writings and Personal Exertions for the Social and Agricultural Improvement of Scotland*, Edinburgh, William and Robert Chambers.

Sinclair, Sir J. (1791-99) *Statistical Account of Scotland drawn up from the Communications of Ministers of the different Parishes*, published in 21 volumes by William Creech, Edinburgh, republished in a new edition by D. Witherington and I. Grant, E.P. Publishing, 1974.

Sinclair, Sir J. (1831), *Analysis of the Statistical Account of Scotland*, Edinburgh, William Tait.

Smiles, S. (1859), *Self-Help. With Illustrations of Character and Conduct*, The World Library.

Smith, D.J. (1977), *Racial Disadvantage in Britain*, Harmondsworth, Penguin.

Smith, H.L. (1930-5), *The New Survey of London Life and Labour*, P.S. King, 9 vols.

Spencer, H. (1904), *An Autobiography*, vol.II, Williams and Norgate.

Spencer, J. (1964), *Stress and Release in an Urban Estate. A Study in Action Research*, Tavistock.

Springrice, M. (1939), *Working Class Wives: their Health and Conditions*, Harmondsworth, Penguin.

Stacey, M. (1960), *Tradition and Change. A Study of Banbury*, Oxford University Press.

Stacey, M. et al. (1975), *Power, Persistence, and Change. A Second Study of Banbury*, Routledge.

Strauss, E. (1954), *Sir William Petty. Portrait of a Genius*, Bodley Head.

Symons, J. (1849), *Tactics for the Times: As Regards the Conditions and Treatment of the Dangerous Classes*, John Oliver.

Therborn, G. (1976), *Science, Class and Society. On the Formation of Sociology and Historical Materialism*, New Left Books.

Thompson, E.P. (1963), *The Making of the English Working Class*, Gollancz.

Thompson, E.P. (1967), 'The Political Education of Henry Mayhew', *Victorian Studies*, vol.XI, pp 42-62.

Thompson, E.P. (1971), 'Mayhew and the Morning Chronicle' in Thompson and Yeo, 1971.

Thompson, E.P. and E. Yeo, (1971), *The Unknown Mayhew. Selections from the 'Morning Chronicle', 1849-1850*, Merlin Press.

Thompson, K. (1976), *Auguste Comte: The Foundation of Sociology*, Nelson.

Thorburn, P. (1977), 'Political Generations: The Case of Class and Party in Britain', *Eur. Jour. Pol. Res.*, vol.5.

Titmuss, R.M. (1960), *The Irresponsible Society*, Fabian Tract no.323, reprinted in *Essays on the Welfare State*, 1963, Allen and Unwin.

Tout, H. (1938), *The Standard of Living in Bristol. A Preliminary Report of the Work of the University of Bristol Social Survey*, Arrowsmith.

Townsend, P. (1957), *The Family Life of Old People*, Routledge.

Townsend, P. (1979), *Poverty in the U.K. A Survey of Household Resources and Standards of Living*, Harmondsworth, Penguin.

Tunstall, J. (1962), *The Fisherman*, McGibbon and Kee.

Vereker, C.H. and J.B. Mays (1960), *Urban Redevelopment and Social Change*, Liverpool University Press.

Webb, B. (1891), *The Cooperative Movement in Great Britain*, Sonnenschein.

Webb, B. (1926), *My Apprenticeship*, Longmans.

Webb, B. (1948), *Our Partnership*, edited by B. Drake and M. Cole, Longmans.

Webb, B. and S. Webb (1894), *The History of Trade Unionism*, Longmans.

Webb, B. and S. Webb (1897), *Industrial Democracy*, Longmans.

Webb, B. and S. Webb (1932), *Methods of Social Study*, Longmans.

Webb, S. (1887), *Facts for Socialists. From the Political Economists and Statisticians*, Fabian Society.

Wells, A.F. (1935), *The Local Social Survey in Great Britain*, Allen and Unwin.

Westergaard, J. (1979) 'In Memory of David Glass', *Sociology*, vol.13, no.2, pp 173-77.

Whyte, W. (1965), *Street Corner Society*, Chicago University Press.

Williams, W.M. (1963), *A West Country Village: Ashworthy*, Routledge.

Willis, P. (1977), *Learning to Labour: How Working Class Kids get Working Class Jobs*, Farnborough, Saxon House.

Wilson, B.R. (1961), *Sects and Society. A Sociological Study of Three Religious Groups in Britain*, Heinemann.

Wiseman, S. (1964), *Education and Environment*, Manchester University Press.

Yeo, E. (1971), 'Mayhew as a Social Investigator' in Thompson and Yeo, 1971.

Young, M. and P. Wilmott (1957), *Family and Kinship in East London*, Routledge.

Young, M. and P. Wilmott (1961), 'Research Report No.3. Institute of Community Studies, Bethnal Green', *Soc. Rev.*, vol.9, pp 203-13.

Young, P. (1939), *Scientific Social Surveys and Research*, New Jersey, Prentice-Hall.

Yule, G.U. (1895), 'On the Correlation of Total Pauperism with the Proportion of Out-relief', *Economic Journal*, vol.V, pp 603-11.

Yule, G.U. (1896), 'Notes on the History of Pauperism in England and Wales from 1850, treated by the method of Frequency Curves, with an Introduction on Method, *Jour. Roy. Stat. Soc.*, vol.59, p.318.

Yule, G.U. (1899), 'An Investigation into the Causes of Changes in Pauperism in England, chiefly during the last two Intercensal Decades', *Jour. Roy. Stat. Soc.*, vol.LXII.

Yule, G.U. (1900), 'On the Association of Attributes in Statistics: with Illustrations from the Material of the Childhood Society, etc.', *Philosophical Transactions*, Series A, CLXXXIV, pp 257-319.

Yule, G.U. (1911), *An Introduction to the Theory of Statistics*, Griffin.

Zweig, F. (1942), *The Planning of Free Societies*, Secker and Warburg.

Zweig, F. (1952), *Women's Life and Labour*, Gollancz.

Zweig, F. (1961), *The Worker in an Affluent Society*, Heinemann.

Zweig, F. (1963), *The Student in an Age of Anxiety*, Heinemann.

Name index

Subject and organisation index

action research, 155-6
American Sociological Association, 121
anthropologists, 134-6

Beveridge Report, 124-5
Bills of Mortality, 15
biometrics, 125. *See also* eugenics
Blue Books, 2
Bourneville Village Trust, 113-4
British Association for the Advancement of Science, 18, 19, 20, 25, 141
British Journal of Sociology established, 139
British Sociological Association, 168; founded, 140-1

capitalism, 42-3
causal analysis, 23, 30. *See also* correlational techniques
Census, 16-7, 18, 23, 53, 57, 142

Centre for Urban Studies, 152
Central Statistical Office, 145
Charity Organisation Society, 64, 99
Chartists, -ism, 31, 32, 38, 45, 47, 64
chi-square, 93
civics, 91-2
class, *see* social class
cohort studies, 129, 174
community studies, 133-9, 143-4
comparative method, 2, 129
computer technology, 141, 200
co-operative societies, 84-5
correlational techniques, 93-7
crime, -inology, 23-4, 26-8, 49
crowding, 57, 107, 111

data bank, *see* survey archive
data-dredging, 200-1
delinquency, 134, 156
demography, early, 15-7

observation, 116. *See also* Mass Observation
Office of Population Censuses and Surveys, 142, 170
old age, 63, 138
overcrowding, *see* crowding
Oxford Mobility Group, 170-5

paid agents, 18-9, 75
paradigms, 190-1
parish, -ochial reports, 14
participant observation, 139, 152-3, 163-5, 176
path analysis, 173
pauperism, 23, 95-7
Pearson's r, 93, 96, 139, 198
pilot survey, 136
Plowden Report, 145, 156-7
political arithmetic, 15-6, 173
political economy, 17-18, 21, 48, 125, 189
political sociology, 142-3, 150-2
polytechnics, sociology in, 182
Poor Law, 31, 38, 89, 99
population controversy, 16
Population Investigation Committee, 125, 127, 129, 152
positivism, 1-2, 168-70, 188
poverty, 31, 43-5, 53-7, 58, 59, 76-8, 79, 81, 103-11, 112, 131-2, 159-63, 178-9. *See also* pauperism
prisons, 152-4
professionalism, 141-52

quantitative techniques, 24, 141, 154, 201. *See also* correlational techniques, statistics
questionnaires: postal, 3, 13-14; interview schedules, *see* interviewing

race relations, 156, 164-6, 175
reform, *see* social reform
Reform Act: 1832, 31
relative deprivation, 47, 150-1
religion, 57-8, 163-4
regression, *see* correlation
replication, 24, 103-10, 173
research techniques/methods, 8, 114-7
Rochdale Pioneers, 31
royal commissions, 30

sampling, 19, 24, 80-2, 102-6, 109-10, 167
school board visitors, 53, 75, 105, 111
scientific revolutions, 192
Scotland, sociology in, 177-8, 186
secondary analysis, 5, 23-4, 142, 178-9
self-help, 64
social accountants, 5, 12-34, 117, 139, 152, 187; social accounting defined, 21
social class, 53-4, 61, 82-3, 105, 137, 139, 144, 148-9, 150-1, 171
Social Democratic Federation, 65
social explorers, 6, 37-67, 134, 187
social mobility, 126-7, 170-5
social reform, 8-9, 18, 22, 29, 124
Social Science Research Council, 141, 152, 157; Survey Unit, 168
Sociological Review, 98, 120, 139, 140
Sociological Society, 6, 89-94, 98, 120, 121
socialism, 59, 64-5, 88